PENGUIN CANADA

HUNGRY FOR COMFORT

Rose (Varty) Murray, a former English teacher, studied cooking techniques at Le Cordon Bleu, La Varenne, and l'Ecole de Gastronomie Ritz-Escoffier in Paris and has studied in Costa Rica, Hong Kong, and Thailand. A contributor to newspapers and national magazines for more than twenty-five years, Rose has written regularly for such publications as *Canadian Living, Elm Street,* and *Homemakers.* She is the author of nine cookbooks, including *A Year in My Kitchen* and *Canadian Christmas Cooking,* and has contributed to more than forty additional cookbooks including the *Canadian Living* series. She lives in Cambridge, Ontario.

Also by Rose Murray

A YEAR IN MY KITCHEN

125 BEST CHICKEN RECIPES
(*First published as* Quick Chicken)

125 BEST CASSEROLES & ONE-POT MEALS
(*First published as* Rose Murrray's New Casseroles and
Other One-Dish Meals)

CELLAR & SILVER

ROSE MURRAY'S COMFORTABLE KITCHEN COOKBOOK

CANADIAN CHRISTMAS COOKING

ROSE MURRAY'S VEGETABLE COOKBOOK

SECRETS OF THE SEA

hungry for comfort

the pleasures of home cooking

rose murray

PENGUIN
CANADA

PENGUIN CANADA

Penguin Group (Canada), a division of Pearson Penguin Canada Inc., 10 Alcorn Avenue, Toronto, Ontario M4V 3B2

Penguin Group (U.K.), 80 Strand, London WC2R 0RL, England
Penguin Group (U.S.), 375 Hudson Street, New York, New York 10014, U.S.A.
Penguin Group (Australia) Inc., 250 Camberwell Road, Camberwell, Victoria 3124, Australia
Penguin Group (Ireland), 25 St. Stephen's Green, Dublin 2, Ireland
Penguin Books India (P) Ltd, 11, Community Centre, Panchsheel Park, New Delhi – 110 017, India
Penguin Group (New Zealand), cnr Rosedale and Airborne Roads, Albany, Auckland 1310, New Zealand
Penguin Books (South Africa) (Pty) Ltd, 24 Sturdee Avenue, Rosebank 2196, South Africa

Penguin Group, Registered Offices: 80 Strand, London WC2R 0RL, England

First published 2003

(WEB) 1 2 3 4 5 6 7 8 9 10

Manufactured in Canada.

_____

NATIONAL LIBRARY OF CANADA CATALOGUING IN PUBLICATION

Murray, Rose, 1941–
    Hungry for comfort : the pleasures of home cooking / Rose Murray.

Includes index.
ISBN 0-14-301599-0

    1. Cookery. I. Title.

TX714.M866 2003   641.5   C2003-904020-8
_____

Visit the Penguin Group (Canada) website at **www.penguin.ca**

for Claire

contents

Introduction viii

RECIPES

comfort year-round

MENUS

the pleasures of entertaining

1959—I was 18 years old, in our farm kitchen.
The whole family as you look at it (from left to right):
Muriel; my father, George; Allen; myself; Helen; my mother, Josephine;
and my brother, John, on the floor. We are on the cot where my father had
a nap every day after lunch.

Introduction

As I finish this manuscript while we experience the coldest winter in years, I am hungry for a steaming-hot bowl of thick, hearty soup; however, I know that by July, when we've had several days of plus-thirty-degree, humid weather, I'll find comfort in a refreshing cold gazpacho. Comfort food can be the psychological woollen scarf that makes you feel warm and well on a cold winter day when the wind is raw and bitter, or it can be the cold hand that soothes a fevered brow when one is under stress. It's food that makes you feel good.

Comfort food may simply be a satisfying meal when you are particularly hungry. It could be just a wonderfully soft, creamy texture that fills your mouth when you are enjoying a favourite food; the joy of biting into the first ripe, juicy peach of the season; pleasure from the heady aroma of muffins baking in the oven; a surprising burst of flavour from a new food.

More frequently, however, we associate comfort food with nostalgia ... memories of pleasant times past and foods we remember with affection. Perhaps we are hungry for the taste of our mothers' butter tarts, our grandmothers' macaroni and cheese, a favourite aunt's date squares. We want to be back in the peace and warmth of those kitchens.

I grew up in a kitchen that exuded comfort. Our farm kitchen with its wood stove (as well as an electric one for the hot summer) was the centre of the house. Everything happened there. At one end, all of the cooking took place, while in the centre was a huge, round table that also served as a work surface and around which we gathered for our meals, frequently with guests. There were rocking chairs at the other end and a day cot along one wall. Over the years, the cot took on the impression of my father because that is where he "rested his eyes" for a few minutes every day after the noon meal. Although not at all lavish, it was a comfortable room ... soothing and calming ... one in which people felt immediately at home.

It was taken for granted that I would spend a great deal of time in that kitchen. During that time, I learned much about food on a farm where we raised our own meat, made our own butter, grew and preserved our own produce, baked our own bread. I don't remember my mother saying, "Now, I'll teach you to make pastry." I just remember doing it.

Over the years, I've passed along many of these techniques and, of course, the recipes themselves to my own children, and often to my readers. This book abounds with Canadian favourites that have found their way into almost every handwritten recipe scribbler that has been tucked away in grandmother's kitchen cupboard: Runny Gooey Butter Tarts, Dutch Apple Pie, Classic Pot Roast.

But I've also explored with my children and readers the traditional dishes of other lands and cultures, food that has nurtured people across the world, and I present a few of those here. Comfort food knows no international boundaries. That perfectly risen Classic Cheese Soufflé has brought satisfaction to generations of cooks and diners. Madeira Tomato and Onion Soup appears on every restaurant menu on that island when there's a chill in the air. Spanish Braised Pork Chops with Peppers and Olives makes a welcome supper after a rainy day in the Spanish mountains, or right here at home.

My brother, John, and I with our farm dog on the lawn. John probably wasn't two yet. I was three years older.

My pal, the minister's son, Wally Downer.
We shared ice cream cones and dolls.
This is our farm lane with its
row of cherry trees.

And not all comfort food comes from the past with memories attached. New ingredients that were never in our mothers' kitchens are available everywhere now; they bring alive classics, enhance flavours and introduce delightful textures.

There are new favourite recipes such as Calico Mussels, Smoky Lentil Salad, Orzo Walnut Pilaf and Blue Cheese, Pear and Radicchio Pizza that mean comfort for me because they are so quick and easy to make and so pleasurable to eat.

On the other hand, there's great pleasure in what we now term Slow Food, a more leisurely kind of cooking that involves ingredients bubbling away for hours, melding flavours and creating melt-in-your-mouth tender textures. The Slow Food movement is a backlash movement started in 1986 by Carlo Petrini, who was horrified by the opening of the first McDonald's restaurant in Rome. It was created to keep safe traditional foods, cooking methods and agricultural heritages and to counter an invasion of American fast food with its homogenization tendencies. Slow Food was intended to "rediscover flavours and savours of regional cooking" and keep rural communities alive.

Now Slow Food is coming to the forefront a bit. People want to experience the satisfaction of this type of cooking, in which ingredients like braising meat, root vegetables and pulses are put together with subtle spicing and slow-released herbs to create complex-tasting dishes with aromas that fill your kitchen. In my mother's era, it was out of necessity that she would use whatever was at hand—often those cheaper cuts of meat and storage vegetables—then put everything together in one pot as a stew or pot roast to burble away while she got on with so many other tasks awaiting her attention. It was the ultimate Slow Food situation. Regardless of the reason, however, there is much good to be said for this kind of cooking, the use of heritage food and a more leisurely enjoyment of it.

Whether the dish is a familiar classic or a recent creation, whether it's international or local, long simmering or quick cooking, the essence of comfort food is that it is homemade.

Too many people, however, are starved for time these days, and for them, cooking can be drudgery. After a busy day at work, no one can wait four hours for a pot roast to finish. But that is one of the joys of this type of food, which often offers one-pot meals that are happy to be cooked ahead and reheated on hectic weeknights. For years, I have been a consultant to the arm of the Ontario government that promotes local seasonal produce, and when putting together its heritage booklet of recipes, I discovered that these recipes we might term old-fashioned were actually quite quick and simple to put together, even if they took a while to cook. Women didn't have a lot of leisure time then either, so these dishes were simple but good and, of course, creations with real food.

So, I have filled many pages here with soothing soups, slow-simmering braised dishes, nurturing stews and other one-pot meals along with heritage desserts such as pies, cakes and puddings that were easy for our mothers to put together and so comforting to eat.

Because we feel that the outside world is becoming a restless place, we are seeking refuge in our own homes and finding a sort of peace in cooking for family and friends. There's nothing as cheering as sharing good food, drink and conversation with our favourite people. It could be as simple as enjoying freshly baked hot-buttered scones with a neighbour or as elaborate as putting together a whole Oriental supper or a Thanksgiving feast for family. Sometimes, I find even the planning, shopping, preparation and serving of such a meal to be comforting; the eating of it is merely a wonderful bonus.

In the last section of the book, I've included a dozen menus for a variety of occasions as you "dine out" at home throughout the year. I hope you are at ease with their preparation and find in them combinations of flavours and textures that will please the palate and soothe the spirit.

My father, George, and my mother, Josephine, just before she was married. She would have made this dress.

RECIPES
comfort year-round

In 1838, Brillat-Savarin said, "The discovery of a new dish does more for the happiness of mankind than the discovery of a star." And when the great chefs and cooks of the world started writing down instructions for the making of a new dish, ordinary household cooks could bring happiness to family and friends.

Through the years, the good recipes have been passed along and around but change very little. In my mother's era, the recipes themselves may have been sketchy. *Everyone* just made delicious pies, date squares, butter tarts, satisfying stews, wonderful bread. There is much comfort even in remembering such good food, but I have adapted these recipes so that they are clear and accurate versions of all-time favourites.

Of course, there are also brand new dishes that I have developed and think will bring you comfort and show you the pleasures of home cooking all year round.

satisfying snacks
and enticing starters

On the farm of my childhood, there was a lot of visiting back and forth with neighbours and friends. I remember a radio program called "Farm Forum" that came on every Monday night. Our farmer friends would often gather at one house to listen to it and to discuss its content.

In 1953, we were among the first people in our county to buy a television set because my father was such a royalist he didn't want to miss seeing the coronation of Queen Elizabeth II. From then on, of course, our visitors increased in number as people called to see if they could watch a favourite television show with us. More often, however, we just happened in on each other after the evening chores were done. Today, sadly, it would seem strange indeed to drop in on friends unannounced. Is it our busy lifestyles that preclude such sociability?

During these spontaneous visits, the coffee pot would go on, and there was always something sweet on hand to serve—some cake left over from supper, a sweet bread, a few cookies. But what I can still taste are the moist fresh sandwiches my mother often made with canned salmon and her homemade white bread. Alongside would go a dish of those crunchy sweet pickles she would pack into a crock when our cucumbers were at their summer best.

This evening lunch (as we called it) was always substantial, but considered necessary fortification if we happened to walk to a neighbour's house in the winter and then trudge home through the snow.

Today, when we get together with family or friends and are not sharing a meal, cocktails and fancier finger food are more apt to be served. Unless it is a very formal occasion, I keep this kind of snack simple and easy to make, and I still like to have a few things on hand ... just in case some friends drop in unannounced.

In this chapter, you'll find easy appetizers to pique dinner appetites, finger food for parties and even snacks to accompany that rented video while you hunker down for an evening at home alone.

stuffed baguette sandwiches

MAKES ABOUT 72 HORS D'OEUVRES

We may not have the same spontaneous visiting back and forth today as we did on the farm, but everyone still loves sandwiches. With these party sandwiches, the farm "lunch" is transformed into a number of hors d'oeuvres that would be at home at any gathering—an anniversary party, an open house, the bridge club. The comfort in these sandwiches is not only in the eating, but in the fact that they can be made ahead. One stuffing is based on a favourite egg salad; the other is inspired by Mediterranean ingredients that are readily available in all supermarkets.

2	thin 20-inch (50 cm) long baguettes 2

EGG SALAD FILLING

6	hard-cooked eggs 6
2 cups	watercress, trimmed and chopped 500 mL
1/4 cup	minced red onion 50 mL
2 tbsp	cream cheese, softened 25 mL
2 tbsp	light mayonnaise 25 mL
1 tbsp	Dijon mustard 15 mL
1/4 tsp	each salt and pepper 1 mL
1/4 tsp	curry powder (optional) 1 mL
Pinch	cayenne pepper Pinch

MEDITERRANEAN FILLING

1	jar (6 oz/170 mL) marinated artichoke hearts 1
1/4 cup	minced black olives 50 mL
1	small clove garlic, minced 1
1	pkg (8 oz/250 g) light cream cheese, softened 1
1	jar (7-1/2 oz/212 g) roasted red peppers, drained and patted dry 1

1. Cut 1 of the baguettes in half crosswise; cut off the ends. Using a wooden spoon, push out the bread from the inside to hollow out each half, leaving 1/2-inch (1 cm) thick walls.

2. Egg Salad Filling: In a bowl, mince eggs; stir in watercress, onion, cream cheese, mayonnaise, mustard, salt, pepper, curry powder (if using) and cayenne. Holding each half of cut baguette on its end, pack the filling into the bread shells with a wooden spoon.

3. Cut off the top third of the remaining baguette lengthwise; hollow out each piece, leaving 1/2-inch (1 cm) thick walls.

4. Mediterranean Filling: Reserving 2 tsp (10 mL) of the marinade, drain artichoke hearts and chop finely; set aside. In a bowl, stir together the olives, reserved artichoke marinade and garlic; spread over the inside of the bread shells. Spread with cream cheese. Arrange peppers and artichoke hearts over the bottom shell; fit top shell over the filling.

5. Wrap each filled loaf tightly in foil; refrigerate for at least 4 hours or up to 24 hours. To serve, cut each loaf with a serrated knife into 1/2-inch (1 cm) thick slices.

tapenade

MAKES 3/4 CUP (175 ML)

I always like to have something on hand that will provide a little extra interest to easy appetizers, sandwiches or main course dishes. This pungent Provençale purée seems to fill that role nicely because it is easy to make, provides a lot of flavour to many different recipes and keeps for ages in the refrigerator. In Provence, you will see both green and black tapenade, but black is more common.

For a quick and easy appetizer, spread this tapenade on toasted country bread or fill miniature tart shells with it. For a knock-out sandwich, slice a baguette in half lengthwise; spread with tapenade and nestle in slices of soft white cheese, sliced cooked chicken or hard-cooked egg, slices of ripe tomato, sweet onion and leaves of fresh basil. Top a hot omelette with a dollop of tapenade or mash it with hard-cooked egg yolks to stuff the cooked egg whites. Mound it in cherry tomatoes, or add it to a warm mussel and potato salad.

Choose good-quality black olives—those that are only slightly wrinkled and cured in oil rather than brine. Usually, lemon juice is not included, but I like the way it cuts the saltiness of the ingredients.

5	anchovy fillets (half a 2-oz/50 g tin) 5
	Milk
3/4 cup	pitted black olives 175 mL
1	clove garlic 1
3 tbsp	capers, rinsed 45 mL
1 tbsp	fresh lemon juice 15 mL
1 tsp	Dijon mustard 5 mL
	Black pepper
1/4 cup	olive oil 50 mL

1. Drain anchovies and soak in milk while preparing the remaining ingredients. (Milk will help eliminate some of the saltiness. The rest of the anchovies will keep well for several days in the refrigerator if left in oil and covered.)
2. In a food processor or blender, purée anchovies, olives, garlic, capers, lemon juice, mustard and black pepper to taste. With the machine running, gradually pour in oil through feed tube.

calico mussels

MAKES 60 HORS D'OEUVRES

Mussels are so affordable and they are utterly impressive in this company appetizer that is a favourite of mine because of its appealing flavour and colour, and the fact that it is better if made ahead.

3 lb	mussels 1.5 kg
1/2 cup	dry white wine or water 125 mL
1	small onion, minced 1
1	lemon, cut in wedges 1
1/4 cup	olive oil 50 mL
3	cloves garlic, minced 3
1/4 cup	chopped fresh parsley 50 mL
3 tbsp	red wine vinegar 45 mL
Half	each sweet red and yellow pepper, diced Half
1	small carrot, shredded 1
1/4 tsp	black pepper 1 mL
Pinch	salt Pinch
	Shredded lettuce

1. Scrub mussels, removing the beards. Discard any that do not close when tapped. In a saucepan, bring wine, onion and 1 lemon wedge to a simmer over medium-high heat. Add mussels; cover and steam until the mussels open, about 5 minutes. Discard any that do not open. With a slotted spoon, transfer mussels to a bowl. Boil the liquid for 5 to 7 minutes or until reduced to 1/2 cup (125 mL). Discard the lemon.

2. In a skillet, heat oil over medium heat; cook garlic for 2 minutes. Add the reduced liquid, parsley, vinegar, sweet peppers, carrot, pepper and salt; pour into a separate bowl.

3. Remove mussels from their shells and add to the marinade in the bowl. Reserve half of each shell. Cover and refrigerate mussels and shells for at least 2 hours or preferably for 24 hours. Arrange shells on a lettuce-lined plate; fill each shell with a mussel. Spoon marinade over top; garnish plate with remaining lemon wedges.

savoury herb cheesecake

MAKES 12 APPETIZER SERVINGS

I love the creamy texture of this easy-to-make savoury cheesecake, and the flavour is so good with the addition of fresh herbs. It makes an excellent dish for a company lunch if served warm in thin wedges on top of dressed mixed salad greens. Or, cut even smaller, set on dressed greens and serve as a first course for a dinner party. What could be more inviting?

1-1/2 cups	fresh bread crumbs	375 mL
2/3 cup	finely chopped walnuts	150 mL
3 tbsp	butter, softened	45 mL
1-1/4 lb	cream cheese, at room temperature	625 g
1/4 cup	freshly grated Parmesan cheese	50 mL
4	eggs	4
2	cloves garlic, minced	2
2 tbsp	each chopped fresh tarragon, basil and oregano	25 mL
1/4 tsp	black pepper	1 mL

1. In a food processor, combine the bread crumbs, walnuts and butter until well mixed. Press onto the bottom of an 8-inch (2 L) springform pan. Bake in a 350°F (180°C) oven for 15 minutes or until golden.

2. Meanwhile, in a bowl and using a hand mixer, beat together the cream cheese and Parmesan cheese until smooth; beat in eggs, 1 at a time, beating well after each addition. Stir in garlic, tarragon, basil, oregano and pepper; pour over base. Bake for about 1 hour or until golden and puffed.

3. Run a sharp knife around the edge of cake; let stand for 15 minutes before carefully removing side of pan. (Cake will fall slightly upon cooling.) Cut into wedges.

prosciutto and fig canapés

MAKES 24 CANAPÉS

Quick and simple appetizers are my very favourite way to start a dinner party. I love the combination of salty prosciutto and succulent juicy figs; here the prosciutto is chopped into sweet butter to top thin slices of crusty baguette as a base for fresh fig pieces, and the result is so delicious you may want to double the recipe.

1/2 cup	unsalted butter, softened 125 mL
1/2 tsp	black pepper 2 mL
1/2 tsp	finely grated lemon zest 2 mL
2 tsp	fresh lemon juice 10 mL
1/4 lb	prosciutto, finely chopped 125 g
24	thin slices of baguette 24
24	tiny flat-leaf parsley leaves 24
3 to 6	fresh figs (depending on size), cut into quarters or wedges to make 24 pieces 3 to 6

1. In a small bowl, beat the butter until soft and creamy. Stir in pepper, lemon zest and lemon juice until well combined. Stir in prosciutto. (Butter can be refrigerated, covered, for up to 24 hours. Bring to room temperature before proceeding with the recipe.)

2. No more than 2 hours before serving, spread butter mixture onto baguette slices, dividing evenly. Arrange a parsley leaf slightly off-centre on each slice; put a piece of fig in the centre of each slice. Let stand at room temperature, loosely covered, until ready to serve.

a trio of tiny tarts

MAKES 2 DOZEN TARTS EACH

This is about as fancy as my appetizers get ... fancy, yes, but easy as pie. Actually, they are tiny tarts with three different flavourful fillings. It's a very good way to offer a variety of finger foods without too many different ingredients.

I was testing these tarts for an article I was writing for *Canadian Living* magazine when we went to an annual dinner at the house of a friend who was on his own. Gerry always treated us with a main course from his Crock-Pot, and these little tarts were just the answer for simple starters that year. Dessert was taken care of when we went to the village's strawberry festival for shortcake we would eat before dinner. Gerry would say, "Life's uncertain; eat dessert first."

You can cheat with tiny, thin and crisp, already-baked tart shells (1-1/4 inches/3 cm in diameter) that are available in some supermarkets, usually around the deli counter. Or, use the easy recipe for Versatile Toast Cups that follows. Each of the fillings can be made and refrigerated for up to 4 hours ahead, and each makes 24 tarts (the number of tart shells in one package). Fill and garnish just before serving.

greek salad tarts

1/2 cup	diced feta cheese	125 mL
1/2 cup	diced cucumber	125 mL
1/4 cup	sour cream	50 mL
2	green onions, minced	2
6	pitted black olives, chopped	6
1/2 tsp	grated lemon zest	2 mL
1 tsp	fresh lemon juice	5 mL
1/2 tsp	dried oregano	2 mL
	Black pepper	
24	baked tartlet shells	24
6	cherry tomatoes, quartered	6
24	thin wedges cucumber	24

1. Stir together the feta, diced cucumber, sour cream, onions, olives, lemon zest and juice, oregano and pepper to taste. Mound into tartlet shells; garnish each with a tomato quarter and cucumber wedge.

shrimp and chive tarts

6 oz	tiny cooked salad shrimp 175 g
3 tbsp	light mayonnaise 45 mL
2 tbsp	minced fresh chives (or green onion tops) 25 mL
1 tsp	fresh lemon juice 5 mL
1/2 tsp	Dijon mustard 2 mL
	Black pepper
24	baked tartlet shells 24
	Strips of chive or green onion

1. Pat shrimp dry; set 24 aside. Chop remaining shrimp. In a bowl, combine chopped shrimp, mayonnaise, minced chives, lemon juice, mustard and pepper to taste. Mound into tartlet shells; garnish with reserved shrimp and strips of chive.

egg salad caviar tarts

4	hard-cooked eggs, chopped 4
2 tbsp	minced green onion 25 mL
1 tbsp	light sour cream 15 mL
1 tbsp	light mayonnaise 15 mL
Pinch	each salt, ground cumin and cayenne Pinch
24	baked tartlet shells 24
2 tbsp	rinsed lumpfish caviar 25 mL
24	each small strips lemon zest and green onion 24

1. Stir together the eggs, minced green onion, sour cream, mayonnaise, salt, cumin and cayenne. Mound into tartlet shells; garnish each with a dollop of caviar, lemon strip and green onion knot.

versatile toast cups

Bite-sized toast cups are perfect for parties—they're easier to make than pastry and easier to eat because they don't crumble. They're also lower in calories and less expensive. Make them days or weeks ahead and serve hot or cold. Look for thinly sliced bread. You can cut the bread to make rounds or merely quarter each slice and press into tart tin cups.

loaf sliced bread 1
Vegetable oil

1. Trim the crusts from the bread and roll each slice until about 1/8 inch (3 mm) thick. Cut each slice into quarters. Or, using a 2-inch (5 cm) round cookie cutter, cut circles from each slice to make 40 rounds, reserving the trimmings for another use such as bread crumbs.

2. Tuck into 1-1/2-inch (4 cm) mini tart tins to form shells; brush each lightly with oil and bake in a 350°F (180°C) oven for 10 to 15 minutes or until crisp and light golden brown. Let cool on racks. (Toast cups can be stored in an airtight container for up to 1 week or frozen for up to 1 month.)

ginger jalapeño shrimp

MAKES ABOUT 24 SKEWERS

Grilled over the coals in the summer or broiled indoors in the winter, these fuss-free seafood skewers are always a hit. It's the kind of recipe I like to make—easy, impressive, very delicious and versatile, working just as well with scallops or chunks of boneless salmon or halibut.

2 lb	large shrimp 1 kg
1/4 cup	vegetable oil 50 mL
1/4 cup	fresh lime juice 50 mL
2 tbsp	minced fresh ginger 25 mL
2	cloves garlic, minced 2
2	small jalapeño peppers, coarsely chopped 2
Pinch	black pepper Pinch
	Lime wedges

1. Peel and devein shrimp leaving tails on; place in a bowl. In a blender, purée half of the oil, the lime juice, ginger, garlic, jalapeño peppers and pepper; pour over the shrimp and toss gently to coat well. Cover and refrigerate for 1 hour.

2. Discarding the marinade, thread 3 or 4 shrimp onto each of 24 soaked wooden skewers. Brush 1 side of the shrimp with some of the remaining oil. Place, oiled side down, on a greased grill over medium heat or under a preheated broiler; close the lid and cook, turning once and brushing with remaining oil, for about 2 minutes per side or until pink and firm to the touch. Transfer to a serving plate; garnish with lime.

black bean hummus

MAKES ABOUT 2 CUPS (500 ML)

Enjoy this easy dip with grilled flatbread or corn chips as you watch your favourite video pick. It's a Caribbean take on a Middle Eastern favourite.

1	can (19 oz/540 mL) black beans, drained and rinsed	1
1/2 cup	tahini (ground sesame paste)	125 mL
1/4 cup	fresh lime juice	50 mL
3 tbsp	vegetable oil	45 mL
1/2 tsp	each ground coriander and ground cumin	2 mL
1/4 tsp	cayenne (or to taste)	1 mL
2	large cloves garlic	2
	Salt and pepper	
2 tbsp	chopped fresh coriander	25 mL

1. In a food processor, purée the beans, tahini, lime juice, oil, coriander, cumin and cayenne until smooth, dropping the garlic through the feed tube with the motor running. Transfer to a bowl and stir in salt and pepper to taste and fresh coriander. (Can be made ahead up to 2 days, then covered and refrigerated.) The dip will thicken upon standing; if you want a thinner dip, stir in 2 to 4 tbsp (25 to 50 mL) water.

homemade caramel popcorn

MAKES 20 CUPS (5 L)

I created this recipe for a Halloween story once because it makes a huge amount and is just right for a party. My daughter-in-law, Cherrie, made it this year for a Super Bowl party where it was such a huge hit I just knew it had to go into my book.

20 cups	freshly popped popcorn	5 L
1 cup	granulated sugar	250 mL
1 cup	packed brown sugar	250 mL
1 cup	butter	250 mL
1/2 cup	corn syrup	125 mL
Pinch	cream of tartar	Pinch
1 tsp	baking soda	5 mL

1. Place popcorn in a large roasting pan; set aside. In a large heavy saucepan, stir together granulated sugar, brown sugar, butter, corn syrup and cream of tartar. Bring to a boil, stirring to dissolve sugar; then boil for 5 minutes without stirring. Remove from the heat; stir in baking soda. Pour over popcorn and mix to coat well. Place in a 200°F (93°C) oven for 1 hour, stirring every 10 minutes. Stir occasionally while mixture cools and store in an airtight container (should it last that long).

VARIATION

ALMOND-PECAN CARAMEL CORN
Combine 2 cups (500 mL) each unblanched almonds and pecan halves with the popped corn and proceed as above.

TIP
You can get about 20 cups (5 L) popped corn from 3/4 cup (175 mL) unpopped corn. If you don't have a roasting pan big enough, divide the mixture between two pans.

salt and pepper almonds

MAKES ABOUT 3 CUPS (750 ML)

If you wish, substitute whole unsalted cashews or unsalted peanuts for this easy snack that goes especially well with champagne! Look for sea salt in specialty food shops and many grocery stores. It gives extra flavour to a very simple recipe.

2 tbsp	butter 25 mL
1 tbsp	each sea salt and coarsely ground black pepper 15 mL
1 cup	each granulated sugar and water 250 mL
3 cups	blanched whole almonds (about 1 lb/500 g) 750 mL

1. Line a large rimmed baking sheet with foil or parchment; grease foil with the butter. Set aside.
2. In a small bowl, mix together the salt and pepper; set aside.
3. In a medium saucepan, combine sugar and water; bring to a boil, stirring until sugar is dissolved. Boil for 5 minutes and remove from heat. Stir in almonds and let stand for 5 minutes, stirring often.
4. Drain nuts in a sieve and return to pan. Stir in half the salt and pepper mixture; then spread out on prepared baking sheet. Sprinkle with remaining salt and pepper; roast in a 350°F (180°C) oven until golden brown, about 20 minutes, stirring once. Let cool on the pan on a rack. (Nuts can be stored in an airtight container at room temperature for up to 2 weeks or frozen for up to 1 month.)

a bowl of comfort

When I asked my younger brother, John, what he remembered of our suppers at home on the farm, his answer came quickly: "I'd ask Mom, 'What's for supper?' and she'd say, 'Chicken ... go kill one.'" This was not his favourite task, and it is beyond the realm of possibility for most kids today who think that chicken is born in Cellophane supermarket wrappers.

Sometimes, if the chicken happened to be what I would call a "spent hen" (one retired from a lifetime of laying eggs), my mother would make a chicken broth, then float small dumplings in the broth. I can still see and taste what we came to call "Chicken and Dumplings," which was not the chunky chicken stew my husband constantly requests.

The other memory of soup from my childhood was of one I never tasted. I studied music with Muriel Stephenson, a blind concert pianist who lived in a huge Victorian house in Collingwood, Ontario. Except for the light by the piano, the interior of the house was dark and gloomy indeed. I can still remember with great vividness that the only comforting thing about it was the pervasive aroma of homemade vegetable soup the housekeeper would cook every Saturday morning.

I never saw the housekeeper nor tasted any of her soup, but I always thought of it when my mother filled one of her big kettles with delicious steaming vegetables and broth that she would always make from scratch (even, sometimes, from that "spent hen").

There is something wonderfully soothing about soup—whether it's hot or cold.

Hearty hot soups will warm family and friends on the coldest winter's day, while cold refreshing ones will comfort a heated brow in the summer.

community cookbooks and
my first published recipe

You don't need to have been born in the forties or raised in the country to know about community fundraising cookbooks. They are still put together by both rural and urban volunteers who want to collect money for schools, hospitals, shelters and an endless list of organizations badly in need of financial assistance.

In the fifties, however, this country produced a huge number of these cookbooks—probably because more people cooked then and were willing to share recipes for family favourites. In that era of affluence, the many households that could manage on one salary allowed wives the luxury of staying at home to look after their families and give volunteer hours to their community. It was the era, too, of getting acquainted with the newest mixes, instants and frozen or canned foods, with much experimenting with these "jet-age" ingredients. What better way to spend your time than swapping recipes and filling books to sell for the benefit of the community?

I have a large pile of these books, but my best-loved community cookbook is one that has on its cover a picture of a village church surrounded by cars of the decade and the words "Duntroon and Glen Huron, Ont. Personal Recipes by Women's Auxiliary of Church of the Redeemer." It was the little Anglican church for which my father acted as warden for many years and the women's auxiliary of which my mother was president at the time the cookbook was put together.

Regrettably, these old community books seldom have a publication date, but I remember well the creation of this one in the fifties. My mother sent out pages on which each women's auxiliary member would write her name, the title of the recipe, the list of ingredients and the method, which in some cases proved quite vague: "Blend all ingredients," "Cook until done." Being a good cook herself, Mom did her best to flesh out such scant instructions. Even recording a reasonable amount for an ingredient was hard work sometimes, especially when dealing with a number of farm cooks who simply knew that their handful of flour worked well. I remember my mother getting the daughter of our neighbour Mrs. Leach in on the job, especially to discover how much flour was in her mother's blue cup with the broken handle. Mrs. Leach was such a wonderful cook; those recipes just had to be recorded.

I have two copies of this book: my mother's, and the one I bought when it was released. The former is falling apart, its coil binding almost broken away with much use. In it are yellowed newspaper clippings of "Today's Recipes" and handwritten additions to pages, passed along by neighbours, relatives and friends.

In the chapter titled "Soups, Salads, Beverages" are recipes for that lovely old-fashioned boiled salad dressing I still make and countless jellied salads (the decade's rage because you no longer had to boil a pot of calves' feet for hours to get jelly) I have never made, but alas, no recipes for soups or beverages. My mother put all the recipes in the right categories, then the North American Press in Kansas City, Missouri, organized them according to some undetermined plan.

In the section called "Miscellaneous—Meat Substitutes, Vegetables" we actually do find some meat, and there is one soup. It is a corn chowder—and the very first recipe I had published in any book. Although the method is quite detailed, the ingredients are not listed in the order used and I don't say whether the onion is chopped, sliced or diced. (I was, after all, just a teenager.)

What follows is the very same recipe, but with thirty years of experience writing recipes.

corn chowder

MAKES 4 SERVINGS

You can substitute side bacon for the salt pork, but the latter (still available in supermarkets) would definitely be my choice. You can, of course, use cooked fresh corn kernels if corn is in season.

1/4 lb	salt pork, diced	125 g
1	small onion, diced	1
4 cups	diced potatoes	1 L
2 cups	boiling water	500 mL
4 cups	milk	1 L
2 cups	corn kernels (canned or frozen)	500 mL
3 tbsp	butter	45 mL
1-1/2 tsp	salt	7 mL
Pinch	black pepper	Pinch
8	soda crackers	8
	Cold milk	

1. In a large saucepan, cook pork over medium heat until crisp, about 5 minutes. Remove with a slotted spoon to drain on paper towels. Pour off all but 2 tbsp (25 mL) of the pan drippings.
2. Add onion; cook until softened, about 5 minutes, stirring often. Add potatoes and water; bring to a boil, reduce heat, cover and cook until potatoes are tender, about 10 minutes.
3. Stir in milk and corn; heat until steaming. Add butter, salt and pepper. Moisten crackers with cold milk. Ladle chowder into warm soup bowls and place 2 crackers on each. Garnish with pork.

hearty chicken noodle soup

MAKES 6 TO 8 SERVINGS

Nothing soothes the body and soul like steaming-hot chicken noodle soup, and this one is packed with lots of healthy vegetables and good flavour. I often use chicken breasts for a soup like this, but legs are less expensive and simply take a bit longer to cook.

3 lb	chicken legs 1.5 kg
	Salt and pepper
2	bay leaves 2
5 cups	chicken broth 1.25 L
3 cups	water 750 mL
1 tsp	dried thyme 5 mL
1/2 tsp	dried sage leaves 2 mL
2	leeks, white and light green parts 2
2 tbsp	butter 25 mL
3	cloves garlic, minced 3
3	carrots, diced 3
3	stalks celery (with leaves), diced 3
1-1/2 cups	thin egg noodles 375 mL
2 tbsp	fresh lemon juice 25 mL
3 tbsp	chopped fresh parsley 45 mL

1. Remove excess fat from chicken and sprinkle legs with salt and pepper. Place in a large saucepan with bay leaves, broth and water; bring to a boil, skimming off any foam. Add thyme and sage; cover and cook over low heat for about 1 hour or until chicken is very tender. Remove bay leaves and chicken. Let chicken cool and remove skin; shred meat from bones, discarding skin and bones.

2. Meanwhile, quarter leeks lengthwise and slice. In a large skillet, melt butter over medium heat; cook leeks until soft, about 5 minutes. Add garlic and stir for 1 minute. Stir in carrots, celery, 1/2 tsp (2 mL) salt and 1/4 tsp (1 mL) pepper; cover and cook for 10 minutes, stirring occasionally, until soft. Stir into broth after chicken is removed and bring to a boil; reduce heat, cover and cook for 10 minutes. Add chicken meat and noodles; cook until noodles are soft, 8 to 10 minutes. Season with lemon juice, and salt and pepper if needed. Stir in parsley to serve.

3. Any leftover soup will thicken upon standing; thin with water or broth.

> **TIP**
> If homemade broth is not available, use two 10-oz (284 mL) cans of chicken broth and 2 cans of water.

hearty double mushroom, beef and barley soup

MAKES ABOUT 8 SERVINGS

Now that so many exotic mushrooms are available in supermarkets, we tend to overlook the dried version, which can lend a wonderful nuttiness to a dish. I must admit that I used some dried porcini I bought in Europe after their heady fragrance lured me into a little store where they were displayed. For the fresh mushrooms needed, buy the white button ones, or exotic if you wish. Usually the brown creminis are the same price as white mushrooms and have more flavour.

1/2 cup	dried mushrooms, such as porcini, cèpes or other (about 1/2 oz/15 g) 125 mL
1 cup	boiling water 250 mL
2 tbsp	vegetable oil 25 mL
1	beef shank (about 1-1/2 lb/750g) 1
3 cups	sliced fresh mushrooms (slightly more than 1/2 lb/ 250 g) 750 mL
2	carrots, finely diced 2
2	onions, chopped 2
1	stalk celery with leaves, chopped 1
2	cloves garlic, minced 2
1/2 tsp	each dried thyme and marjoram 2 mL
1	bay leaf 1
1/2 cup	Madeira, Marsala or medium sherry (or additional beef broth) 125 mL
5 cups	beef broth 1.25 L
	Salt and pepper
1/2 cup	pot or pearl barley 125 mL
1/2 cup	chopped fresh parsley 125 mL

1. Combine dried mushrooms with boiling water; let stand for 30 minutes. Drain in a sieve set over a bowl. Slice mushrooms and strain liquid to remove any grit; set aside mushrooms and liquid.
2. In a large heavy saucepan or Dutch oven, heat oil over medium-high heat. Brown beef well and remove to a plate.
3. Add fresh mushrooms, carrots, onions and celery to the pan; cook, stirring, for 5 minutes. Add garlic, thyme, marjoram and bay leaf; cook, stirring, for 2 minutes.
4. Stir in Madeira and bring to a boil, scraping up any brown bits from the bottom of the pan.
5. Add beef shank, broth and 1/2 tsp (2 mL) each salt and pepper. Bring to a boil, reduce heat and simmer, covered, for 1-1/2 hours or until beef is very tender. Remove shank, discard bone and dice beef.
6. Stir in reserved mushrooms and their liquid, diced beef and barley. Cover and simmer for 30 minutes or until barley is tender. Discard bay leaf; taste and adjust seasoning. Stir in parsley and serve. Any leftover soup will thicken upon cooling; thin with broth or water.

> **TIP**
> Barley is a grain that is widely available. Both pot and pearl barley are polished (pearl more so) and can be used interchangeably.

madeira tomato and onion soup

MAKES 6 SERVINGS

For the most part, the Madeiran cuisine reflects the good, simple food you find on the Portuguese main-land, but this Atlantic island has a few specialties. The Bolo da Madeira, or yeast-raised fruitcake that's drizzled with Madeira wine to serve, and the skewers of tender beef grilled and hung from a hook at your table are two you often encounter on restaurant menus. This simple soup with its garnish of poached egg, however, is on almost every menu. It gets its rich flavour from the beautiful ripe tomatoes and sweet onions that grow in the island's volcanic soil.

When our tomatoes are at their ripe seasonal best, use seven or eight peeled and chopped fresh tomatoes and an extra 1 cup (250 mL) water. Don't even consider using insipid, pale, hard, out-of-season tomatoes. Instead of poaching the eggs separately, you can place raw eggs gently on top of the simmering soup, cover and poach for 15 minutes.

Although we found many versions and textures when we tried the soup in Madeira, I like it almost puréed, but with a few chunks of tomato.

1/4 cup	olive oil 50 mL
4	onions, coarsely chopped 4
1	can (28 oz/796 mL) diced tomatoes, undrained 1
1	can (5-1/2 oz/156 mL) tomato paste 1
4	cloves garlic, minced 4
5 cups	chicken broth 1.25 L
1 tsp	granulated sugar 5 mL
	Salt and pepper
6	warm poached eggs 6
1/4 cup	finely chopped fresh parsley 50 mL

1. In a large saucepan, heat oil over medium heat and cook onions for 15 minutes until softened and light brown, stirring often. Add tomatoes, tomato paste, 2 tomato paste cans of water and garlic. Bring to a boil, reduce heat, cover and simmer for 1 hour. Uncover and simmer for 30 minutes, stirring occasionally.
2. Stir in broth, sugar, and salt and pepper to taste. Bring to a boil, reduce heat and simmer, uncovered, for 1-1/2 hours or until flavours are well blended. If you wish, purée part or all of the soup. (If you have an immersion blender, this works well.) Cool, cover and refrigerate for at least 1 hour or up to 24 hours.
3. Bring soup to room temperature. Bring slowly to a simmer. Ladle into large shallow bowls; top each with an egg and a sprinkling of parsley.

> **NOTE**
> Pick the freshest eggs you can for poaching. Since the yolk membrane is stronger and the white is thicker in a fresh egg, the yolk will stay together and the white will cling better to it.

thai red curry beef noodle soup

MAKES 6 SERVINGS

I felt no need for piping-hot soup in Thailand when the temperatures reached a humid 35°C, but this interesting and colourful soup brings much comfort to a cold, windy day here. Serve it as the first course of an Asian dinner, or on its own as a light lunch or supper.

You can find most of the Asian ingredients in a regular supermarket, but you might have to seek out fish sauce in an Asian store where you can also find Thai basil, a more pungent version of our sweet basil; either will do nicely here.

1/2 lb	dried rice stick noodles 250 g
1 lb	sirloin steak 500 g
1 tbsp	vegetable oil 15 mL
2 tsp	Thai red curry paste 10 mL
1/2 lb	green beans, trimmed and cut into 1-inch (2.5 cm) pieces 250 g
5 cups	chicken broth 1.25 L
1 tbsp	fish sauce (approx.) 15 mL
1 tsp	granulated sugar 5 mL
2 tbsp	each rice vinegar and soy sauce 25 mL
1 cup	bean sprouts 250 mL
1/2 cup	fresh coriander leaves 125 mL
1/2 cup	roasted unsalted peanuts, coarsely chopped 125 mL
	Additional fish sauce
4	green onions, sliced 4
1/4 cup	slivered fresh basil leaves 50 mL

> **TIP**
> If homemade broth is not available, use two 10-oz (284 mL) cans of chicken broth and 2 cans of water.

1. Put noodles in a large bowl, add enough boiling water to cover them, and set aside for 10 minutes. Drain noodles in a colander, rinse them under cold running water and drain again.

2. Meanwhile, heat a well-seasoned heavy skillet over medium-high heat. Grease lightly. Add steak; cook for 3 to 5 minutes on each side for rare. If steak is thicker than 3/4 inch (2 cm), cook it over medium heat for 4 to 6 minutes on each side. Remove steak to a cutting board, tent loosely with foil and let stand for 5 minutes. Slice steak into very thin strips across the grain, reserving any juices that have accumulated under steak. Cut steak strips into 2- x 1/4-inch (5 cm x 5 mm) pieces, then set aside.

3. Heat oil in a large saucepan over medium heat. Add curry paste, then cook, stirring, for 1 minute, until fragrant. Add beans; stir-fry for 1 minute. Stir in broth, 1 tbsp (15 mL) fish sauce and sugar. Bring to a boil over high heat. Reduce heat to medium-low and simmer, uncovered, for 10 minutes, until beans are tender-crisp.

4. Meanwhile, stir together vinegar and soy sauce in a small bowl. Put bean sprouts, coriander leaves and peanuts in 3 separate small bowls. Pour some fish sauce into another small bowl. Arrange these condiments on the table so each person can add to the soup as desired.

5. Divide steak strips among 6 large warm soup bowls. Stir noodles and reserved steak juices into soup. Heat until piping hot. Stir green onions and basil into soup, then taste and add more fish sauce if necessary. Ladle soup into bowls, using tongs to divide noodles evenly among bowls. Serve at once.

chorizo, bean and coriander soup

MAKES 4 TO 6 SERVINGS

Hearty enough to be a main course, this colourful soup needs only fresh crusty bread as an accompaniment. Look for cooked chorizo—a spicy sausage—in the deli section of your supermarket. We are lucky here in Cambridge, Ontario, because our large Portuguese population uses this sausage in many dishes, and good chorizo is available in most stores.

2 tbsp	olive oil (approx.) 25 mL
2	slices side bacon, diced 2
1/2 lb	cooked chorizo (mild or hot), coarsely chopped 250 g
2	boneless skinless chicken breast halves, diced 2
3	small leeks (white and light green parts only), cleaned and thinly sliced 3
2	stalks celery, diced 2
2	carrots, diced 2
1 tsp	ground coriander 5 mL
1/2 tsp	black pepper 2 mL
1/4 tsp	hot pepper flakes 1 mL
5 cups	chicken broth 1.25 L
1	bunch fresh coriander (stems and leaves), finely chopped 1
1	can (19 oz/540 mL) white kidney beans, drained and rinsed 1

1. Heat 1 tbsp (15 mL) oil in a large saucepan over medium-high heat. Add bacon, then cook, stirring often, until crisp, about 2 minutes. Remove bacon to a paper towel-lined plate. Add chorizo and chicken to fat remaining in saucepan; cook for 3 to 5 minutes, stirring often, until browned. Using a slotted spoon, remove chorizo and chicken to a bowl and set aside.

2. Reduce heat to medium. Add remaining oil to the saucepan if necessary. Add leeks, celery and carrots; cook for 5 minutes, stirring to scrape up any brown bits from the bottom of the saucepan, until leeks are soft. Stir in ground coriander, pepper and hot pepper flakes; cook, stirring, for 1 minute.

3. Return chorizo and chicken to saucepan, along with any juices that have accumulated in the bowl. Stir in broth and half the fresh coriander. Bring to a boil over high heat. Reduce heat to low, then simmer, covered, for 40 minutes, until vegetables are very soft.

4. Stir in beans, then cook for 5 minutes, until piping hot. Taste and add more pepper if necessary. Ladle into warm bowls, then serve sprinkled with bacon and remaining fresh coriander.

> **TIP**
> If homemade broth is not available, use two 10-oz (284 mL) cans of chicken broth and 2 cans of water.

gazpacho

MAKES ABOUT 6 SERVINGS

Gazpacho originated in the southern part of Spain, in Andalusia, but is now universally loved as the cold soup that soothes and refreshes on hot summer days. Originally made by farm workers using whatever was in the fields, this "liquid salad" always showcases field-ripened tomatoes, cucumbers and peppers.

The traditional recipe often calls for bread in the soup, but I prefer making croutons to serve on top. Most gazpachos are processed only until chunky, but in Spain, I have on occasion enjoyed the soup puréed and sieved into a tall glass as a pre-meal drink.

3	tomatoes, peeled and coarsely chopped 3
1	each sweet green and red pepper, coarsely chopped 1
1	English cucumber, peeled and coarsely chopped 1
1	small fresh hot pepper, diced (or 1/2 tsp/2 mL hot pepper sauce) 1
1	small onion, coarsely chopped 1
·3	cloves garlic, chopped 3
2 tbsp	each red wine vinegar and olive oil 25 mL
1 tbsp	Worcestershire sauce 15 mL
3 cups	vegetable cocktail 750 mL
	Salt and pepper

GARNISH

Croutons (recipe follows)
Diced cucumber, green pepper, tomato and onion

1. In a food processor or blender, process in batches the tomatoes, peppers, cucumber, hot pepper, onion, garlic, vinegar, oil and Worcestershire sauce until vegetables are finely chopped. Transfer to a large bowl; stir in vegetable cocktail, and salt and pepper to taste. Cover and refrigerate for several hours to be well chilled or up to 5 days.
2. Taste and add more vinegar, salt or hot pepper or sauce if needed.
3. Serve soup in chilled bowls, passing small bowls of croutons, diced cucumber, green pepper, tomato and onion for garnish.

croutons

MAKES ABOUT 1-1/2 CUPS (375 ML)

2 tbsp	butter 25 mL
1	clove garlic, crushed 1
6	slices white bread, crusts removed and finely cubed 6

1. In a large skillet, melt butter over low heat. Add garlic, then bread cubes, stirring to coat. Cook for 30 minutes or until golden and crunchy, stirring occasionally.

spinach and potato soup

MAKES 4 TO 6 SERVINGS

I love the satisfying addition of potatoes in soup, especially when combined with bright, flavourful spinach or asparagus. Use the egg as a garnish or top each serving with a dollop of sour cream and some snipped chives.

1/4 cup	butter	50 mL
1	large leek (white and light green parts), sliced	1
4	cloves garlic, minced	4
4	potatoes, peeled and sliced	4
5 cups	chicken broth	1.25 L
2 tbsp	fresh lemon juice	25 mL
1 tsp	salt	5 mL
1/2 tsp	dried marjoram	2 mL
1/4 tsp	black pepper	1 mL
1	pkg (10 oz/284 g) fresh spinach	1
1 cup	18% cream or milk	250 mL
2	hard-cooked eggs, whites and yolks chopped separately	2

1. In a large saucepan, over medium heat, melt butter. Add leek and garlic; cook over low heat for 10 minutes, stirring often, until softened but not brown.
2. Stir in potatoes and toss to coat with butter. Stir in broth, lemon juice, salt, marjoram and pepper. Bring to a boil, reduce heat and simmer mixture, covered, for about 15 minutes or until potatoes can be pierced easily with a fork.
3. Stir in spinach; bring back to a boil and simmer for 5 minutes, uncovered. Purée with an immersion blender or in a blender in batches, holding down the lid. (Soup can be cooled, covered and refrigerated for up to 24 hours.)
4. Reheat slowly, add cream and gently heat without boiling. Taste and adjust seasoning, adding more salt, pepper or lemon juice if necessary. Ladle into hot soup bowls and garnish each with a mound of chopped egg white on which you place a mound of egg yolk.

VARIATION

ASPARAGUS AND POTATO SOUP
Substitute 1 lb (500 g) asparagus, trimmed and cut into 1-inch (2.5 cm) lengths, for the spinach.

---

carrot and red lentil soup with parsley cream

MAKES 4 SERVINGS

Simple but comforting and delicious—this soup is just right for either company or family. If you want to skip the Parsley Cream garnish, just top with croutons. (See page 28 for recipe.)

2 tbsp	olive oil 25 mL
1 lb	carrots (about 6 small), sliced 500 g
1	onion, chopped 1
1	small sweet red pepper, chopped 1
2	cloves garlic, minced 2
2 tsp	ground ginger 10 mL
1 cup	red lentils, picked over and rinsed 250 mL
6 cups	chicken broth 1.5 L
	Salt
2 tsp	fresh lemon juice (approx.) 10 mL

PARSLEY CREAM
1/2 cup	parsley leaves 125 mL
1	green onion, sliced 1
1/3 cup	sour cream 75 mL
Pinch	cayenne Pinch

1. In a large saucepan, heat oil over medium heat; cook carrots, onion, red pepper, garlic and ginger for 5 minutes, stirring often.
2. Add lentils and broth; bring to a boil and simmer, covered, for 15 to 20 minutes or until carrots are very tender. Purée with an immersion blender or transfer to a standard blender and purée in batches, holding down the lid. Return to saucepan and bring to a simmer. Season with salt and lemon juice.
3. Parsley Cream: Finely chop parsley and green onion in a mini-chopper; add sour cream and cayenne and process until well combined. Or, finely chop parsley and onion by hand and stir in sour cream and cayenne.
4. Serve soup hot, garnished with a dollop of Parsley Cream.

roasted squash soup with sage and pancetta

MAKES 8 TO 10 SERVINGS

Pancetta is an Italian bacon that is salt-cured but not smoked. Look for it in delis or Italian grocery stores.

1	butternut squash (about 2-3/4 lb/1.25 kg) 1
4 oz	pancetta, coarsely chopped 125 g
2	onions, coarsely chopped 2
2	cloves garlic, minced 2
1-1/2 tbsp	chopped fresh sage (or 1-1/2 tsp/7 mL crumbled dried sage) 22 mL
1/4 tsp	hot pepper flakes (or to taste) 1 mL
6 cups	chicken broth 1.5 L
	Salt and pepper
	Sour cream
1	large ripe tomato, diced 1
8 to 10	sage leaves, fresh or dried (optional) 8 to 10

1. Cut squash in half, remove seeds and roast, cut side down and covered with foil, in a greased or parchment-lined baking pan in a 400°F (200°C) oven for about 45 minutes or until tender. When cool enough to handle, scrape flesh from rind.

2. Meanwhile, in a large saucepan, cook pancetta over medium heat until crisp, about 5 minutes. With a slotted spoon, transfer to paper towels to drain.

3. In the pan drippings, over medium-low heat, cook onions, garlic, chopped sage and hot pepper flakes for about 10 minutes or until very soft, stirring occasionally. Add roasted squash, broth and salt and pepper to taste; bring to a boil, reduce heat, cover and simmer for 20 minutes for flavours to blend.

4. Purée in blender (holding down lid) in batches. (Soup can be prepared to this point, then cooled, covered and refrigerated for up to 3 days.) Return to saucepan and reheat gently. Taste and adjust seasoning.

5. Serve in heated bowls, garnishing each serving with a dollop of sour cream, a sprinkle of diced tomato and pancetta and a sage leaf (if using).

cream of rutabaga soup

MAKES 4 TO 6 SERVINGS

The rutabaga is one of our most delicious storage vegetables. Often confused with its small, white-purple, thin-skinned friend, the summer turnip (and indeed often called a yellow turnip), the rutabaga has much more substance and flavour. Cooked and mashed, rutabaga is the perfect side dish for roast chicken, turkey or pork. I also often dice it into a vegetable soup, but this simple, creamy soup features rutabaga at its mildest and sweetest.

1/4 cup	butter 50 mL	
1 cup	sliced leeks 250 mL	
3 cups	diced peeled rutabaga 750 mL	
4 cups	chicken broth 1 L	
1 cup	whipping or 18% cream 250 mL	
2 tbsp	maple syrup 25 mL	
	Salt and pepper	
	Chopped chives or green onion	

1. In a large saucepan, melt butter over low heat; cook leeks, covered, for 5 minutes. Add rutabaga and cook, covered, for 5 minutes. Stir in broth and bring to a boil. Reduce heat to low; cook, covered, for about 35 minutes or until rutabaga is very tender.

2. Transfer to a blender or food processor and purée in batches. (A blender makes a smoother purée.) Pass through a food mill or sieve for an even smoother soup. (Soup can be prepared a day ahead to this point, then cooled, covered and refrigerated.)

3. Return to the saucepan and heat through; stir in cream, maple syrup and salt and pepper to taste. Gently heat through; serve in warmed soup bowls or tureen. Garnish with chives or green onion.

country garlic soup with poached eggs

MAKES 4 SERVINGS

Our best vacations in Europe always include renting an apartment or house so I can pretend to live in that country, visit all the local markets and cook. September 2002 found us in an old farmhouse in Gard in the mid-south region of France—just a few miles from Provence. It also found us in the worst flood the area had seen for decades. The fierce thunder, lightning and torrential rains started early one Sunday morning and didn't let up until late Monday, with twenty-seven people killed as the swollen rivers angrily overshot their banks.

Fortunately, our farmhouse was on a hill, and although the village below was hit hard, we were safe. The disaster did, however, curtail travel for a time, and since the restaurants were closed and many roads impassable, we were lucky we could cook our own meals.

A visit to the local market is always first on the list of activities when we settle into a place. Because we had arrived before the storm, we had managed to buy some vegetables, cheese, sausage, eggs and a good supply of local garlic.

On one of the days we couldn't travel out, I had to make do with such supplies and made this soul-warming, easy soup. It is actually a soup found all over Spain, but since there were eggs, garlic and part of a baguette on hand, I didn't think anyone would mind a cross-cultural lunch. It's a great soup to make when you are housebound in any country.

2 tbsp	olive oil	25 mL
6	cloves garlic, minced	6
4	baguette slices	4
1 tsp	paprika	5 mL
5 cups	chicken broth	1.25 L
4	eggs	4
	Salt and pepper	
4	large sprigs fresh parsley or coriander	4

1. In a large deep skillet, heat oil over low heat and cook garlic until light golden, about 8 minutes, stirring often. Remove garlic with a slotted spoon and set aside. Add bread to the skillet and cook over medium heat, turning once and moving around in the pan, until browned, about 4 minutes. Place a slice in each of 4 heatproof soup bowls, sprinkle each with some of the paprika and keep warm in a low oven.
2. Add broth and cooked garlic to the skillet; bring to a simmer. Break 1 egg into a cup and slip into the simmering broth. Repeat with the remaining eggs. Cover and poach at a bare simmer until the whites are firm but yolks are still runny, 3 to 4 minutes.
3. With a slotted spoon, transfer eggs to the toasts and sprinkle with salt and pepper. Ladle soup into the bowls and garnish with parsley. Serve at once.

smoked fish and celery root chowder

MAKES ABOUT 6 SERVINGS

If smoked rainbow trout is unavailable, substitute other smoked fish fillets, such as mackerel, in this hearty chowder.

2 tbsp	butter 25 mL
1	onion, chopped 1
2	stalks celery, thinly sliced 2
2	cloves garlic, minced 2
1	celery root, peeled and cut into 1/2-inch (1 cm) cubes 1
3/4 tsp	dried thyme 4 mL
2	bottles (8 oz/240 mL each) clam juice 2
1 cup	each water and dry white wine 250 mL
2	red-skinned potatoes, unpeeled and cut into 1/2-inch (1 cm) cubes 2
3/4 lb	smoked rainbow trout fillets, skinned and flaked 375 g
1 cup	frozen corn kernels, thawed 250 mL
1 cup	whipping cream 250 mL
1/4 tsp	each salt and black pepper 1 mL
1/4 cup	chopped fresh parsley 50 mL
2 tbsp	fresh lemon juice 25 mL
	Celery leaves and paprika

1. In a large heavy saucepan, over medium heat, melt butter. Add onion, celery and garlic; cook for 5 minutes, stirring often, until onion is soft but not brown. Add celery root and thyme; cook, stirring, for 1 minute. Stir in clam juice, water and wine. Bring to a boil over high heat. Reduce heat to medium-low and simmer, covered, for 15 minutes. Add potatoes; simmer, covered, for 15 minutes until all vegetables are very tender.
2. Stir in fish, corn, cream, salt and pepper. Cook, covered, over low heat for 5 minutes. Stir in parsley and lemon juice. Taste and add more salt and pepper if necessary. Ladle into warm soup bowls, then garnish with celery leaves and serve sprinkled with paprika.

old-fashioned fish chowder

MAKES 8 SERVINGS

Fish chowder is one of the simplest of all soups—wholesome fish, gently sautéed vegetables and a broth enriched with cream. Make it a cozy supper with freshly baked biscuits and a salad, just right for eating in front of the fire after a day on the ski hill.

2 lb	fresh or thawed haddock, halibut or cod fillets 1 kg
1/4 lb	salt pork, diced 125 g
1/4 cup	butter 50 mL
2	large onions, thinly sliced 2
2	small leeks, thinly sliced 2
1/2 cup	sliced celery 125 mL
4 cups	thinly sliced, peeled potatoes (about 6 small) 1 L
1 tsp	dried thyme 5 mL
	Salt and pepper
4 cups	boiling water 1 L
2 cups	milk 500 mL
2 cups	18% cream 500 mL
2 tbsp	chopped fresh parsley or chives 25 mL
	Paprika

1. Remove any small bones from the fish; cut into large bite-sized pieces. Set aside.
2. In a large heavy pot, cook salt pork until crisp. Drain on paper towels; set aside. Drain off any fat.
3. In the same pot, melt butter over low heat; cook onions, leeks and celery, stirring occasionally, for about 15 minutes or until softened but not browned. Stir in potatoes, thyme, and salt and pepper to taste; pour in boiling water and bring to a boil.
4. Reduce the heat, cover and simmer for about 10 minutes or until potatoes are barely tender. Add fish; simmer, covered, for about 10 minutes or just until fish flakes easily when tested with a fork.
5. Stir in milk, cream and salt pork. Gently heat through but do not boil. Ladle into warm bowls; sprinkle with parsley and paprika.

the staff of life and more

While in elementary school, I carried my lunch from home and envied those friends whose sandwiches had the neat corners only store-bought bread could provide. I always thought my sandwiches were rather scruffy looking because they featured my mother's homemade bread.

As time has a habit of reversing things, my daughter's experience with homemade bread was just the opposite. While she was in elementary and high school, Anne missed my baking all of our bread when I started doing more and more writing and didn't have the time any more. In fact, she missed it so much that she readily agreed to learn to bake our family's bread herself. While still quite young, Anne would spend a part of each Saturday mixing and kneading a number of loaves for the coming week.

Bread is a metaphor for life itself, and a golden, crusty homemade loaf with its enticing aroma exudes contentment and well-being. Even now, when plenty of decent bread is available, there is much satisfaction in the very act of kneading and producing food that shows we are nurturing our families and ourselves.

Bread is much revered in various parts of the world. Ukrainians have a charming custom of greeting honoured guests with bread and salt. In fact, to them, bread is one of the holiest of all foods. Older Ukrainians consider it most disrespectful when leftover pieces are thrown carelessly about. In Morocco, too, such reverence is shown for bread that it should never touch the floor or be wasted in any way. We don't have quite the same strict view here in North America, but we do appreciate the good taste and comfort of freshly baked bread made from honest ingredients.

nutty crunch bread

MAKES 1 LOAF, 12 SLICES

There's nothing more satisfying than the aroma of bread baking in the oven or even in a bread machine, and for those who want to wake up to this wonderful fragrance, this loaf done on the overnight cycle of your machine is just the answer.

1-1/2 cups	water	375 mL
2 tbsp	vegetable oil	25 mL
2 tbsp	liquid honey	25 mL
1/3 cup	dry milk powder	75 mL
1-1/2 tsp	salt	7 mL
2 cups	all-purpose flour	500 mL
1-1/4 cups	whole wheat flour	300 mL
1/3 cup	each wheat germ, rolled oats and sunflower seeds	75 mL
3 tbsp	sesame seeds	45 mL
2-1/2 tsp	bread machine yeast	12 mL

1. Into the pan of a 1-1/2- to 2-lb (750 g to 1 kg) bread machine, add (in order) water, oil, honey, milk powder, salt, all-purpose flour, whole wheat flour, wheat germ, rolled oats, sunflower seeds, sesame seeds and yeast. (Do not let yeast touch liquid.) Choose whole wheat setting.
2. Let baked loaf cool on a rack.

By Hand:
1. Substitute active dry yeast for bread machine yeast.
2. In a saucepan, heat water to 105 to 115°F (40 to 45°C). Add yeast and 1 tsp (5 mL) of the honey; let stand for 10 minutes or until frothy.
3. In a large bowl and using a wooden spoon, stir together yeast mixture, oil and remaining honey. Stir in all-purpose and whole wheat flours, dry milk powder, wheat germ, rolled oats, sunflower seeds, sesame seeds and salt until soft dough forms.
4. Turn out onto lightly floured surface. Knead for 10 minutes or until smooth and elastic. Transfer to a large greased bowl, turning to grease all over. Cover and let rise in a warm, draft-free place for about 1 hour or until doubled in bulk.
5. Punch down dough. Form into a loaf and fit into a greased 9- x 5-inch (2 L) loaf pan. Cover and let rise for about 1 hour or until 1 inch (2.5 cm) above pan.
6. Bake in the centre of a 375°F (190°C) oven for about 45 minutes or until bottom of the loaf sounds hollow when tapped. Turn out onto a rack and let cool.

> **TIP**
> A heating pad turned to low and placed under the dough makes an excellent spot for it to rise.

rye bread

MAKES 3 LOAVES

Despite not making bread on a regular basis as I used to, I still find that kneading dough and producing a fragrant, lightly risen loaf gives me as much satisfaction as ever. But I do miss the satisfaction of teaching others to make a perfect loaf as I once did at Conestoga College in Waterloo, Ontario.

This easy rye bread is one I make every year to serve with the side of smoked salmon my brother-in-law brings from Vancouver at Christmastime. No matter what other bread I offer with the salmon, slices of this fine-textured loaf will go first. I find people eating it without the salmon ... just to savour the taste of the bread itself.

Many of the bread recipes I make I have developed over the years or I received initially from my mother, but I honestly don't know where I gleaned the idea behind this one. At one time, I thought the germ of the recipe might have come from James Beard, but I could not find it in his collection of bread recipes. All I know is that it is very old, easy and absolutely delicious. As a bonus, it freezes well for up to eight months.

2 cups	rye flour	500 mL
2 cups	boiling water	500 mL
3/4 cup	molasses	175 mL
1/3 cup	shortening or butter	75 mL
1 tbsp	salt	15 mL
1	pkg active dry yeast	1
1/2 cup	warm water	125 mL
6-1/4 cups	all-purpose flour (approx.)	1.55 L
	Cornmeal	

1. In a large bowl, combine rye flour, boiling water, molasses, shortening and salt; stir until shortening melts. Let cool.
2. In a measuring cup, sprinkle yeast on warm water and let stand for 10 minutes until bubbly. Stir and add to rye flour mixture. Gradually add enough all-purpose flour to make a stiff dough. Turn out onto a floured surface and knead for 3 or 4 minutes or until the dough springs back when you poke it with a finger. Divide into 3 pieces and shape each third into a round loaf. Place loaves on 2 cookie sheets sprinkled with cornmeal. Cover and let rise in a warm place (a heating pad on low works well) until doubled in bulk, about 2 hours.
3. Bake in a 350°F (180°C) oven for 40 to 50 minutes or until dark brown and hollow-sounding when rapped on the bottom with your knuckles. Remove to racks to cool.

whole wheat soda bread with currants and cardamom

MAKES 1 LOAF, 6 WEDGES

For a breakfast or brunch treat, butter warm wedges of this easy, delicious bread and serve with a selection of cheeses.

1 cup	each whole wheat and all-purpose flour 250 mL
2 tbsp	granulated sugar 25 mL
1-1/2 tsp	baking powder 7 mL
1/2 tsp	each baking soda and salt 2 mL
1/2 tsp	ground cardamom or cinnamon 2 mL
2 tbsp	butter 25 mL
1/2 cup	dried currants 125 mL
1 cup	buttermilk 250 mL

TOPPING
2 tsp	all-purpose flour 10 mL

1. In a large bowl, whisk together whole wheat and all-purpose flours, sugar, baking powder, baking soda, salt and cardamom. Using a pastry blender or 2 knives, cut in butter until crumbly. Stir in currants. Add buttermilk all at once; stir with a fork just until combined.

2. On a lightly floured surface and with floured hands, press dough into a ball; knead lightly 10 times. Place on a greased baking sheet or in a 9-inch (23 cm) pie plate. Gently pat into a 5-inch (12 cm) circle.

3. Topping: Sprinkle with flour. With a sharp knife, cut 1/2-inch (1 cm) deep cross on top of loaf. Bake in the centre of a 375°F (190°C) oven for 35 to 40 minutes or until tester inserted in the centre comes out clean. Slice into wedges and serve warm.

hot skillet cornbread

MAKES 6 SERVINGS

In the American South, this is a staple lunch and dinner bread used to sop up gravies and sauces. It's also delicious as a breakfast treat, served hot with butter and maple syrup or honey.

1-1/2 cups	cornmeal	375 mL
1/2 cup	all-purpose flour	125 mL
1 tsp	granulated sugar	5 mL
1 tsp	baking soda	5 mL
3/4 tsp	salt	4 mL
1	egg	1
1-1/2 cups	buttermilk	375 mL
2 tbsp	butter	25 mL

1. Heat a cast-iron or ovenproof 9-inch (23 cm) skillet in a 425°F (220°C) oven. In a large bowl, stir together cornmeal, flour, sugar, baking soda and salt. In a separate bowl, whisk egg with buttermilk.
2. Remove skillet from the oven. Quickly add butter to melt; whisk into buttermilk mixture. Return skillet to the oven.
3. Add buttermilk mixture to dry ingredients; stir just until moistened. Pour into the hot skillet and return to the centre of the oven; bake for 15 to 20 minutes or until tester inserted in the centre comes out clean. Cut into wedges and serve hot.

TIP

Use the same batter to make muffins, using melted butter. Divide among 12 greased muffin cups. Bake in the centre of a 400°F (200°C) oven for 18 to 20 minutes or until golden and tops are firm to the touch. Makes 12 muffins.

VARIATIONS

BACON AND CHEDDAR CORNBREAD

In the skillet, over medium-high heat, cook 5 strips of bacon until crisp. Drain on paper towels; chop. Drain drippings from skillet. Add bacon and 1 cup (250 mL) shredded Cheddar cheese to dry ingredients before combining with liquid.

RED PEPPER CORNBREAD

Add 1/2 cup (125 mL) diced sweet red pepper and 1 cup (250 mL) frozen corn kernels, thawed, to dry ingredients before combining with liquid.

CHORIZO AND GREEN PEPPER CORNBREAD

Add 3/4 cup (175 mL) diced cooked chorizo or other spicy cooked sausage and 1/2 cup (125 mL) diced sweet green pepper to dry ingredients before combining with liquid.

biscuits and scones

On the farm, we always had our own cream on hand, and when we'd see my mother disappear with a cup and come back with cream from the basement, we knew there would be flaky, hot tea biscuits for lunch. She would make them in a flash ... the best way, of course, to ensure that tea biscuits are light and tender.

We had all our own meat on the farm as well, and after a pig was butchered, my mother would render down the fat to make homemade pure lard that she would use for baking. One great treat after such an activity was having "scrap cakes," our name for biscuits made with the crisp pork bits left after rendering the fat. A few of these bits were added before the dough was kneaded. I found out later that such biscuits were called Pork Buns in Newfoundland, where salt pork would provide the crisp bits they called scrunchions or scuncheons.

The English cousin of tea biscuits is the scone, made very much the same way, but usually cut into triangular shapes rather than circles as biscuits are, and often brushed with a bit of egg or cream glaze.

buttermilk scones

MAKES 8 LARGE SCONES

I usually have a container of buttermilk on hand since I like to use it for such treats as pancakes and these tender scones. There is absolutely no problem now, but years ago my husband would get quite worried when he saw a carton of buttermilk in our refrigerator since each time I was pregnant I craved buttermilk!

Quick to make, these melt-in-your-mouth scones are just as suitable for an afternoon tea party as for breakfast. Accompany with your favourite jam and butter or Devon cream (if you dare).

2 cups	all-purpose flour	500 mL
2 tbsp	granulated sugar	25 mL
2 tsp	baking powder	10 mL
1/2 tsp	baking soda	2 mL
1/2 tsp	salt	2 mL
1/4 cup	each butter and shortening	50 mL
3/4 cup	buttermilk	175 mL
1	egg, beaten	1

1. In a large bowl, whisk together flour, sugar, baking powder, baking soda and salt. Using a pastry blender or 2 knives, cut in butter and shortening until the mixture resembles coarse crumbs. Make a well in the centre; pour in the buttermilk. With a fork, stir just until soft dough forms, being careful not to overmix.
2. On a lightly floured surface and with floured hands, knead dough gently about 5 times or until the dough comes together. Pat into a 1/2-inch (1 cm) thick round. With floured knife, cut into 8 wedges. Transfer to an ungreased baking sheet. Brush tops with egg.
3. Bake in the centre of a 400°F (200°C) oven for 20 minutes or until golden and crusty. Transfer to a rack; let cool for 10 minutes. Serve warm.

VARIATION

FRUITED BUTTERMILK SCONES
Add 1/2 to 1 cup (125 to 250 mL) currants, chopped dried apricots, raisins or dried cranberries to dry ingredients before adding buttermilk.

TIPS

Always shake the container of buttermilk well before using it.
If you don't have buttermilk on hand, place 2 tsp (10 mL) lemon juice or vinegar in a liquid measuring cup and pour in milk level to 3/4 cup (175 mL) and stir. Let stand for 15 minutes to produce sour milk.

angel biscuits

MAKES 48 BISCUITS OR ABOUT 2 DOZEN BIGGER ROLLS

These old-fashioned biscuits are a cross between a yeast bread and a baking powder biscuit. In the nine-teenth century, since leavening agents could be unreliable, cooks would often use more than one type in the same recipe—just for insurance—and no doubt that is how this recipe developed. The name probably came about because these are lighter than regular biscuits and have a nice fine crumb and lovely flavour, a good reason for making them even though our modern leavening agents are pretty foolproof.

I like them not only for their lovely texture, but also for the fact that they can be made up to 3 days ahead to be baked whenever you need nice fresh rolls. I remember my mother often having these on hand and either cutting them into biscuits or forming larger rolls from the dough. Mom used to make homemade hamburger buns as well; I'm not sure if this is the dough she used for them, but it certainly would do.

1	pkg active dry yeast (about 2-1/2 tsp/12 mL) 1
1/4 cup	lukewarm water 50 mL
5 cups	all-purpose flour 1.25 L
3 tbsp	granulated sugar 45 mL
4 tsp	baking powder 20 mL
2 tsp	salt 10 mL
1 cup	shortening, in bits 250 mL
1 tsp	baking soda 5 mL
2 cups	buttermilk 500 mL

1. In a measuring cup, sprinkle yeast into lukewarm water and let stand for 5 minutes or until foamy. Stir with a fork.
2. In a large bowl, whisk together the flour, sugar, baking powder and salt; cut in the shortening until the mixture resembles coarse meal. Stir the baking soda into the buttermilk and add to the flour mixture with the yeast mixture, stirring just until ingredients are moistened. Knead slightly to form a dough. Cover and refrigerate for at least 1 night and up to 3 days.
3. On a lightly floured surface, knead the dough lightly 12 times and roll out to a 1/2-inch (1 cm) thickness. With a 2-inch (5 cm) round cutter, cut out biscuits and place 1 inch (2.5 cm) apart on greased baking sheets. Or, shape by hand into bigger rolls. Cover and let rise in a warm place for about 1 hour or until doubled.
4. Bake in a 400°F (200°C) oven for about 15 minutes or until golden brown. Serve warm.

rhubarb streusel muffins

MAKES 24 MUFFINS

Years ago, every yard seemed to have a rhubarb patch. This reliable perennial would sprout up untended each spring in the corner of the garden. Those long, rosy stalks were so versatile that if you grew your own, you had the makings of many economical cakes, cobblers, muffins, preserves and pies, the latter lending the nickname "pie plant" to rhubarb.

Raw rhubarb freezes well washed and cut into 1-inch (2.5 cm) pieces. For most recipes, there's no need to thaw rhubarb; use straight from the freezer and lengthen the cooking time slightly. For baked goods like these muffins, thaw the rhubarb almost completely—leaving some ice crystals—and pat dry with paper towels before using.

STREUSEL TOPPING

1/4 cup	chopped pecans	50 mL
1/4 cup	all-purpose flour	50 mL
1/4 cup	granulated sugar	50 mL
1/4 cup	chilled butter, cubed	50 mL

MUFFINS

3	eggs	3
1 cup	vegetable oil	250 mL
1-1/2 cups	packed brown sugar	375 mL
1-1/2 tsp	vanilla	7 mL
2-1/2 cups	finely diced rhubarb (3/4 lb/375 g)	625 mL
1/2 cup	chopped pecans	125 mL
3 cups	all-purpose flour	750 mL
2 tsp	baking soda	10 mL
1-1/2 tsp	cinnamon	7 mL
1/2 tsp	each salt, baking powder, nutmeg and ground allspice	2 mL

1. Streusel Topping: In a food processor, process pecans until finely chopped. Add flour, sugar and butter; process until well combined. Transfer to a small bowl and set aside.

2. Muffins: In a large bowl and using an electric mixer, beat eggs, oil, sugar and vanilla until thick and foamy. Stir in rhubarb and pecans.

3. In a separate large bowl, combine flour, baking soda, cinnamon, salt, baking powder, nutmeg and allspice. Gradually stir dry ingredients into rhubarb mixture, just until no dry spots remain. Spoon batter into 24 greased or paper-lined muffin cups. Sprinkle streusel topping evenly over each muffin. Bake in a 350°F (180°C) oven for 25 to 30 minutes or until a tester inserted in the centre of a muffin comes out clean. Let muffins cool in the pan for 2 minutes. Remove from pan and let cool completely on a wire rack.

the best banana muffins

MAKES 12 MUFFINS

Banana muffins are my daughter's favourite, and she would often make them even when she was very young. Every time I start to make banana muffins myself, I remember the evening she set out a couple of very ripe bananas and got all of the dry ingredients ready so she could put the muffins together first thing in the morning; my husband, thinking the fruit was well past its prime, tossed the bananas out, much to Anne's chagrin. I doubt if he will ever do that again.

This particular version comes to me from my husband's sister, Alene Clark, a good cook and an excellent muffin maker. She sat down one wintry day and wrote out all of her favourite recipes for me, including this one from a Winnipeg friend for wonderfully moist muffins with crisp, sugary crowns. If Anne were making these, she might add 1/2 cup (125 mL) chocolate chips to the batter, just as she did as a child.

3 tbsp	granulated sugar 45 mL
1/2 tsp	cinnamon 2 mL
2	very ripe bananas 2
1/2 cup	packed brown sugar 125 mL
1/3 cup	shortening 75 mL
1	egg 1
1 tsp	vanilla 5 mL
1-1/2 cups	all-purpose flour 375 mL
1 tsp	each baking powder and baking soda 5 mL
1/2 tsp	salt 2 mL
1/4 cup	water 50 mL
1/2 cup	coarsely chopped walnuts or pecans 125 mL

1. In a small bowl, mix together the granulated sugar and cinnamon; set aside.

2. In a large bowl, mash the bananas well. Stir in brown sugar, shortening, egg and vanilla; beat until well mixed. Sift or stir together the flour, baking powder, baking soda and salt. Stir half the dry ingredients into the banana mixture until barely mixed; stir in water and the remaining dry ingredients just to combine. Do not overmix. Add nuts and stir just to blend them in. Spoon into twelve 2-1/2-inch (6 cm) greased muffin cups. Sprinkle tops evenly with cinnamon sugar (it will seem like a lot, but use it all) and bake in a 350°F (180°C) oven for 25 minutes or until golden and a tester inserted in the centre comes out clean.

ready-to-bake bran muffins

MAKES ABOUT 5 DOZEN MUFFINS (DEPENDING ON SIZE OF THE MUFFIN CUPS)

The only aunt I have left on both sides of my family is now in her late nineties, but still very much interested in my cookbooks and writing. When I was just starting to cook, Aunt Lexie would send me Christmas presents of cookbooks that were usually put together by church women. I loved looking through these, and I remember one of my favourite recipes was a six-week refrigerator bran muffin mix that I kept on hand when the kids were small. The recipe that made 72 muffins did keep in the refrigerator for many days, making it easy to scoop out and bake a dozen muffins whenever the need arose ... very comforting for a busy young mother to have on hand.

Many years later, when I was writing an article about Stratford, Ontario, for *Canadian Living* magazine, I interviewed many locals who ran bed and breakfast establishments around the town and gleaned some breakfast recipes for my article. The ingredients in the delicious ready-to-bake bran muffin mix that came from Flint's Inn were almost identical to those in the muffins I had been making for years. To me, this proved that really good recipes withstand the test of time.

Feel free to replace the raisins with other dried fruits such as cranberries, chopped dates or apricots and add a touch of grated orange or lemon zest.

4 cups	100% bran cereal 1 L
2 cups	boiling water 500 mL
5 cups	all-purpose flour 1.25 L
2 cups	natural bran 500 mL
2 cups	raisins 500 mL
5 tsp	baking soda 25 mL
1 tsp	salt 5 mL
2 cups	packed brown sugar 500 mL
1 cup	vegetable oil 250 mL
4	eggs 4
4 cups	buttermilk 1 L

1. In a bowl, combine the cereal and boiling water; let cool.
2. In a very large bowl, combine flour, natural bran, raisins, baking soda and salt. In a separate bowl, whisk together sugar, oil and eggs; blend in buttermilk. Pour over dry ingredients; add cereal mixture. Stir together just until moistened. (Batter can be refrigerated in an airtight container for up to 10 days.)
3. Spoon into greased or paper-lined muffin cups. Bake in a 350°F (180°C) oven for about 30 minutes or until tops are firm to the touch.

the heart
of the meal

On a cold day, when you walk into a warm house, there is an immediate sense of welcome. And if it's quiet and there's an inviting aroma coming from the kitchen, a feeling of peace and contentment surrounds you like a cozy blanket.

This is certainly one of the pleasures of cooking long-simmering stews and oven roasts or braises. It's a particularly comforting activity on a weekend day when there is time to be at home getting on with other chores.

When my children were young, I might have been working on a half-dozen magazine articles at a time. I did all the testing for these articles in my own kitchen at home. Of course, I never liked to waste anything, and my family had to eat all of the test cases ... whether they turned out well or not. It was my son who made the now-famous statement that "we only got the good stuff once." Sometimes even the good stuff was a bit on the weird side, but my family was very good about trying everything. One Sunday, I decided to dispense with testing and put a prime rib beef roast in the oven with roast potatoes and, later, Yorkshire pudding. Both Allen and Anne remarked on what an unusual dinner this was ... and how delicious.

Nothing is easier than popping a roast of beef, pork, lamb or a whole chicken into the oven, and there are a few such glorious roasts in this chapter. Pot roasts and stews are not much more demanding and have so much going for them too. Since they are good make-ahead meals, gaining more flavour if made one day and reheated another, they are perfect for preparing on the weekends so weekday meals can be quick and easy without relying on processed supermarket fare. You can be your own personal chef with complete control over the ingredients.

Many of these recipes are also economical, best made with the least expensive meat and vegetables.

Although the skillet suppers I've included here are essentially fuss free, I like to oven-bake most long-simmering one-pot meals because they need little or no stirring. With long cooking, too, the oven means more even cooking since the pot is fully surrounded by heat. For oven-baking, it's convenient to have a Dutch oven or a flameproof casserole that can go both onto the stove-top and into the oven.

There are a few casseroles in this chapter, and you'll find more throughout the menus. In the fifties, during the height of the can-opener era, the casserole was at its prime. The term "casserole" might still connote that ubiquitous tuna–noodle–mushroom soup–potato chip concoction, but we've come a long way since then. Casseroles are friendly, soothing and convenient to prepare and serve. They may take a little longer to make and dirty a few more dishes than a stew, but those dishes can be washed and put away and the casserole can be happily on its way to the family table or a potluck supper or tucked away in the refrigerator or freezer for future use.

glazed pork pot roast with tomato sauce

MAKES 6 TO 8 SERVINGS

A spicy rub goes over an inexpensive pork roast that slowly braises to moist tenderness on top of a tomato-onion sauce, and the whole thing smells so inviting as it happens. It's sheer comfort food in every respect, especially if served with Creamy Mashed Potatoes (see page 203), crisp green beans and Mary Lou's Old-Fashioned Cabbage Salad (see page 101).

1	pork shoulder or butt roast (4 to 5 lb/1.8 to 2.2 kg), boneless or bone-in 1
2	cloves garlic, slivered 2
1/4 cup	packed brown sugar 50 mL
1 tsp	each dried sage and dry mustard 5 mL
1/2 tsp	each dried thyme and salt 2 mL
1/4 tsp	each cayenne and black pepper 1 mL
2	onions, thinly sliced 2
1	can (28 oz/796 mL) crushed tomatoes* 1
1 cup	water 250 mL
1/2 cup	ketchup 125 mL
1 tbsp	Worcestershire sauce 15 mL

1. With the point of a sharp knife, make slits in the pork and insert the garlic. Combine the sugar, sage, mustard, thyme, salt, cayenne and black pepper. Rub all over the pork.
2. In a large roasting pan, combine the onions, tomatoes, water, ketchup and Worcestershire sauce. Set pork on top, cover and roast in a 350°F (180°C) oven for 2-1/4 hours.
3. Uncover and roast in a 400°F (200°C) oven for 45 minutes longer, basting pork occasionally with the sauce.
4. Remove roast to a carving board, tent with foil and let rest for 10 minutes, then carve into thick slices.
5. Meanwhile, if the sauce is too thick, thin with water and heat through. Season to taste and serve in a heated sauceboat.

* If crushed tomatoes are unavailable, use canned whole tomatoes and their juice; put them in the roasting pan and mash well with a potato masher. You may need to simmer the sauce to thicken it since these tomatoes won't make the sauce as thick as a can of crushed tomatoes will.

herbed roast pork with bread stuffing

MAKES 8 TO 10 SERVINGS

There's nothing more flavourful and succulent than a roast of pork, and this one has a classic bread stuffing. Choose a long, narrow roast to accommodate all of the stuffing. Use kitchen scissors to chop the dried apricots. The stuffing would be delicious in a small chicken as well.

2 tbsp	butter 25 mL
1	onion, chopped 1
1	stalk celery, diced 1
2 cups	cubed bread
	(2-1/2 slices) 500 mL
1 cup	chopped dried apricots 250 mL
1/4 cup	chopped fresh parsley 50 mL
3 tbsp	minced fresh sage (or 1 tbsp/
	15 mL crumbled dried) 45 mL
1 tbsp	minced fresh marjoram
	(or 1 tsp/5 mL dried) 15 mL
1/4 tsp	each salt and pepper 1 mL
4 lb	long narrow boneless (double)
	pork loin roast 1.8 kg
2 tbsp	each vegetable oil and fresh
	lemon juice 25 mL
1 tsp	each dry mustard and
	paprika 5 mL
2	cloves garlic, minced 2
1 cup	dry white wine or chicken stock
	(approx.) 250 mL
1 tbsp	cornstarch 15 mL

1. In a large skillet, melt butter over medium heat. Add onion and celery; cook, stirring, for 5 minutes, until onion starts to soften. Stir in bread, apricots, parsley, 2 tbsp (25 mL) sage, marjoram, salt and pepper. (Stuffing can be made ahead, covered and refrigerated for up to 1 day.)

2. Cut strings on roast, if any. Open out roast; pat and mound stuffing evenly over inside surface of half of the roast. Place other half on top; tie tightly in several places with string. Place roast on a rack in a roasting pan.

3. In a small bowl, stir together oil, lemon juice, mustard, paprika, garlic and remaining sage. Spread mixture over top of roast; pour wine or stock into the pan. Roast, uncovered, in a 325°F (160°C) oven for 1-1/2 to 2 hours, adding more wine or stock as necessary, until a meat thermometer registers 160°F (70°C). Remove roast to a warm platter; tent loosely with foil and let stand for 15 minutes before slicing.

4. Meanwhile, pour 1 cup (250 mL) water into pan drippings and bring to a boil, scraping up any browned bits from the bottom of the pan. In a small bowl, stir together 2 tbsp (25 mL) cold water and cornstarch, until smooth. Stir cornstarch mixture into gravy and cook, stirring, until thickened and smooth. Pour gravy (straining if desired) into a warmed pitcher or gravy boat and serve with the pork.

honey-garlic barbecued ribs

MAKES 4 SERVINGS

Since Europeans use a knife and fork for every kind of food, our Belgian exchange student was intrigued when we introduced her to a few meals we eat with our fingers—hamburgers and corn on the cob, for example. By the time we served barbecued ribs, Sofie had been with us long enough to make this comment: "You Canadians certainly eat with your hands a lot!" It's quite true that food like these "finger-licking-good" ribs are enjoyed most by picking them up and forgetting about those knives and forks. Just provide a lot of serviettes.

3 lb	pork back or meaty side ribs 1.5 kg
3/4 cup	ketchup 175 mL
4	cloves garlic, minced 4
1/4 cup	liquid honey 50 mL
2 tbsp	each Worcestershire sauce and soy sauce 25 mL
1 tbsp	each vinegar and Dijon mustard 15 mL
1 tsp	hot pepper sauce (or to taste) 5 mL

1. Remove excess fat from ribs and cut them into 2- or 3-rib pieces. Place in a large saucepan. Cover with cold water and bring to a boil, skimming off any froth; reduce heat, cover and simmer for 40 to 45 minutes or until meat is tender. Drain well and arrange in a single layer in a large shallow glass dish. Set aside.

2. Combine ketchup, garlic, honey, Worcestershire sauce, soy sauce, vinegar, mustard and hot pepper sauce. Pour over ribs, turning to coat well. Cover and marinate in the refrigerator for 4 hours or up to 24 hours, turning occasionally.

3. Reserving marinade in the dish, place ribs on a greased grill over medium-high heat; cook, brushing often with marinade and turning once, for about 10 minutes or until hot and glazed.

NOTE
Since the ribs are cooked when you pour the marinade over them, you can use it to brush over the ribs as they heat on the grill without any danger of cross-contamination as you would have with raw meat.

VARIATION

OVEN-BARBECUED RIBS
Instead of boiling the ribs, place in a roasting pan, sprinkle with salt and pepper and bake, uncovered, in a 400°F (200°C) oven for 30 minutes. Pour ketchup mixture over ribs, cover pan and roast in a 350°F (180°C) oven for 1 hour or until ribs are tender, basting once or twice.

pork chop skillet stroganoff

Now that there are only two in our household, I like simple recipes like this one to cook on busy weeknights. As quick accompaniments, cook two nests of egg noodles, adding frozen green peas for the last three minutes of cooking time.

2	loin pork chops (about 1 lb/ 500 g total) 2	
2 cups	sliced mushrooms 500 mL	
1	clove garlic, minced 1	
	Salt and pepper	
1/3 cup	light sour cream 75 mL	
2 tsp	Worcestershire sauce 10 mL	
2 tsp	Dijon mustard 10 mL	

1. Trim excess fat from chops. In a large skillet, over medium heat, melt just enough fat to lightly grease the bottom. Add chops and cook over medium heat for 5 minutes without turning or lifting.

2. Add mushrooms and garlic to 1 side of skillet; cook for 5 minutes, stirring mushroom mixture only. Turn chops over; sprinkle with salt and pepper to taste. Cover and cook over low heat for 2 to 5 minutes or until chops are no longer pink inside. Stir in sour cream, Worcestershire sauce and mustard; heat through without boiling.

spanish braised pork chops with peppers and olives

MAKES 4 SERVINGS

Good cooks around the world have known for years that inexpensive cuts of meat can be delicious when gently braised to tender succulence.

The basics of braising are easy: brown the meat well, add a small amount of liquid, add aromatic seasonings to the pan, cover and simmer gently over very low heat until the meat is deliciously tender.

4	pork shoulder butt chops (about 2 lb/1 kg total) 4
	Salt, pepper and all-purpose flour
2 tbsp	olive oil (approx.) 25 mL
1	onion, thickly sliced 1
1	bay leaf 1
1-1/2 cups	coarsely chopped canned tomatoes with juice 375 mL
1/2 cup	water 125 mL
1	red or yellow sweet pepper, sliced 1
4 oz	prosciutto, coarsely chopped 125 g
4	cloves garlic, thinly sliced 4
1 tsp	paprika 5 mL
1/4 tsp	hot pepper flakes 1 mL
12	pitted black olives, cut lengthwise into halves 12
2 tbsp	chopped fresh parsley 25 mL

1. Trim fat from the edges of the chops. Sprinkle chops on both sides with salt and pepper; dust with flour. In a large skillet, over medium-high heat, heat 1 tbsp (15 mL) oil (less if using a nonstick pan). Brown the chops, 2 at a time, adding a little more oil if necessary. Remove chops to a plate. Discard all but 1 tbsp (15 mL) fat from the pan. Add onion and bay leaf; cook over medium heat, stirring often, for 5 minutes or until onion is softened.

2. Stir in tomatoes, water, sweet pepper, prosciutto, garlic, paprika and hot pepper flakes; bring to a boil. Return chops to the skillet, spooning sauce over the meat. Add olives, reduce heat to low, cover and simmer for 30 to 40 minutes or until chops are very tender. Stir in parsley.

> **VARIATION**
>
> **SPANISH BRAISED LAMB CHOPS WITH PEPPERS AND OLIVES**
> Substitute lamb shoulder chops for the pork and reduce the cooking time to about 20 minutes.

satisfying stews

When you are in a country that you think is always warm, but the weather turns cold, you feel even colder than you would at home at the same temperature. This is what happened near the end of November one year when we were renting a villa in the south of Spain. At the beginning of the month, we were wearing shorts and cooling off with refreshing gazpacho. Later in the month, the cold wind outside demanded heartier fare.

Since we were entertaining the neighbours one weekend, I decided to attempt to make Cocido Madrileno (a kind of stew of boiled beef and chickpeas—and almost everything else you might find at a market). Cocido rivals paella and gazpacho in popularity, but our neighbours—who were from England—had never tasted it.

Cocido began as a staple meal in central Spain because of its inexpensive and easy-to-obtain ingredients. Now, however, it has become a special-occasion meal that takes a couple of days to make and some searching for the ingredients.

Most of those ingredients were to be found at a butcher shop, and since I had a favourite one in the market of a nearby town, I set about to devise a list of what I needed. I gathered around me all the dictionaries and phrase books the villa contained, and as I wrote down the Spanish words for each type of meat (chicken, beef, bacon, chorizo sausage, blood sausage, cured ham and beef bones), I drew a little picture of the animal that would have given up such a part.

The butcher was a big, handsome, pleasant-looking man who took my list very seriously. Each time he came to a sketch for a different animal, he would make the noise of the animal; by the time we finished, despite my poor attempts at art, I left with exactly what I needed for my stew. As the butcher pored over my list, I took his picture, which I used in a newspaper article later. The next year, when friends brought him a copy of the article, he remembered the Canadian with her poor Spanish and interesting shopping list.

I'm not including the recipe for Cocido Madrileno here since it would be difficult for readers to collect all of the necessary ingredients without the help of my friendly Spanish butcher, but there are plenty of easier stews and other braised dishes that will fill your kitchens with the comforting aroma of good food to come.

classic beef stew

MAKES 8 SERVINGS

The secret to good stew is to let it cook for a long time at a very low heat, preferably in the oven since that method requires no stirring.

I always check the price of beef stewing cubes, pot roasts such as blade or cross rib and simmering steaks and buy the least expensive. Never use a more expensive oven roast or grilling steak since the texture and flavour won't be as good for this type of slow cooking.

2 lb	stewing beef 1 kg
1/2 cup	all-purpose flour 125 mL
	Salt and pepper
4	carrots 4
3	stalks celery 3
Half	rutabaga Half
3	onions 3
1	leek (or an additional onion) 1
1/4 cup	vegetable oil (approx.) 50 mL
3	cloves garlic, minced 3
2-1/2 cups	beef stock 625 mL
1-1/4 cups	dry red wine (or additional stock) 300 mL
1	can (5-1/2 oz/156 mL) tomato paste 1
2 tbsp	Worcestershire sauce 25 mL
1 tsp	dried thyme 5 mL
1	bay leaf 1
Pinch	hot pepper flakes Pinch
3	potatoes, peeled and cubed 3
1/2 lb	mushrooms, halved or quartered 250 g
2 tbsp	chopped fresh parsley 25 mL

1. If not using stewing cubes, cut beef into 1-1/2-inch (4 cm) cubes. In a sturdy plastic bag, combine beef, flour and 1 tsp (5 mL) each salt and pepper; set aside.
2. Cut carrots and celery into 2-inch (5 cm) chunks. Peel rutabaga and cut into 2-inch (5 cm) chunks. Keeping them separate from the other vegetables, quarter onions and thickly slice leek.
3. In a large skillet, heat 1 tbsp (15 mL) oil over medium heat. Add onions and leek; cook for 5 minutes, stirring often. With a slotted spoon, remove to a large, heavy ovenproof saucepan or casserole.
4. Increase the heat under the skillet to medium-high and add 1 tbsp (15 mL) more oil. Shaking off excess flour, brown floured beef in batches, adding more oil as necessary and removing browned meat to the onion pan. Reserve extra flour.
5. Add carrots, celery, rutabaga and garlic to the skillet; cook for 3 minutes over medium heat, adding a bit more oil if needed. With a slotted spoon, remove to onion pan. Stir reserved flour into skillet and cook, stirring, for 1 minute. Add stock and bring to a boil, stirring up any brown bits from the bottom of the pan. Whisk in the wine, tomato paste, Worcestershire sauce, thyme, bay leaf and hot pepper flakes. Bring to a boil, whisking. Pour over meat mixture, bring to a boil, cover tightly and place in a 325°F (160°C) oven for 1-1/2 hours. (Alternatively, simmer over low heat on top of the stove for about 1 hour, stirring often.)
6. Stir in potatoes and mushrooms; bake, covered, for 60 to 75 minutes longer or until beef and vegetables are fork-tender. (Alternatively, simmer over low heat on top of the stove for about 30 minutes, stirring often.) Remove bay leaf; taste and adjust seasoning. (Stew can be made, cooled, covered and refrigerated for up to 2 days or frozen for up to 1 month.) Sprinkle with parsley to serve.

the magic of christmas

Each year, sometime before December 25, we'll pull out the worn boxes of garlands and coloured lights. I'll take my collection of Santas out of their year-round hiding places and crowd them onto the hall table. We'll receive a mountain of cards from friends and relatives we haven't seen for decades. I'll find my mother's spattered fruitcake recipe, hoping to duplicate what nostalgia remembers so deliciously. My daughter-in-law, Cherrie, and I will spend a Saturday baking all of the Christmas cookies on my son, Allen's, list of favourites (not that he gets to eat many of them since we give boxes to neighbours and friends). My daughter, Anne, will keep in touch, telling us what cookies she's made or about the fresh tree shipped to her home in Bermuda from Quebec. And, of course, the most exciting Christmas was in 2002 when Anne's husband, Rob, e-mailed us pictures of our first grandchild born four days earlier.

We'll put up the tree just where it was last year, and decorate it to the sound of Dylan Thomas reading "A Child's Christmas in Wales." If my husband, Kent, has trouble getting the tree to stand upright, I'll retire to the kitchen to make another batch of shortbread. There will be decorations the kids made when they were little, the funny antique Santas my mother had on her childhood tree one hundred years ago, and zany new decorations my friends know I love. Not a designer tree for certain, but an eclectic Murray version.

There will be the same activities and visiting—calling on friends, having Kent's family here for a Clark Christmas around December 18, and my family here on Christmas Day, when the food will be the traditional Murray fare: roast goose, whipped potatoes, rutabaga and fiddleheads.

Every year, I will think, too, of my childhood Christmases of so long ago. As I now do, my mother would start preparing weeks in advance. The fruitcakes and steamed puddings would have to be made early so they could "ripen" for the best flavour and texture.

My father would have been raising his special flock of turkeys all year for the big day, but when the time came for him to get them "ready" for his select customers (some of whom turned out to be my future husband's family), he would have nothing to do with their killing. He was just too attached to this feathery bunch he used to greet each time he walked near their pen, receiving the appropriate *gobble gobble* back.

Christmas Eves were particularly memorable on the farm. After our usual poking around to see what was under the tree (my father right in there on his knees with all the kids), we would head off to the late-night church service in the brisk, cold winter air. I remember one year having to go by horse and sleigh because the roads were all blocked with snow, but braving the cold seemed worthwhile when we gathered inside our wee candlelit church with our good friends and neighbours. Once home, we would set out big flat soup bowls for Santa to fill instead of hanging stockings ... maybe because we didn't have a fireplace, or maybe because this was a tradition in my mother's family, and holidays are all about traditions.

big batch slow-cooked beef stew

MAKES ABOUT 15 SERVINGS

I was asked to appear on a live television show in Toronto on the same day we had planned to have my husband's family for our traditional Christmas get-together. The show started at one, and since it was the Friday before the holidays I had no idea how long it would take me to get home after it finished at two o'clock. This meant I would be away for most of the day ... with thirteen people coming for supper. When I told my friends the Slimmons about this dilemma, they passed along a recipe they had used for a family gathering just the week before. It was from a friend of theirs who had found it in an American magazine some years ago.

When recipes are passed along like this it is often impossible to find their origin. The unusual method of not browning the meat and letting it stew away for hours in the oven was apparently first found in an old community cookbook and probably called something like Busy Day Stew. I obviously cannot take credit for the method, but I did put my own stamp on the ingredients, and the stew turned out to be absolutely delicious and just the answer for a very busy day ... even busier than I had imagined since my daughter in Bermuda went into labour that day with our first grandchild.

This would also be a comforting meal to come home to after a day of play, perhaps on the ski hills. All you need is a crusty loaf of bread or two and a green salad to go alongside, and supper is ready for the gang.

5 lb	lean stewing beef, in cubes 2.2 kg	1 cup	dry red wine 250 mL
1-1/2 lb	mini carrots 750 g	1/2 cup	minute tapioca 125 mL
10	small onions, quartered 10	1/4 cup	packed brown sugar 50 mL
8	large parsnips, cubed 8	2 tbsp	Worcestershire sauce 25 mL
8	potatoes, peeled and cubed 8		
6	cloves garlic, minced 6		
4 tsp	each dry mustard and black pepper 20 mL		
2 tsp	each salt, celery seeds and dried thyme 10 mL		
4 cups	vegetable cocktail 1 L		
1	can (10 oz/284 mL) consommé, diluted 1		

1. In a very large roasting pan, combine beef, carrots, onions, parsnips, potatoes, garlic, mustard, pepper, salt, celery seeds and thyme. In a bowl, stir together vegetable cocktail, consommé, wine, tapioca, brown sugar and Worcestershire sauce until brown sugar is dissolved. Stir into meat mixture until everything is well distributed. Cover tightly and cook in a 275°F (140°C) oven for 7 hours without lifting the lid.

classic pot roast

MAKES 6 TO 8 SERVINGS

A pot roast is the ultimate comfort food. Turn any leftovers into a beef pie by dicing the beef and vegetables, then stirring those into the gravy and topping with biscuits or a puff pastry crust.

1	boneless cross rib or blade beef roast (4 lb/1.8 kg) 1
	Salt and pepper
2 tbsp	vegetable oil 25 mL
3	onions, thickly sliced 3
4	carrots, thickly sliced 4
2	stalks celery, thickly sliced 2
4	cloves garlic, minced 4
1	can or bottle (12 oz/355 mL or 11 oz/341 mL) beer (or 1-1/2 cups/375 mL beef broth) 1
1 cup	crushed or diced canned tomatoes 250 mL
2 tsp	Dijon mustard 10 mL
1/2 tsp	dried thyme 2 mL
1	bay leaf 1
6	potatoes, peeled and quartered 6
3	parsnips, thickly sliced 3
2 tbsp	cornstarch 25 mL
1/4 cup	cold water 50mL

1. Sprinkle the beef all over with salt and pepper. Place on a rack in a shallow pan and roast in a 450°F (230°C) oven for 20 minutes.
2. Meanwhile, in a large Dutch oven or ovenproof casserole, heat oil over medium heat. Cook onions, stirring often, for 8 minutes. Add carrots and cook for 3 minutes. Add celery and garlic; cook for 1 minute. Stir in beer, tomatoes, mustard, thyme and bay leaf. Bring to a boil, stirring. Add beef and any drippings from the roasting pan; cover pan tightly. Place in a 325°F (160°C) oven and roast for 2 hours.
3. Turn roast over; add potatoes and parsnips. Cover and roast another 60 to 70 minutes or until vegetables are tender and meat is very tender. (Recipe can be completed a day ahead of serving. Cool, cover and refrigerate. Remove any fat and gently reheat to serve.)
4. Remove beef to a cutting board and tent with foil to keep warm. Remove vegetables to a warm platter and keep warm. Heat gravy to simmering. Dissolve cornstarch in cold water and stir into gravy; cook over medium heat, stirring, until thick and smooth. Slice the beef, add to platter and pass gravy in a warm sauceboat.

mushroom barbecued pot roast

MAKES 6 SERVINGS

You don't think of cooking on the grill when someone mentions pot roast, but less-than-tender cuts, wrapped in foil with herbs and mushrooms, roast to fork-only perfection on the barbecue.

1-1/2 tsp	each dried thyme and dry mustard 7 mL
1/2 tsp	black pepper 2 mL
1	chuck short rib or blade beef roast (4 lb/1.8 kg) 1
6 cups	sliced mushrooms (about 1 lb/500 g) 1.5 L
2 tbsp	dry sherry or beef stock 25 mL
1 tbsp	each vegetable oil and Worcestershire sauce 15 mL

SAUCE

	Beef stock
1 tbsp	cornstarch 15 mL
2 tbsp	cold water 25 mL

1. Combine thyme, mustard and pepper; rub all over meat.
2. Sprinkle half of the mushrooms in the middle of a piece of heavy-duty foil large enough to wrap roast; place roast on top. Sprinkle with remaining mushrooms; drizzle with sherry and half of the oil. Loosely wrap foil over roast, sealing tightly; wrap with a second piece of foil.
3. Place roast on a greased grill over medium heat; close the lid and cook, turning often, for about 2 hours or until meat thermometer registers 170°F (75°C) for well done.
4. Remove roast from the foil, reserving mushrooms and juices in a measuring cup for the sauce. Place roast on the grill; cook, turning once and brushing with remaining oil and Worcestershire sauce, for about 10 minutes longer or until browned. Remove roast to a cutting board and tent with foil; let stand for 10 minutes before carving.
5. Sauce: Meanwhile, add enough stock to the mushrooms and juices to make 2 cups (500 mL); pour into a saucepan and bring to a boil. Dissolve cornstarch in cold water; stir into pan and cook, stirring, for about 1 minute or until thickened and bubbly. Serve with the roast.

oven-barbecued brisket

MAKES 8 SERVINGS

The aroma of this easy-to-put-together and even-easier-to-tend brisket will have helpers rushing to the kitchen to mash the potatoes and cook the carrot and broccoli side dishes.

6	onions 6
4	cloves garlic, chopped 4
1 tbsp	vegetable oil 15 mL
1	beef brisket (5 to 6 lb/2.2 to 2.7 kg) 1
1 tsp	each salt, pepper and paprika 5 mL
2 cups	beef stock 500 mL
2/3 cup	each ketchup and red wine vinegar 150 mL
3 tbsp	packed brown sugar 45 mL
2 tbsp	each Worcestershire sauce and soy sauce 25 mL
1 tsp	Dijon mustard 5 mL
1/2 tsp	hot pepper sauce 2 mL

1. Slice onions thinly; separate into rings. Toss with garlic and oil; arrange over the bottom of a roasting pan. Top with brisket, fat side up; rub salt, pepper and paprika over top of the meat.
2. Combine beef stock, ketchup, vinegar, sugar, Worcestershire sauce, soy sauce, mustard and hot pepper sauce; pour over the meat. Cover and bake in a 325°F (160°C) oven, turning over halfway through, for 3-1/2 to 4 hours or until meat is very tender.
3. Transfer meat to a serving platter and tent with foil; let stand for 10 minutes. Skim fat from the sauce. Slice meat thinly and serve with the sauce in a sauceboat.

braised beefsteak with red wine

MAKES 6 TO 8 SERVINGS

This comfort classic is an update on Swiss steak, which I made often in the sixties when I was first married. Browning the meat well and cooking the onions until they are caramelized enriches the flavour and colour. Serve with Creamy Mashed Potatoes (see page 203).

2 lb	round steak 1 kg	
3 tbsp	all-purpose flour 45 mL	
2 tbsp	vegetable oil (approx.) 25 mL	
	Salt and pepper	
3	onions, thinly sliced 3	
1 cup	dry red wine 250 mL	
1 cup	beef stock 250 mL	
1 lb	mini carrots 500 g	
1	celery stalk, diced 1	

1. Pat steak dry with paper towels and trim off fat. Sprinkle one side with half of the flour and pound in with the side of a plate. Repeat on the other side. Cut steak into 6 to 8 serving-sized pieces.

2. In a large ovenproof skillet or casserole, heat half the oil over medium-high heat. Working in batches, brown beef on both sides, sprinkling with salt and pepper. Add a little more oil between batches if necessary. Remove steak to a plate.

3. Reduce heat to medium and add 1 tbsp (15 mL) oil. Add onions and cook for about 10 minutes until softened and browned. Add wine, increase heat and bring to a boil, stirring up any bits in the bottom; boil until liquid is reduced by half. Stir in stock and bring to a boil. Add carrots and celery; place steak (and any juices) on top. Cover tightly. Transfer to a 325°F (160°C) oven for 1 to 2 hours or until meat is very tender.

meat and cheese loaf

MAKES 4 SERVINGS

In the eighties, I wrote a whole article for *Homemakers* magazine on meat loaf with half a dozen recipes that used everything from sausage to salmon. In fact, my children claim they knew there would be meat loaf for dinner on the day I cleaned out the fridge. It seems that this inexpensive family-style supper staple will never go out of style. Actually, meat loaf, a hold-over from "the good old days," still fits into today's lifestyle because it's convenient and easy to make. You can put it together in the morning or even the night before. In fact, meat loaf is better if you can refrigerate it for at least one hour to allow the flavour to develop and the loaf to firm up.

In cool weather, meat loaf is a cozy focal point for an easy oven meal. Just pop in some potatoes and squash to bake alongside it, put your feet up and wait for the delicious aroma to waft your way. In summer, cold meat loaves are perfect for a salad plate, and slices of cold loaf make awesome sandwiches.

My favourite aunt, Lexie Armstrong, gave me one of the recipes in my meat loaf article. Lexie was married to my Uncle George, who wanted only plain meat and potatoes—and lots of them. I can imagine Aunt Lexie, who was an excellent cook and perhaps a little tired of preparing the same old meals all the time, sneaking in a few cubes of cheese and bits of green pepper to overcome culinary boredom.

It is no wonder this old recipe has survived over the years; it is quick, easy, moist and delicious.

1	egg	1
1 cup	milk	250 mL
1/2 cup	fine cracker crumbs	125 mL
Half	onion, chopped	Half
Half	sweet green pepper, chopped	Half
1/2 tsp	salt	2 mL
1/4 tsp	black pepper	1 mL
Pinch	groud mace*	Pinch
1 lb	lean ground beef	500 g
3/4 cup	diced mild Cheddar cheese	175 mL

1. In a large bowl, beat egg with a fork; blend in milk, cracker crumbs, onion, green pepper, salt, pepper and mace.
2. Gently mix in the beef, then the cheese; pack into a 9- x 5-inch (2 L) loaf pan and bake in a 350°F (180°C) oven for 1 hour and 15 minutes or until browned and a meat thermometer registers 170°F (75°C). Let stand for 5 minutes; drain off any fat.

* Mace is the orange outer web on the nutmeg shell. Since you probably won't use it often, buy a small amount of ground mace in a bulk store.

> **TIPS**
> To keep it tender, don't overwork ground beef. To make cracker crumbs, place 12 soda crackers in a plastic bag, close the bag and roll with a rolling pin.

italian meatball shepherd's pie

MAKES 4 SERVINGS

Creamy mashed potatoes enriched with Parmesan cheese top a layer of Italian-style meatballs. This is the ultimate in comfy casseroles.

1 lb	lean ground beef 500 g
2	cloves garlic, minced 2
	Salt and pepper
2 tbsp	cold water 25 mL
2 tbsp	all-purpose flour 25 mL
1 tbsp	olive oil 15 mL
1	small onion, chopped 1
1-1/2 cups	canned tomatoes with juice 375 mL
1/2 tsp	each dried basil and oregano 2 mL
3	large baking potatoes, peeled and quartered 3
1	egg, beaten 1
1 cup	freshly grated Parmesan cheese 250 mL
2 tbsp	chopped fresh parsley 25 mL

1. In a bowl, mix together the beef, half of the garlic, 1/4 tsp (1 mL) each salt and pepper, and cold water; gently form into 1-1/2-inch (4 cm) balls.
2. In a shallow dish, combine flour with a pinch each salt and pepper; roll meatballs in flour to coat.
3. In a large nonstick skillet, heat half of the oil over medium heat; cook meatballs, in batches, until browned all over. Remove to a plate and set aside.
4. Add remaining oil to the skillet; cook onion and remaining garlic, stirring occasionally, for 5 minutes. Stir in tomatoes, basil, oregano and meatballs; simmer, uncovered and stirring often, for 15 minutes.
5. Meanwhile, in a saucepan of boiling water, cook potatoes for 20 minutes or until tender. Drain well; mash until smooth. Stir in egg, 3/4 cup (175 mL) of the Parmesan cheese, and salt and pepper to taste. Stir in parsley.
6. Spoon meatball mixture into an 8-inch (2 L) square baking dish. Spread potato mixture over top. Sprinkle with remaining Parmesan. (Casserole can be prepared to this point, covered and refrigerated for up to 1 day; bring to room temperature before baking.)
7. Cover and bake in a 350°F (180°C) oven for 45 minutes. Uncover and bake for 10 minutes. Broil for 1 minute or until cheese is golden.

braised veal chops, osso bucco style

MAKES 4 SERVINGS

Traditionally made with veal shanks, this Italian classic is equally delicious and cooks more quickly with veal shoulder chops. Serve with polenta, pasta or mashed potatoes.

4	veal shoulder chops (about 2 lb/1 kg total) 4
	Salt, pepper and all-purpose flour
2 tbsp	olive oil (approx.) 25 mL
1	onion, chopped 1
2	each carrots and celery stalks, finely diced 2
2	cloves garlic, minced 2
1	strip lemon zest (about 4 inches/10 cm) 1
1/2 cup	dry white wine or vermouth 125 mL
1 cup	chicken stock 250 mL
1 cup	chopped canned plum tomatoes with juice 250 mL
3	sprigs Italian parsley 3
1	bay leaf 1

GREMOLATA

2 tbsp	finely chopped Italian parsley 25 mL
1	clove garlic, minced 1
2 tsp	minced lemon zest 10 mL

1. Sprinkle both sides of chops with salt and pepper; dust with flour. In a large skillet, heat 1 tbsp (15 mL) olive oil over medium-high heat. Brown chops, 2 at a time, adding a little more oil if needed. Remove chops to a plate. Add 1 tbsp (15 mL) oil to the skillet.

2. Reduce heat to medium. Add onion, carrots and celery; cook, stirring often, for about 10 minutes or until softened. Add garlic, lemon zest, wine, stock, tomatoes, parsley, bay leaf, and a little salt and pepper. Bring to a boil, stirring; reduce heat to a simmer. Return chops to the skillet, spooning sauce over meat. Cover and simmer for 40 minutes or until very tender. Discard bay leaf.

3. Gremolata: Mix parsley with garlic and lemon zest. Sprinkle over chops.

VARIATION

BRAISED LAMB CHOPS, OSSO BUCCO STYLE
Substitute lamb shoulder chops for the veal chops and reduce cooking time to about 20 minutes.

TIP

I keep a bottle of vermouth in the cupboard and use it when a recipe calls for white wine. Vermouth stores well and is generally less acidic in recipes.

liver en brochette

MAKES 4 SERVINGS

When we moved from Owen Sound to Cambridge, Ontario, our children were quite young and seemed to love our beautiful tree-lined street. It was filled with friendly, lovely people, one of whom asked us in for tea shortly after our move. At the time, I was in the middle of writing a rather long article for *Canadian Living* magazine on organ or variety meats. After a diet of tripe, sweetbreads, liver, tongue and heart for several days, my daughter decided to take matters into her own hands. She went to our new friend's house, knocked on the door and asked, "Mrs. Dunning, what are you having for supper?" Chicken appealed to her more at that point than liver again, so she stayed when invited. I'm sure our friend Fredda wondered what kind of household had moved in after Anne's litany of our last few meals. Now, of course, one of Anne's favourite foods in the whole world is foie gras, and I still remember her ordering sweetbreads in a restaurant in Paris during a trip there when she was sixteen.

On the farm, we butchered our own animals, so we used every part of them, from the nose to the tail. As a result, I grew up enjoying the best and freshest of organ meats. Liver is especially good if it is just hours old. The cardinal rule in cooking liver is not to toughen it with overcooking.

1 lb	calves' liver 500 g
8	slices bacon, halved 8
2	onions, quartered 2
1	small green pepper, cut in 1-1/2 inch (4 cm) pieces 1
1/2 lb	mushrooms 250 g
4	tomatoes, quartered 4
	Salt

MARINADE

2 tbsp	vegetable oil 25 mL
2 tbsp	white vinegar 25 mL
2 tsp	Dijon mustard 10 mL
1 tsp	Worcestershire sauce 5 mL
	Black pepper

1. Wipe liver with paper towel and remove any tubes. Cut into 1-1/2-inch (4 cm) cubes.
2. Using skewers, thread liver pieces with bacon piece by weaving bacon in and out between liver pieces; then skewer pieces of onion, green pepper and mushroom. Repeat with liver, bacon and vegetables (leaving room for tomatoes to be added later since they take less time to cook) until all are used. Place skewers in a shallow baking pan.
3. Marinade: In a small bowl, stir together oil, vinegar, mustard, Worcestershire sauce and pepper to taste. Brush over meat and vegetables. Marinate for 30 minutes at room temperature or longer in the refrigerator.
4. Preheat broiler and grill brochettes 4 inches (10 cm) from the heat for about 3 minutes on each side. As you turn skewers, add 1 tomato piece to the end of each. Sprinkle with salt and serve immediately.

braised lamb chop curry

MAKES 4 SERVINGS

Lamb shoulder chops don't take long to simmer to a nice tenderness. If I have leftover roast lamb, I will make the sauce, starting with cooking the onion, and let it simmer for 10 minutes, then add cubed cooked lamb to heat through for about 5 minutes. Serve the curry with rice, chutney and a cucumber salad dressed with yogurt.

4	lamb shoulder chops (about 1-1/2 lb/750 g total) 4
2 tbsp	olive oil 25 mL
1	onion, chopped 1
2	stalks celery, chopped 2
1	large apple, peeled and chopped 1
1	clove garlic, minced 1
1/3 cup	raisins 75 mL
2 tbsp	curry powder 25 mL
1 cup	beef stock 250 mL
1/2 cup	tomato sauce 125 mL
1 tbsp	cider vinegar 15 mL
1	bay leaf 1

1. Trim excess fat from chops. In a large deep skillet, over medium-high heat, heat oil and brown chops well on both sides. Remove to a plate.
2. Add onion to the skillet and cook over medium heat until softened. Add celery, apple, garlic, raisins and curry powder. Cook, stirring often, for 3 minutes.
3. Stir in stock, tomato sauce and vinegar; add bay leaf and bring to a boil. Return chops to the pan, spooning sauce over the meat. Reduce heat to low, cover and simmer for about 20 minutes or until chops are very tender. Discard bay leaf.

moroccan lamb shanks with chickpeas

MAKES 6 SERVINGS

There is something so satisfying about a slow-cooked, braised dish like these lamb shanks burbling away for hours, melding flavours and creating a mouth-watering, tender texture. Serve with couscous and a crisp green salad.

2 tbsp	olive oil (approx.) 25 mL
6	small lamb shanks 6
	Salt and pepper
2	onions, chopped 2
1 tbsp	minced fresh ginger 15 mL
4	cloves garlic, minced 4
2	jalapeño peppers, minced 2
1 tbsp	ground cumin 15 mL
1 tbsp	ground coriander 15 mL
2 tsp	paprika 10 mL
1 tsp	black pepper 5 mL
1 cup	chopped drained canned tomatoes 250 mL
2-1/2 cups	chicken broth 625 mL
1	can (19 oz/540 mL) chickpeas, drained and rinsed 1
1/4 tsp	saffron threads 1 mL
1	piece (1 inch/2.5 cm) cinnamon stick 1
6	carrots, sliced lengthwise and cut into 2-inch (5 cm) lengths 6
1 cup	dried apricots (6 oz/175 g) 250 mL
2 tsp	honey 10 mL
	Chopped fresh coriander

1. In a large Dutch oven or ovenproof casserole, heat half the oil over medium-high heat. Brown shanks in batches, adding more oil as needed. Remove to a plate and sprinkle with salt and pepper.

2. Reduce heat to medium. Add onions and more oil if needed; cook until soft, about 5 minutes.

3. Stir together ginger, garlic, jalapeño peppers, cumin, coriander, paprika and pepper. Stir half into the onions and cook for 1 minute. Stir in tomatoes and chicken broth; bring to a boil. Return shanks and any juices. Bring back to a boil. Cover tightly and bake in a 325°F (160°C) oven for 1-1/2 hours.

4. Stir in chickpeas, remaining ginger-spice mixture, saffron, cinnamon, carrots, apricots and honey. Cover and return to the oven for 45 to 60 minutes or until lamb and carrots are very tender. Serve sprinkled generously with coriander.

> **TIP**
>
> Usually, the method for making couscous is on the box. If not, bring 1-1/2 cups (375 mL) water to a boil in a medium saucepan; add 1 cup (250 mL) couscous and 1/2 tsp (2 mL) salt. Remove from the heat. Let stand, covered, for 5 minutes or until couscous is tender and the water is absorbed; fluff with a fork.

traditional roast leg of lamb

MAKES 6 TO 8 SERVINGS

Although I do remember, as a child on our farm, feeding young lambs with a bottle, I really don't recall our eating much lamb then ... perhaps a good thing. I did, however, acquire a love of roast leg of lamb while attending university. My landlady often roasted lamb for Sunday dinner in the traditional British way. Despite creating hundreds of lamb recipes for magazine articles and for a special client over the years, I still like this way of cooking lamb best.

My English friend Catherine Betts always makes Yorkshire pudding with leg of lamb, and crisply roasted potatoes are an excellent accompaniment. Sometimes, I'll toss thinly sliced potatoes with a bit of olive oil, salt and pepper and put them in the roasting pan right under the rack on which the lamb sits.

1	leg of lamb (5 to 6 lb/2.2 to 2.7 kg), bone in 1
4	cloves garlic, minced 4
1 tbsp	chopped fresh rosemary (or 2 tsp/10 mL dried, crumbled) 15 mL
1 tsp	each coarse salt and black pepper 5 mL

1. Trim the lamb of excess fat, but leave the parchment-like covering or fell on it. Pierce the leg in 8 to 10 places with a sharp paring knife.
2. In a small bowl, combine garlic, rosemary, salt and pepper. Rub over the lamb, pressing it into the incisions with your fingers.
3. Place the leg, fat side up, on a rack in a shallow roasting pan. Roast, uncovered, in a 500°F (260°C) oven for 20 minutes. Reduce heat to 375°F (190°C) and roast another 40 to 60 minutes or until a meat thermometer registers 130°F (55°C) to 140°F (60°C) for rare. (It will continue to cook somewhat after it is removed from the oven; for mildest and best flavour, serve rare.) Transfer to a heated platter and tent with foil; let rest for 15 minutes before carving.

how do you tell a young chick from an old hen?

In the poultry world, it's not a matter of wrinkles, but it *is* a matter of weight.

Broilers are 2-1/3 to 3 pounds (1.17 to 1.5 kg) and are best broiled, fried or braised. Fryers, weighing in at 3 to 4 pounds (1.5 to 1.8 kg) are basically used the same way as broilers.

Roasters, on the other hand, at 4 to 6 pounds (1.8 to 2.7 kg) or more, have more meat per pound than smaller birds, are good for such uses as frying or broiling and are excellent for roasting as well. You sometimes have to go directly to a small farmer for these birds.

Now, capons, at 6 to 9 pounds (2.7 to 4.2 kg) are interesting. They were cocks or males that were desexed when young. They grew big and fat and were therefore delicate and tender, with lots of white meat and a mild flavour. Higher in price per pound than chicken, they were worth seeking out at farmers' markets and delicatessens because they were perfect for stuffing and roasting. Alas, they seem to be no more. Since the fast food industry demands birds of a certain size, large-scale chicken farmers are filling those needs, feeding their chicks a certain way and getting them out of the barn faster. Capons no longer fit into this scheme.

Stewing hens are just that. These older, 3- to 7-pound (1.5 to 3.1 kg) gals are only good for stew or soup because they're tough without long braising.

Free-range chickens are raised outside any confines and are generally firmer with richer chicken flavour, but they may not be quite as tender as supermarket poultry because of the extent of their travels and unpredictable food. Even the federal chicken farmers' group cannot define what is actually meant by the term "free range."

Look for air-chilled poultry since it will not have the water content of water-chilled fowl and will have better colour.

country roast chicken

MAKES 8 TO 10 SERVINGS

In our fast-moving world, we yearn for comfort foods such as the plump roast chicken that was so often the focus of Grandmother's Sunday supper. I don't mean one of those scrawny supermarket chicks or the "spent hens" my mother used for soup, but the kind of nice meaty bird you might find at a farmers' market. For some unknown reason, we always call them "farm chickens"—as if other chickens are raised in the city!

If I'm cooking a little 3-pound (1.5 kg) chicken for a quick weeknight supper, I use the fast roast method. I rub the bird with butter, sprinkle with salt and pepper and roast it at 450°F (230°C) for 45 minutes.

However, a good-sized chicken like the one in this recipe, especially with an old-fashioned stuffing inside, merits a longer, slower roast. For a bigger chicken, add about 20 minutes per pound (500 g) to the roasting time; for slightly smaller birds, reduce the time by the same formula. Either stuff the chicken or pop the onion in it and bake the stuffing alongside in a casserole; the stuffed bird will take a bit longer to cook.

The stuffing would be great for pork roasts as well.

1	roasting chicken (about 8 lb/3.5 kg) 1
Half	lemon (cut crosswise) Half
	Salt and pepper
1	onion, quartered (optional) 1
1 tbsp	each butter, softened, and Dijon mustard 15 mL
1 cup	chicken stock (approx.) 250 mL
1 tbsp	cornstarch 15 mL

FRUIT AND BREAD STUFFING

1/2 cup	coarsely chopped pitted prunes or dried apricots 125 mL
1/2 cup	chicken stock 125 mL
2 tbsp	butter 25 mL
1	apple, peeled and diced 1

1. Fruit and Bread Stuffing: Soak prunes in 1/2 cup (125 mL) stock for 30 minutes.
2. Meanwhile, in a large skillet, melt butter over medium heat; cook apple and celery for 5 minutes, stirring often. Remove from heat; stir in bread, prunes with stock, green onions, parsley, thyme, sage, and salt and pepper to taste. Let cool. (Stuffing can be made 1 day ahead, covered and refrigerated.)
3. Remove neck and giblets from chicken if present. Rinse and pat dry inside and out. Rub with lemon half inside and out and sprinkle with salt and pepper. Stuff loosely with bread mixture, putting any extra in a greased casserole or enclosing in a piece of foil to be added to the oven for the last 30 minutes of roasting. (Alternatively, place the onion in the cavity and transfer all of the stuffing to an 8-cup (2 L) casserole; drizzle with pan drippings later, cover and bake in a 325°F (160°C) oven for the last 30 minutes or so, or until heated through.)

2	stalks celery, chopped	2
6 cups	cubed stale bread*	1.5 L
4	green onions, sliced	4
2 tbsp	chopped fresh parsley	25 mL
1/4 tsp	each dried thyme and sage	1 mL
	Salt and pepper	
2 tbsp	pan drippings or melted butter (optional)	25 mL

4. Tie legs together with string; tuck wings under the back. Place, breast side up, on a rack in a roasting pan. In a small bowl, combine butter and mustard. Spread over the chicken.

5. Roast, uncovered, in a 325°F (160°C) oven for about 2-1/2 to 3 hours or until juices run clear when chicken is pierced and a meat thermometer inserted in the thigh registers 185°F (85°C); baste occasionally with pan drippings. Transfer chicken to a warm platter and tent with foil; let stand for about 15 minutes before carving so juices can settle into the meat. Remove stuffing to a heated bowl.

6. Discard any fat from pan drippings. Place pan over high heat; add 1 cup (250 mL) stock and bring to a boil, stirring to scrape up any brown bits. Dissolve cornstarch in a small amount of cold water; add to the pan and cook, stirring, until thickened and bubbly. Season to taste with salt and pepper. For thinner gravy, add more stock or some cooking water from potatoes or other vegetables. Serve gravy in a heated sauceboat.

* If you don't have stale bread, place slices of bread out on a counter for 1 hour or so to dry.

coq au vin

MAKES 8 SERVINGS

When I was writing a "sixties menu" for *Elm Street*, the staff at the magazine had fun remembering what they or people they knew cooked for company in that decade. My menu started with shrimp cocktail and French onion soup, ended with crêpes Suzette and had this classic stew as its focus. Most of us agreed that Coq au Vin was the first "grown-up" dish many cooks learned to make in the sixties, and it tastes just as good today. Use two frying chickens, or the equivalent weight in legs and breasts, and serve it with plenty of crusty French bread to soak up the plentiful, delicious gravy. To add to the stew—and to drink with the finished dish—choose a young, full-bodied red Burgundy, Beaujolais or Côtes du Rhône.

8 oz	lean salt pork	250 g
24	peeled pearl onions	24
1 lb	small mushrooms	500 g
5 to 6 lb	chicken pieces	2.2 to 2.7 kg
	Salt and pepper	
1/4 cup	cognac or brandy	50 mL
1	bouquet garni of 4 parsley sprigs and 1 bay leaf tied together with string	1
2	cloves garlic, crushed	2
1/2 tsp	dried thyme	2 mL
2 cups	dry red wine	500 mL
1 cup	beef or chicken stock	250 mL
2 tbsp	all-purpose flour	25 mL
1 tbsp	tomato paste	15 mL
2 tbsp	chopped fresh parsley	25 mL

1. Cut salt pork into 1-1/4 x 1/4-inch (3 cm x 5 mm) strips. To remove excess saltiness, blanch in 2 cups (500 mL) simmering water for 5 minutes, then drain well and pat dry. Cook pork in a 20-cup (5 L) flameproof casserole over medium heat for 5 minutes, until crisp. Transfer to paper towels to drain. Drain off all but 1 tbsp (15 mL) of the fat from casserole, reserving a further 1 tbsp (15 mL) for later use.

2. Add onions to fat in casserole and cook, stirring, over medium-high heat for 3 to 5 minutes, until browned. Remove onions with a slotted spoon, transfer to a plate and set aside. Add mushrooms to the casserole and cook, stirring, for 3 minutes, until softened. Remove with a slotted spoon and add to the plate with the onions.

3. Season chicken pieces with salt and pepper, removing skin first if you prefer. Heat remaining 1 tbsp (15 mL) reserved pork fat in the casserole. Cook chicken, a few pieces at a time, over medium-high heat for 5 to 7 minutes, until browned, removing to a plate as each batch browns. Return browned chicken to the casserole and set aside.

4. Warm cognac in a medium saucepan, light with a match and pour over the browned chicken, shaking the casserole until the flame dies. Add bouquet garni, garlic and thyme to the casserole.

5. In the same saucepan you used for the cognac, boil wine until it is reduced to 1-1/2 cups (375 mL). In a small bowl, whisk together stock, flour and tomato paste. Gradually whisk stock mixture into reduced wine. Bring to a boil, whisking constantly, and cook for 1 to 2 minutes, until thickened and smooth. Pour wine mixture over chicken in casserole. Bring contents of casserole to a boil over high heat, then cover tightly and bake in a 350°F (180°C) oven for 45 minutes.

6. Gently stir onions and mushrooms into chicken, moistening them with the sauce. Cover and bake for a further 10 to 15 minutes, until chicken is no longer pink inside. Discard bouquet garni. (Coq au Vin can be prepared up to this point, cooled, covered and refrigerated for up to 1 day. Reheat in a 350°F/180°C oven for 30 to 40 minutes, stirring occasionally, or simmer gently on top of the stove, occasionally basting chicken with sauce.) Taste and adjust seasoning, then serve sprinkled with parsley and salt pork.

oven-barbecued chicken

MAKES 6 SERVINGS

Here's an easy dinner that gives you the taste of a summer barbecue in the middle of winter, but is delicious year-round. Serve with creamy mashed potatoes and a green vegetable such as peas or broccoli.

3 lb	chicken pieces 1.5 kg	
1-3/4 cups	Zesty Barbecue Sauce (recipe follows) 425 mL	

1. In a shallow baking dish large enough to hold the chicken pieces in a single layer, arrange chicken skin side down. Pour Zesty Barbecue Sauce over top and bake, uncovered, in a 350°F (180°C) oven, basting occasionally. After 30 minutes, turn chicken pieces over, baste and bake for 30 minutes longer, continuing to baste occasionally, until chicken is tender when pierced with a fork.

zesty barbecue sauce

MAKES 1-3/4 CUPS (425 ML) SAUCE, ENOUGH FOR 3 LB (1.5 KG) CHICKEN PIECES OR 4 LB (1.8 KG) SPARERIBS

This spicy sauce will keep for several days in the refrigerator or it can be frozen for longer storage.

2 tbsp	vegetable oil 25 mL
1	large onion, finely chopped 1
1/4 cup	lightly packed brown sugar 50 mL
3/4 cup	ketchup 175 mL
1/4 cup	fresh lemon juice 50 mL
1 tbsp	Worcestershire sauce 15 mL
1 tbsp	Dijon mustard 15 mL
1 tsp	chili powder 5 mL
Pinch	cayenne pepper Pinch

1. In a small saucepan, heat oil; cook onion until softened but not browned. Stir in brown sugar and cook over low heat, stirring constantly, until sugar has dissolved. Remove from the heat and stir in ketchup, lemon juice, Worcestershire sauce, mustard, chili powder and cayenne.

> ### VARIATION
>
> #### OVEN-BARBECUED RIBS
> Substitute 4 lb (1.8 kg) meaty spareribs or back ribs for the chicken. Sprinkle with salt and pepper and roast, uncovered, in a 400°F (200°C) oven for 30 minutes. Pour Zesty Barbecue Sauce over top, cover, reduce heat to 350°F (180°C) and roast for 1 hour, turning once and basting occasionally with sauce. Makes 6 servings.

crispy oven-fried chicken legs

MAKES 4 SERVINGS

Crunchy on the outside, moist on the inside—no wonder everyone loves fried chicken. With this version, you get all the satisfaction of the crunch without the fat of frying. It is one of my favourite ways to cook inexpensive legs.

1-1/2 cups	fine fresh white bread crumbs 375 mL
1/2 cup	grated Parmesan cheese 125 mL
1 tsp	grated lemon zest 5 mL
1/2 tsp	dried basil 2 mL
2	eggs 2
4	whole chicken legs (thighs and drumsticks) 4
	Salt, pepper and all-purpose flour
2 tsp	each butter and vegetable oil 10 mL
2 tbsp	fresh lemon juice 25 mL

1. In a shallow bowl, combine the bread crumbs, cheese, lemon zest and basil. In a separate shallow bowl, beat eggs lightly to blend.
2. Sprinkle chicken with salt and pepper; dust lightly with flour. Dip each chicken leg into eggs to coat well, then dredge all over with the bread crumb mixture, pressing crumbs so they adhere to chicken. (Recipe can be prepared ahead to this point, covered and refrigerated for up to 8 hours.)
3. In a 13- x 9-inch (3.5 L) baking dish, combine the butter and oil. Place in a 375°F (190°C) oven for 1 to 2 minutes or until butter melts. Tilt the dish to coat the bottom evenly with the butter/oil mixture.
4. Arrange chicken in the dish, skin side down. Drizzle with lemon juice. Bake, uncovered, for 20 minutes. Turn the chicken over. Bake for 20 to 25 minutes longer, or until juices run clear when the thigh is pierced.

> **TIP**
> To make bread crumbs, process 2 slices of bread in the food processor until fine.

codfish cakes

MAKES 3 TO 6 SERVINGS, DEPENDING ON MENU

When a gale comes to Bermuda, you wonder how the winds can blow any harder or the rain can pelt down with any more severity to turn the weather into a full-fledged hurricane. It was such a gale that kept us all inside one Good Friday morning when we should have been watching the kites fly over Horseshoe Bay. But since Kent and I were visiting our daughter and son-in-law, who live in Bermuda, I really didn't mind being indoors and taking comfort in helping to make and share the Good Friday breakfast the country traditionally enjoys.

If the weather had been good enough for the kite festival, we would have savoured not only a wonderful display of homemade tissue-paper kites sailing overhead but also the codfish cakes served up in the local snack bar, as well as having enjoyed the Gombey dancers who lead everyone out of the area when the festival is over.

These are our daughter Anne's own version of the popular Bermudian recipe. Serve them for breakfast with sour cream and hot sauce, or put them in a bun with tartar sauce and tomato slices for a lovely lunch.

1 lb	salt cod 500 g
2	potatoes, peeled and quartered 2
1 tbsp	butter 15 mL
1	onion, chopped 1
1	egg 1
1/4 cup	chopped fresh parsley 50 mL
1/2 tsp	hot pepper sauce 2 mL
	Black pepper
	All-purpose flour or fine dry bread crumbs
	Vegetable oil

1. Rinse salt cod and place in a bowl of cold water, covered, in the refrigerator for at least 12 hours, changing the water 3 or 4 times. Drain and rinse well.

2. In a large saucepan of boiling water, cook fish and potatoes, covered, for about 20 minutes or until very tender. Drain well. When cool enough to handle, pick out any bones from fish and shred with fingers; place in a large bowl. Mash potatoes and add to fish.

3. In the skillet in which you will fry the cakes, melt butter over medium heat and cook onion until softened, about 5 minutes. Add to fish mixture; beat in egg, parsley, hot pepper sauce and a generous amount of pepper. Form into 6 patties about 3/4-inch (2 cm) thick. Place a thick layer of flour on a platter; season with pepper and dredge each patty in the mixture. (Patties can be prepared several hours ahead, covered and refrigerated.)

4. Pour a layer of oil into the bottom of the skillet and heat over medium-high heat. Cook patties until golden brown, about 6 minutes a side.

savoury prosciutto and cheese bread pudding

MAKES 6 TO 8 SERVINGS

Layered dishes like this with bread and custard are often called stratas and make excellent company breakfasts because they have to sit for several hours before they are baked. This easy version, with just one layer of bread, is a bit different from the usual strata. You could, of course, substitute cooked bacon, sausage or ham for the prosciutto, and feel free to use up any bits of different kinds of cheese you might have in the refrigerator. It's also a great way to use up leftover slices of baguette you might have cut to go with last night's stew. Ordinary white bread will also do the trick; just quarter each slice.

12 to 16	slices baguette, preferably stale 12 to 16
1/2 lb	prosciutto, chopped 250 g
1/2 lb	cheese (Jarlsberg, Fontina or old Cheddar, or a combination), shredded 250 g
1/2 lb	mushrooms, sliced 250 g
1/4 cup	minced onion 50 mL
6	eggs 6
3 cups	milk 750 mL

1. Place bread in a single layer in the bottom of a greased 13- x 9-inch (3 L) glass baking dish. Top with a layer of prosciutto, a layer of cheese and a layer of mushrooms. Sprinkle mushrooms with onion. Whip eggs and milk in a blender and pour over top. Cover and refrigerate overnight.
2. Uncover and bake in a 350°F (180°C) oven for about 1 hour or until the centre is set.

macaroni and cheese

MAKES 4 SERVINGS

There's nothing more satisfying than this old-fashioned pasta casserole. My family still prefers it with tomatoes—the way my mother used to make it.

2 cups	macaroni (8 oz/250 g) 500 mL
3/4 lb	Cheddar cheese, preferably old 375 g
1	can (19 oz/540 mL) tomatoes, undrained and chopped 1
1 tsp	each granulated sugar, dry mustard and Worcestershire sauce 5 mL
1/2 tsp	each dried thyme, salt and Tabasco sauce 2 mL
1/4 tsp	black pepper 1 mL
1	egg, beaten 1
1/2 cup	milk 125 mL

1. In a large pot of boiling salted water, cook macaroni until al dente, about 8 minutes. Drain and transfer to a greased 8-cup (2 L) deep casserole.
2. Shred three-quarters of the cheese and cut remainder into thin slices; set aside. Stir together tomatoes, shredded cheese, sugar, mustard, Worcestershire sauce, thyme, salt, Tabasco sauce and pepper. Pour over macaroni and mix well. Top with cheese slices.
3. In a small bowl, blend egg with milk; pour over cheese-covered macaroni but do not stir. Bake, uncovered, in a 350°F (180°C) oven for 40 to 50 minutes or until top is golden brown.

tomato baked beans

MAKES 6 SERVINGS

On the farm, my mother actually grew and dried the beans with which she would make baked beans during the winter months. I buy dried beans in a store now, but this simple, old-time favourite still appears quite often on our table as an easy but satisfying supper. It's our traditional Halloween supper too ... I guess it's the start of hearty oven-meals that are so welcome when cold weather hits.

My mother used to add strips of side pork (sliced pork belly) to the top, but I like to cook the side pork in a pan alongside the casserole of beans for the last hour so it is crisp and all the fat is rendered out of it. I add a creamy cabbage salad (see page 101), chili sauce and perhaps some brown bread to the meal.

1 lb	dried white pea (navy) beans (2 cups/500 mL) 500 g
6 cups	cold water 1.5 L
1	can (28 oz/796 mL) crushed tomatoes* 1
4 oz	salt pork, diced 125 g
1/2 cup	molasses 125 mL
1/4 cup	packed brown sugar 50 mL
1	onion, chopped 1
1 tbsp	cider vinegar 15 mL
2 tsp	each dry mustard and black pepper 10 mL
1 tsp	salt 5 mL

1. Sort and rinse the beans. In a medium saucepan, cover beans with cold water and let soak overnight in the refrigerator. (Or, cover with water and bring to a boil; boil for 2 minutes. Remove from the heat, cover and let stand for 1 hour.)

2. Drain beans; cover again with fresh cold water and bring to a boil; reduce heat and simmer, covered, for about 40 minutes or until tender. Reserving cooking water, drain beans and transfer to a bean pot or heavy 12-cup (3 L) casserole. Stir in tomatoes, pork, molasses, brown sugar, onion, vinegar, mustard, pepper and salt. Stir in 1 cup (250 mL) of the cooking liquid. Cover and bake in a 300°F (150°C) oven for 3 hours. Uncover, stir well and bake for about 1 hour longer or until the sauce thickens.

* Crushed tomatoes are available in most grocery stores; if you cannot find them, use a can of whole tomatoes and break them up in the food processor.

cheese mushroom potatoes

MAKES 4 SERVINGS

When I'm tired and hungry, there is something about a baked potato that really soothes my soul, especially when it's topped with vegetables such as broccoli or mushrooms and oozing with melted Cheddar cheese. These stuffed potatoes are simple to make, and you can have them on hand when you need an easy pick-me-up. They are an especially homey main course to take to the office if it has a microwave oven.

4	baking potatoes 4
2 tbsp	butter 25 mL
1	onion, finely chopped 1
2 cups	sliced mushrooms (slightly less than 1/2 lb/250 g) 500 mL
1/2 tsp	dried thyme 2 mL
1 tsp	fresh lemon juice 5 mL
	Salt and pepper
1-1/2 cups	shredded Cheddar cheese 375 mL
2	slices crisply cooked bacon, crumbled 2

1. Scrub potatoes and prick with a fork; bake in a 400°F (200°C) oven for 45 to 60 minutes or until soft when pierced with a fork. Cut each potato in half and scoop out the pulp, leaving 1/4-inch (5 mm) thick shell; arrange shells on a baking sheet. Mash potato pulp and set aside.

2. In a large skillet, melt butter over medium heat. Brush some of the butter inside the potato shells; place baking sheet in the oven to keep shells warm. In the remaining butter, cook onion until softened, about 3 minutes. Add mushrooms and thyme; cook for 3 minutes. Sprinkle with lemon juice, and salt and pepper to taste. Stir in mashed potato and 1 cup (250 mL) of the cheese. Pack mixture into shells, mounding tops. Sprinkle with remaining cheese; garnish with bacon bits. (Stuffed potatoes can be wrapped and refrigerated for up to 1 day or frozen for up to 2 months. Cool and wrap individually in plastic wrap and then foil. If frozen, thaw in the refrigerator and bake, uncovered, in a 350°F (180°C) oven for about 20 minutes or until heated through. Or, heat each in the microwave at Medium (50%) for about 1 minute or until heated through.) Bake at 400°F (200°C) for about 15 minutes or until filling is steaming hot.

> **VARIATION**
>
> **CHEESE BROCCOLI POTATOES**
> Substitute 4 cups (1 L) small broccoli florets for the mushrooms and cook, uncovered, in a large pot of boiling water for 2 to 3 minutes or until tender-crisp. Stir into the skillet after the mashed potatoes.

egg and potato skillet supper

MAKES 4 SERVINGS

Like a frittata cooked in a skillet, but also resembling a crustless quiche with a more custard-like texture, this easy supper is comfort itself ... both in its making and in its eating. Be sure to bake or boil two extra potatoes the night before so they are cold to dice.

3	Italian sausages, thinly sliced (about 1/2 lb/250 g) 3
1	onion, chopped 1
2	cold cooked potatoes, diced 2
6	eggs, beaten 6
2/3 cup	18% cream or milk 150 mL
	Salt and pepper
Pinch	hot pepper flakes Pinch
1 cup	cooked broccoli, chopped 250 mL
1 cup	grated Cheddar cheese, preferably old 250 mL

1. In a large ovenproof nonstick skillet, cook sausages and onion over medium heat until sausage is no longer pink, about 10 minutes. Add potatoes and cook for 5 minutes.

2. Reduce heat to medium-low. In a bowl, whisk together eggs, cream, 1/2 tsp (2 mL) salt, 1/4 tsp (1 mL) pepper and hot pepper flakes. Stir in broccoli; pour into the skillet and cook, stirring gently, for 1 minute. Stir in cheese and place in a 375°F (190°C) oven for 15 to 20 minutes or until eggs are just set in the centre. Let cool for 5 minutes, then cut into wedges to serve.

> **TIP**
> If you don't have leftover cooked broccoli, thaw 1-1/2 cups (375 mL) frozen broccoli and pat dry.

soufflés

There is a certain peace to a perfectly risen soufflé. There is also a definite feeling of achievement and confidence if it is of your doing. For this reason, I always started my International Cooking course by having the students make a soufflé, perceived by all as a difficult task, but actually very easy if a few simple steps are followed.

Although I had taught high-school English, it seemed a natural progression for me to teach cooking when I switched careers from grammar to food. I started teaching basic cooking at night-school classes for the Public Utilities Commission in London, Ontario; then started an International Cooking ten-week course for the school board when we moved to Owen Sound, Ontario. In the Waterloo region, where we now live, I taught courses at Conestoga College and was part-owner of a cooking school in Kitchener for a time, but now do only guest appearances at schools and festivals throughout the country.

Just as there was great satisfaction for the students when they each pulled a perfectly risen soufflé from the oven, I have always had a lovely feeling of accomplishment in teaching people anything new regarding food and its preparation.

classic cheese soufflé

MAKES 4 TO 6 SERVINGS

In my own household, when the children were young, I would sometimes make a cheese soufflé for a lunch treat with the warning that it would fall if there was any roughhousing while it was in the oven ... ensuring a very quiet morning.

No one's soufflé repertoire is complete without this traditional recipe. Served with a green salad and white wine for the adults, it can be a most satisfying lunch despite its light texture. I've called for Cheddar here, but experiment with other kinds and combinations of cheeses if you wish, such as Fontina, provolone, Swiss, Asiago or a little bit of blue. You can even use up those unidentifiable pieces of dehydrated cheese lurking in the back of your refrigerator.

	Softened butter and freshly grated Parmesan cheese
3 tbsp	butter 45 mL
3 tbsp	all-purpose flour 45 mL
1 cup	hot milk 250 mL
1/2 tsp	salt 2 mL
1/4 tsp	each black pepper and dry mustard 1 mL
4	egg yolks 4
5	egg whites 5
1/4 tsp	cream of tartar 1 mL
3/4 cup	coarsely grated sharp Cheddar cheese 175 mL

1. Grease a 6-cup (1.5 L) soufflé or other straight-sided dish with softened butter, then sprinkle Parmesan cheese over the base and sides. Fold a 24-inch (60 cm) length of waxed paper in half horizontally and tie tightly around the outside of the dish to make a collar (this will support the soufflé as it rises). Butter the inside of the paper that protrudes above the dish, then sprinkle with Parmesan cheese.

2. In a large saucepan, melt the butter over medium heat. Add the flour, then reduce the heat to low and cook, stirring constantly, for 1 to 2 minutes, until the flour mixture looks dry but is not browned. Remove the saucepan from the heat, then gradually whisk in the hot milk, whisking vigorously until blended and smooth. Whisk in salt, pepper and dry mustard.

3. Return the saucepan to medium heat, then bring the sauce to a boil, whisking constantly. Simmer for about 1 minute, whisking constantly, until smooth and thickened. Remove from the heat, then beat in egg yolks, 1 at a time, whisking thoroughly after each addition. Set aside.

4. In a large bowl and using an electric mixer with clean beaters, beat egg whites until foamy. Add cream of tartar, then continue beating until whites are stiff but not dry. Stir a large spoonful of beaten egg whites into the sauce to lighten it; stir in all but 1 tbsp (15 mL) of the Cheddar. With a rubber spatula, lightly fold in the remaining egg whites, using an over-and-under cutting motion rather than a stirring motion. Do not overmix.

5. Spoon mixture into the prepared dish. Gently smooth the surface with the spatula, then sprinkle the remaining Cheddar on top. To make a decorative cap, run your thumb around the mixture at the edge of the dish to a depth of 1 inch (2.5 cm). Place the soufflé in a 400°F (200°C) oven and immediately reduce the temperature to 375°F (190°C). Bake for 30 to 35 minutes or until golden brown and a long thin knife inserted in the side of the soufflé where it has risen above the top of the dish comes out clean. (Don't open the oven door during the first 20 minutes of baking.) Serve immediately.

TIPS

Eggs separate more easily when they are cold, but you get more volume in beating room-temperature egg whites. Always separate each egg over a small bowl before adding the white to a large bowl containing the rest of the whites so that if you happen to break a yolk, it will not contaminate the whole bowl of whites. Any little bit of egg yolk will prevent the whites from increasing in volume.

Never use a plastic bowl for beating egg whites since it may harbour some fat from another time. Any fat will prevent the whites from increasing in volume. Leftover egg yolks, covered with cold water, will keep up to 3 days in the refrigerator and can be used in omelettes or scrambled eggs.

grilled cheese french toast

MAKES 2 SERVINGS

If you've been out and are just too tired to cook, this soul-warming hot sandwich will be just the answer. Serve it with chunky salsa or sliced ripe tomatoes.

4	slices bread 4
1 tbsp	Dijon mustard 15 mL
4 oz	Cheddar or Swiss cheese, sliced 125 g
2	thin slices ham 2
2	eggs 2
1/4 cup	milk 50 mL
Pinch	each salt and pepper Pinch
2 tsp	butter 10 mL
1 tsp	vegetable oil 5 mL

1. Spread 1 side of each bread slice with mustard. Evenly arrange Cheddar and ham over 2 of the slices; sandwich with remaining bread.
2. In a shallow dish, whisk together eggs, milk, salt and pepper. Add sandwiches, 1 at a time, turning to soak up the mixture.
3. In a large skillet, melt butter with oil over medium heat; cook sandwiches for about 3 minutes on each side or until golden brown and cheese has melted.

smoky lentil salad

MAKES 4 SERVINGS

Serve this easy salad with rye bread and pickled beets for a quick and delicious supper, just right when time is at a premium but you still want something satisfying, homemade and good.

3 tbsp	cider vinegar 45 mL
2 tbsp	sweet mustard 25 mL
1	clove garlic, minced 1
Dash	Worcestershire sauce Dash
	Salt and pepper
1/3 cup	olive oil 75 mL
2 tbsp	each chopped fresh parsley and snipped chives 25 mL
1	can (19 oz/540 mL) lentils, drained and rinsed 1
3 cups	shredded cabbage 750 mL
1/2 cup	slivered red onion 125 mL
1 lb	kielbasa sausage 500 g

1. In a small bowl, whisk together vinegar, mustard, garlic, Worcestershire sauce, 1/2 tsp (2 mL) salt and 1/4 tsp (1 mL) pepper. Gradually whisk in oil; stir in parsley and chives and set aside.
2. In a large bowl, combine lentils, cabbage and onion; stir in dressing to coat well, cover and set aside.
3. Grill or broil sausage until browned, 15 to 20 minutes. Cut into thick diagonal slices. Mound salad on a platter and top with sausage slices.

comfy
accompaniments

A succulent, freshly cut stalk of asparagus cooked until tender-crisp nestles beside a lamb chop. Tiny just-shelled peas cozy up to a slice of roast chicken. Fresh in-season vegetables need little to endear them to our use. There is no need for fancy sauces that would, in fact, mask the flavour of freshly harvested vegetables.

For that reason, I've concentrated more on embellishing storage vegetables, including my favourite comfort food, the potato. I've added a few simple salads and couldn't resist touching on preserves, one of the ways to ensure that we have good local, seasonal ingredients throughout the year.

I believe completely in the philosophy that food is an important part of a region, that it is to everyone's benefit to enjoy the produce that is grown nearby, especially by farmers you know ... one of the reasons I think farmers' markets are so necessary. Today, people are so cut off from their roots they often don't know where food comes from, only recognizing it in Cellophane supermarket bags. We should be able to see the connection between growing, harvesting, cooking and enjoying food; eating should be a celebration of these gifts of the land.

After cold, harsh winter has frozen the land through and through, it is always a delight to see the first green fiddlehead fronds appearing along the rivers in the country. Then, asparagus shoots its spears through the earth, followed by a long list of fresh vegetables such as beans, beets, corn and vine-ripened tomatoes that tumble upon one another throughout the growing season and far into the fall, with crops such as kale and Brussels sprouts surviving through the first snows. Wonderful tastes to celebrate, indeed.

potatoes

I find almost no other food as satisfying as a potato. It's such a simple vegetable dug out of the earth, but it brings great comfort—whether baked to steamy softness inside crunchy skin and slathered with sour cream or yogurt, perfectly mashed to creaminess with milk and butter, deep-fried to golden crispness, dressed in a tangy salad or made into a soothing soup.

There must be others who share my love of potatoes because it is the country's most important vegetable crop, with the Maritimes leading the way in production since potatoes were first cultivated in Port Royal, Nova Scotia, in 1623.

My one big complaint about the way that potatoes are sold is that when we buy them in a super-market, we don't always know what kind we are buying. At a farmers' market, however, vendors should be able to say exactly what varieties they have to offer. We are starting to see a bit of labelling—sometimes just a general-use name such as "baking" or a specific variety such as "Yukon Gold"—and I did buy a bag that was clearly named "russets" the other day. As a general rule, without knowing any of the names for potatoes, you can discover their best use by looking at them. Round, smooth potatoes are best for boiling, scalloped potatoes or salads. Oblong potatoes with a faint criss-cross kind of pattern on the skin usually have a floury texture that's best for baking, deep-frying, mashing and scalloped potatoes if you like soft, melting slices rather than distinct slices.

scalloped potatoes french-style (gratin dauphinois)

MAKES 4 SERVINGS

There's nothing nicer to accompany baked ham or roasted lamb racks than soft, buttery scalloped potatoes. I used to make this French version with a lot of whipping cream, but I find it just as delicious made with milk alone.

1 tbsp	butter 15 mL
1	large shallot, minced (or 1/4 cup/50 mL minced onion) 1
4	large baking potatoes, peeled and thinly sliced 4
2 cups	milk 500 mL
	Salt and pepper
Pinch	nutmeg Pinch
1	clove garlic, halved 1
1 cup	shredded Swiss Gruyère cheese 250 mL

1. In a medium saucepan, melt butter over medium heat; cook shallot until softened, about 3 minutes. Add potatoes and milk.
2. Bring to a simmer over medium heat and cook, uncovered, for 20 minutes, lowering heat as necessary and stirring often to prevent scorching. Season to taste with salt, pepper and nutmeg.
3. Meanwhile, rub cut sides of garlic over a greased shallow 6-cup (1.5 L) baking dish. Mince garlic and sprinkle in the dish. Top with potato mixture and sprinkle with cheese. (Potatoes can be cooled, covered and refrigerated for up to 2 days.)
4. Bake, uncovered, in a 375°F (190°C) oven for about 30 minutes (longer if really cold) or until golden brown on top and bubbly.

old-fashioned potato salad

I could make a whole meal of this type of delicious potato salad, but it does go awfully well with ribs or barbecued chicken.

2-1/2 lb	potatoes (6 to 8) 1.25 kg
2 tbsp	white wine vinegar 25 mL
1 tsp	granulated sugar 5 mL
	Salt and pepper
8	large radishes, sliced 8
4	green onions, sliced 4
3	hard-cooked eggs, chopped 3
1/2 cup	chopped dill pickle 125 mL
1/4 cup	diced celery 50 mL
3/4 cup	light mayonnaise 175 mL
1/4 cup	light sour cream 50 mL
1 tbsp	Dijon mustard 15 mL
Pinch	cayenne pepper Pinch

1. Peel and quarter potatoes. Cook in boiling salted water until tender, about 20 minutes. Drain well and coarsely chop. Place in a big bowl and, while still hot, combine with vinegar, sugar, 1/2 tsp (2 mL) salt and 1/4 tsp (1 mL) pepper.
2. Add radishes, green onions, eggs, dill pickle and celery; toss gently.
3. In a small bowl, stir together mayonnaise, sour cream, Dijon mustard and cayenne. Stir into potato mixture to coat well. Taste and adjust seasoning. Serve right away or refrigerate for up to 8 hours; bring to room temperature to serve.

colcannon

MAKES 6 TO 8 SERVINGS

A favourite dish of Irish, Scottish and German settlers in the Maritimes, colcannon is perfect comfort food for cold winter days. Colcannon or Kohl Cannon is made in various ways. The Irish just mash potatoes, cooked cabbage and onion together, while the Lunenburg Germans include rutabaga, and the Scots add carrots. Whatever you include, colcannon is creamy, soothing and oh, so satisfying.

Half	small rutabaga Half
5	medium potatoes 5
Half	small head cabbage Half
1	leek (white and light green part only) or small onion 1
1/2 cup	butter 125 mL
1 tbsp	chopped fresh parsley 15 mL
Pinch	ground mace Pinch
	Salt and pepper

1. Peel rutabaga and potatoes; cut into 1-inch (2.5 cm) cubes. Shred cabbage coarsely. Clean leek and chop coarsely.
2. Place rutabaga and potatoes in a large saucepan with enough salted water to cover. Bring to a boil. Reduce heat to medium-low; simmer, covered, for 20 to 30 minutes or until tender. Add cabbage and leek for the last 10 minutes of cooking time.
3. Drain vegetables in a colander and return to the pan; mash well. Stir in butter, parsley, mace, and salt and pepper to taste. Serve immediately.

corn and potato pancakes

MAKES SIXTEEN 3-INCH (8 CM) PANCAKES

Pancakes of any sort are homey and delicious, but in an article on pancakes I wrote for *Homemakers* magazine, these were a particular hit. As the editor and test kitchen staff said, "These light-textured pancakes are positively addictive—as we found out when we sampled them in our test kitchen. While they're perfect alongside bacon and sausages, they also make a great vegetable accompaniment to roast chicken." If you have any leftover mashed potatoes, substitute 2 cups (500 mL) for the baking potatoes.

2	baking potatoes (about 1 lb/ 500 g total) 2
1 cup	frozen or canned corn kernels (thawed and/or drained) 250 mL
3	eggs, separated 3
1/4 cup	sour cream 50 mL
2 tbsp	all-purpose flour 25 mL
1/2 tsp	black pepper 2 mL
1/4 tsp	each salt and baking powder 1 mL
2 tbsp	vegetable oil (approx.) 25 mL

1. Peel potatoes; cut into small pieces. Cook in boiling salted water over medium-high heat about 10 minutes, until very tender. Drain well; transfer to a medium bowl. Mash potatoes roughly. With an electric mixer, beat potatoes until smooth. Stir in corn, egg yolks, sour cream, flour, pepper, salt and baking powder.

2. In a separate bowl, using clean beaters, beat egg whites until stiff peaks form; gently fold into potato mixture until well combined.

3. Heat oil in a large skillet over medium-high heat. Drop heaping table-spoonfuls (15 mL) of batter into the skillet, spacing them well apart. Cook for 3 to 4 minutes, until bubbles appear on the surface. Turn pancakes; cook for 3 minutes or until well browned. Repeat with remaining batter, adding more oil as necessary. Serve at once.

golden rutabaga casserole

MAKES 8 SERVINGS

For years, everyone called the big yellow-fleshed rutabaga "turnip," and some still do, often calling it "Swede turnip." The real turnip, the white globe-shaped summer vegetable with a purple crown, is in fact a member of the mustard family and has been around since ancient times, while the bigger storage vegetable came along in the 1700s, originating in Scandinavia. Rutabagas are usually waxed to prevent dehydration, and if this wax proves to be a problem when using the vegetable, you can remove it by piercing the rutabaga in several places with the point of a knife and placing the root on a double thickness of paper towel in the microwave oven; heat at High for 3 to 4 minutes until the wax dissolves on the paper. Doing this will also make it easier to cut and peel the rutabaga.

To prepare a rutabaga, slice off the top, then set it cut side down on a board and slice in two. Place each half, cut side down, on the board and cut into slices. Peel off the thick skin from each slice, including the bitter band that runs underneath.

Full of flavour, rutabaga marries well with sweet carrots and fruit in this company casserole that would be a perfect side dish to roast poultry or pork.

1	orange 1	
3 cups	water 750 mL	
6	carrots, chopped 6	
5 cups	cubed peeled rutabaga 1.25 L	
1/2 cup	dried apricots 125 mL	
2 tbsp	maple syrup 25 mL	
2 tbsp	butter 25 mL	
	Salt and pepper	
1/2 cup	sour cream 125 mL	
Pinch	each cinnamon and nutmeg Pinch	

1. Remove rind from orange; cut into julienne strips. Cut white pith from orange and chop orange.
2. In a large saucepan, combine water, orange rind, orange, carrots, rutabaga, apricots, maple syrup, butter, and salt and pepper to taste; bring to a boil. Reduce heat and simmer, uncovered, for 30 to 40 minutes or until water evaporates and vegetables are tender.
3. In a food processor, purée mixture in batches, adding sour cream, cinnamon and nutmeg to the last batch. Transfer to a warmed vegetable bowl and stir. (To make ahead, transfer to a greased oven dish, cool, cover and refrigerate for up to 1 day. Bring to room temperature for 30 minutes before reheating. Bake, covered, in a 350°F/180°C oven for about 30 minutes or until heated through.)

parsnip currant puffs

MAKES 8 SERVINGS

These individual puffs with a dab of red currant jelly hidden in their centres will be a hit with even those who say that parsnips are not on their list of favourite vegetables, as they are on mine.

2 lb	parsnips	1 kg
2	eggs, separated	2
1/2 tsp	ground ginger	2 mL
	Salt and pepper	
3 tbsp	red currant jelly	45 mL

1. Peel parsnips and cut into about 6 pieces each. Cook, covered, in a small amount of boiling salted water for 10 minutes or until soft. Drain well. Place in a food processor, in batches if necessary, and purée. Add egg yolks, ginger, and salt and pepper to taste. Process until light and fluffy. (Recipe can be prepared ahead to this point, covered and refrigerated for up to 1 day. Bring to room temperature before proceeding.)

2. Whip egg whites in a medium bowl until stiff but still moist. Fold into parsnip mixture. Divide most of the mixture among 8 buttered 6-oz (175 mL) custard cups or individual soufflé dishes. Make a well in each, spoon one-eighth of the jelly into each and cover with remaining parsnip mixture, smoothing the top. Place filled dishes in a shallow pan with boiling water halfway up the sides of the dishes. Bake in a 325°F (160°C) oven for about 20 minutes or until slightly puffed and set on top. Serve immediately.

parsnip crumble

MAKES 4 SERVINGS

My friend Diane Slimmon, an excellent cook and obviously a good detective, tasted this homey side dish in a restaurant, paid very good attention to what she was eating, then went home to recreate it. Sharing Diane's great love of parsnips, I couldn't wait to make a version of what she had described. It makes an excellent accompaniment to roast chicken or pork.

6	parsnips, peeled, trimmed and thinly sliced (about 1-1/2 lb/ 750 g total) 6
3 tbsp	butter 45 mL
3 tbsp	sour cream 45 mL
1/4 tsp	nutmeg 1 mL
1/2 cup	rolled oats 125 mL
1/3 cup	packed brown sugar 75 mL
1/3 cup	all-purpose flour 75 mL
1 cup	fresh or frozen* cranberries, chopped 250 mL

1. In a medium saucepan, in just enough boiling salted water to cover them, cook parsnips until very tender, 20 to 25 minutes. Drain well and place over low heat for a few seconds to dry them.

2. Mash parsnips with 1 tbsp (15 mL) of the butter. Stir in sour cream and half the nutmeg; transfer to a greased shallow 6-cup (1.5 L) casserole.

3. In a small bowl, stir together rolled oats, sugar, flour and remaining nutmeg. Cut in remaining butter until crumbly. Stir in cranberries and sprinkle over the parsnip mixture. (Casserole can be covered and refrigerated up to 6 hours. Bring to room temperature before reheating.) Bake, uncovered, in a 350°F (180°C) oven for 30 minutes or until golden brown on top and heated through.

* If using frozen cranberries, chop while frozen; then thaw slightly.

steamed fiddleheads with lemon beurre blanc

MAKES 4 SERVINGS

When most people move to a new town, they seek out a doctor, a dentist and maybe a hairdresser soon after their arrival. Not my husband, Kent. He goes looking for a fern patch. He's been picking those lovely, green, nutritious fiddleheads (the unopened frond of the ostrich fern) ever since his grandfather showed him how. His grandfather told him the story of how natives taught his ancestors that this wild vegetable would help keep them alive after a long winter had used up all other resources.

Every spring, Kent goes out to his secret patch and brings home enough fiddleheads so we can enjoy them while they are fresh and put some in our freezer for treats during the year. I always save a bag of them for Christmas dinner.

In season, fiddleheads are now often available in supermarkets, but if you do find your own patch, remember that the only unopened frond you should eat is the ostrich fern, and if you pick them in the wild, always leave a couple of fronds on each plant. Pick them when they are very young with the head tightly curled and the stalk tender.

Fresh fiddleheads are best enhanced with only butter, salt and pepper and a sprinkling of fresh lemon juice. This simple, classic sauce uses these flavours to add a crowning touch to the succulent green vegetable.

8 oz	fresh fiddleheads (or 10.6-oz/300 g pkg frozen) 250 g
1	small shallot, minced 1
2 tbsp	dry white wine 25 mL
1/4 cup	cold unsalted butter, in small pieces 50 mL
	Salt and pepper
	Zest of 1 lemon

1. Clean fiddleheads by removing the brown scales left from last year's fronds by pulling out each curl and shaking off this husk. Wash in several changes of water. Trim off any dark ends (caused by natural oxidization).
2. In a basket steamer or bamboo tray set over water in a wok, steam fresh or frozen (not thawed) fiddleheads 6 to 8 minutes or until tender. Drain well and transfer to a warm serving dish.
3. Meanwhile, in a small saucepan over medium heat, cook shallot in the wine until the shallot is soft and the wine has almost evaporated, about 3 minutes.
4. Remove pan from the heat and whisk in butter, 1 piece at a time, so it blends well. Season to taste with salt and pepper. Whisk in zest; spoon over fiddleheads and serve immediately.

mary lou's old-fashioned cabbage salad

MAKES 8 TO 12 SERVINGS

My husband, Kent, talked for years about having a pig roast; finally, last year, we celebrated Canada Day (the hottest day of the year) by serving roast pork to fifty-six people in our backyard. Everyone loved the pork, which we served with salads, roast new potatoes and the last of the season's asparagus. The favourite salad was this simple, old-fashioned coleslaw that my friend Mary Lou Ruby Jonas brought along. Mary Lou has an Old Order Mennonite background, and her recipes reflect the homey flavours of Mennonite cooking.

1 cup	whipping cream 250 mL
1/3 cup	granulated sugar 75 mL
1/3 cup	white vinegar 75 mL
	Salt and pepper
8 cups	shredded cabbage 2 L
4	stalks celery, diced 4
4	green onions, thinly sliced 4

1. In a blender, combine cream, sugar, vinegar and 1/2 tsp (2 mL) salt. Blend until thick like whipped cream. (The dressing can be made and refrigerated for up to 1 week in a covered glass jar.)
2. In a large bowl, combine the cabbage, celery and green onions. Toss with dressing just before using. Season to taste with salt and pepper.

spinach caesar with pine nuts

MAKES 6 TO 8 SERVINGS

I love spinach raw or cooked, and this variation on an old favourite is not only delicious but also healthy. Baby spinach costs a bit more than regular spinach, but it's worth it.

3 tbsp	light mayonnaise 45 mL
2 tbsp	fresh lemon juice 25 mL
2 tsp	each Dijon mustard and anchovy paste 10 mL
2	cloves garlic, minced 2
1/2 tsp	each salt, pepper and Worcestershire sauce 2 mL
3 tbsp	olive oil 45 mL
1/3 cup	freshly grated Parmesan cheese 75 mL
8 cups	baby spinach 2 L
4	slices bacon, crisply cooked and crumbled 4
1/2 cup	toasted pine nuts 125 mL

1. In a small bowl, whisk together mayonnaise, lemon juice, mustard, anchovy paste, garlic, salt, pepper and Worcestershire sauce. Gradually whisk in oil. Stir in cheese. Taste for seasoning.
2. In a large bowl, toss spinach with half the bacon and half the pine nuts. Toss with enough dressing to coat spinach (any extra can be kept for several days, covered and refrigerated). Sprinkle with remaining bacon and pine nuts.

> **TIPS**
> If you wish, you can reduce the saturated fat by replacing bacon with 1/4 cup (50 mL) finely chopped sun-dried tomatoes.
> To toast pine nuts, spread out on a baking sheet in a 350°F (180°C) oven for about 5 minutes or until fragrant. I find a toaster oven handy for this job.

tomato salad provençale

MAKES 4 SERVINGS

I love combining sliced tomatoes with chopped basil and a drizzle each of balsamic vinegar and olive oil for a quick salad when tomatoes are at their sun-ripened best. This salad is an easy variation on that theme.

2	large tomatoes 2
1/4 cup	finely chopped black olives 50 mL
1/4 cup	finely diced celery 50 mL
4 tsp	chopped fresh parsley 20 mL
2 tbsp	olive oil 25 mL
2 tsp	fresh lemon juice 10 mL
1	clove garlic, minced 1
	Salt and pepper
	Thin strips lemon zest

1. Cut tomatoes in half crosswise; scoop out seeds from each half. Place tomatoes, cut side up, in a serving dish. Sprinkle with olives, celery and parsley.
2. Whisk together oil, lemon juice, garlic, and salt and pepper to taste; spoon over tomatoes. Garnish with lemon zest.

microwave old-fashioned salad dressing

MAKES ABOUT 3-1/2 CUPS (875 ML)

One of my favourite uses for the microwave oven is to make sauces and creamy cooked dressings. This old-fashioned cooked dressing is like my mother's, but without the 10 minutes of constant stirring on top of the stove. I like to keep it on hand in the summer for salads of potatoes, greens or cabbage. I've discovered that it is one of my daughter's favourites; right now, while she is living in Bermuda, she has it in her refrigerator year-round.

1/2 cup	granulated sugar	125 mL
3 tbsp	all-purpose flour	45 mL
1 tbsp	dry mustard	15 mL
1 tsp	salt	5 mL
2	eggs	2
1 cup	each milk and water	250 mL
3/4 cup	white vinegar	175 mL

1. In an 8-cup (2 L) microwaveable measuring cup, combine sugar, flour, mustard and salt; beat in eggs. Stir in milk, water and vinegar.
2. Microwave at Medium-High (70%) for 6 minutes. Stir and microwave at High for 5 minutes or until bubbly and thickened, stirring halfway through.
3. Let cool at room temperature for a few minutes, stirring often. (Dressing can be stored in a covered jar in the refrigerator for up to 2 weeks.)

preserving pleasures

I remember, as a child, going down to the cellar in our farmhouse always with a feeling of awe. Within its cool, thick walls were shelves and tables lined with a colourful array of pickled fruits and vegetables, crystal-clear jellies, bright jams and perfectly ripe fruit suspended in syrup. Foods from our garden and the surrounding woods were preserved for our enjoyment through the meagre months of winter.

Even now, when time is at a premium and there is no longer a vegetable garden outside my door, I can't resist buying fresh produce at our local farmers' market and putting up a few jars. Preserving is a nostalgic pleasure, in the doing *and* in the eating. It is also a way of controlling the ingredients; no additives are necessary. And locally grown food harvested at its peak will be more economical and have better flavour and more nutrients than winter imports.

For thousands of years, people have preserved foods by drying, fermenting, salting, pickling or saturating them with sugar or alcohol. Before canning became widespread with the 1858 patenting of the Mason jar, long cold winters forced early North American settlers to rely on brine-curing, smoking, drying and their less-than-effective root cellars in order to preserve the harvest. My 95-year-old aunt has told me of my grandmother brine-curing their own hams and smoking them in barrels, and I can remember tasting those hams as a child.

Even though we no longer need to fill our cellars with enough jars, crocks and barrels to see us through winter, I find preserving fruits and vegetables to be a satisfying activity, especially when we make a bee of it with good friends or when my daughter-in-law, Cherrie, suggests our making some jam or chili sauce together. I'm very pleased that she wants to learn this old-fashioned art that's worth preserving!

preserving basics

Use scratch- and nick-free canning jars with new two-piece lids. Wash jars in soapy water and, if the filled jars are to be processed in a boiling water bath for fewer than 10 minutes, sterilize the empty jars by placing them in the rack of your boiling water canner filled with cold water; let jars fill with water. Bring to a boil and boil for 10 minutes.

Just before using, place flat metal disks in a pan of water and heat through to 180°F (82°C) to soften the sealing compound. It is no longer recommended that you boil the lids for 5 minutes. It's not necessary to heat the band part of the lid.

Fill the jars, leaving the recommended headspace and avoiding any spillage on the rims. Wipe clean if there is any spillage. Centre disk on the jar and apply the screw band until just fingertip-tight; do not overtighten.

Fill a boiling water canner about two-thirds full of water and start to heat as the preserve nears the end of its cooking. Place the filled jars, right side up, in the rack of a boiling water canner; lower into the hot water and pour in enough extra hot water to cover jars by at least 1 inch (2.5 cm). Cover canner and time the processing after the water returns to a boil.

Using a jar lifter, transfer the hot jars to a rack or folded towel. Do not be tempted to tighten the lids. As they cool, check for the seal. If the lid has snapped down, curving downward, it has sealed. If not, refrigerate the jar and use as soon as possible.

If you wish, you can remove the screw band from sealed jars and reserve for use again.

homemade hot dog relish

MAKES 14 JARS

I love haunting farmers' markets where vendors often grow the produce they are selling. That way, they can tell you exactly what type of potatoes they have, the breed of corn or how to cook any of it. I often ask for their recipes, especially from those people who sell the produce and a few preserved jars of it. Shirley Plumtree has been a vendor at the Cambridge market ever since anyone can remember, and she shared this old-fashioned relish recipe with me. I think you will agree that it has a wonderful full flavour that far surpasses the astringent taste of that nasty green commercial stuff.

7	large (unpeeled) cucumbers, seeded 7
5	onions 5
2	sweet red peppers 2
1 tbsp	pickling salt 15 mL
3 cups	white vinegar 750 mL
3 cups	granulated sugar 750 mL
3/4 tsp	turmeric 4 mL
1/2 tsp	black pepper 2 mL
1/4 tsp	ground ginger 1 mL

1. In a food processor or meat grinder, chop cucumbers, onions and peppers. Combine with salt in a nonreactive bowl; refrigerate overnight.
2. Drain well. In a large saucepan, combine vinegar, sugar, turmeric, pepper and ginger. Bring to a boil; add cucumber mixture and simmer, stirring occasionally, for 5 minutes.
3. Pour into hot 1-cup (250 mL) jars, leaving 1/2 inch (1 cm) headspace. Seal with 2-piece metal lids. Process in a boiling water canner for 15 minutes. Remove jars to a folded towel on the counter and let cool for 24 hours. Check seals, label and store in a cool, dark place.

lady rose pickles (from point ideal)

MAKES 25 JARS

Our friends Diane and Gary Slimmon brought us a hostess gift of a bright sealer of Lady Rose pickles one evening. Already intrigued by the name, I couldn't wait to taste this interesting relish that I knew was an old-fashioned Canadian favourite. We opened the jar a few days later, and the contents disappeared quickly indeed when we discovered how delicious these pickles are.

The Slimmons had helped make them with a friend in Waterloo, and it took very little coaxing for Steven Boothby to let me in on the next year's production. When local vegetables were at their summer best, we met one morning in Steven's kitchen: Steven; Gary; Diane; my husband, Kent; Steven's wife, Bonnie; and I. The six of us started peeling, chopping, stirring and bottling, and by mid-afternoon we had twenty-five glorious pints to divide among the three families.

I find making a bee of preserving is not only easier but also much more fun than going it alone. Even more fun was learning about the recipe we were using. It seems that Steven's family had a resort on Lake of Bays called Point Ideal Resort. According to a little handwritten book on Muskoka, the resort in its prime had a "very fine garden, both of vegetables and flowers; they had their own cows with plenty of good milk and cream and in the early days, always had a flock of sheep so their guests could have delicious lamb, for which Muskoka was noted."

Steven Boothby had worked at the resort as a boy, helping out at the marina, in the garden and carrying wood to supply the cottages. Steven's aunts, Helen Crosson and Lilian Boothby, both worked there as well, and it was their recipe we were using to make this wonderful relish.

We chopped the cauliflower, celery and peppers by hand, but took advantage of the food processor to chop the cucumbers and onions.

12 cups	chopped cucumber (about 16 cucumbers, peeled and seeded) 3 L
12 cups	chopped onions (12 large) 3 L
4	bunches celery, finely diced 4
4	sweet red peppers, diced 4

1. Combine vegetables in a large kettle; sprinkle with salt and mix well. Let stand for 2 hours.
2. Meanwhile, in another large kettle, combine vinegar, sugar and mustard seed; bring to a boil. In a small bowl, stir together the flour, mustard and turmeric; add enough cold water to make a paste. Stir into the vinegar mixture until smooth and thickened. Drain vegetables well and add to

3	large heads cauliflower, finely chopped 3
1/2 cup	pickling salt 125 mL
10 cups	white vinegar 2.5 L
15 cups	granulated sugar 3.75 L
4 tsp	mustard seed 20 mL
1-1/2 cups	all-purpose flour 375 mL
1/2 cup	dry mustard 125 mL
4 tsp	turmeric 20 mL
1/4 cup	cornstarch (optional) 50 mL

the boiling vinegar solution. Bring back to a boil, reduce heat and simmer for 5 minutes. (There should be a bit of crunch left in the vegetables.) If not thick enough, dissolve cornstarch in a bit of the liquid and stir back into the pickles.

3. Pour into hot 2-cup (500 mL) jars, leaving 1/2 inch (1 cm) headspace. Seal with 2-piece metal lids. Process in boiling water canner for 10 minutes. Remove and place on folded towel on the counter and let cool 24 hours. Check seals, label and store in a cool, dark place.

red pepper jelly

MAKES 5 JARS

Because the juice is not extracted after cooking, the result is closer to a gelled relish in this delicious condiment that is excellent with roast pork, poultry or cream cheese and crackers. You can substitute hot peppers for up to one-quarter of the sweet ones, but use rubber gloves when handling the spicy variety. Do not use overly ripe peppers, which will present problems in gelling.

Years ago, I made cases of this popular jelly for a friend who had a craft store in Kitchener; Joan could never keep enough of it on her shelves.

6	small sweet red peppers (1-1/2 lb/750 g total)	6
1/2 cup	each lemon juice and cider vinegar	125 mL
2 tbsp	grated lemon zest	25 mL
1 tsp	chili powder	5 mL
1/2 tsp	pickling salt	2 mL
Pinch	cayenne	Pinch
1	pkg (2 oz/57 g) fruit pectin crystals	1
5 cups	granulated sugar	1.25 L

1. Remove cores and seeds from peppers; chop coarsely. In batches, finely chop peppers in a food processor or a meat grinder. Measure out 3 cups (750 mL) peppers and juice.

2. In a large nonreactive pot, combine peppers with lemon juice, vinegar, lemon zest, chili powder, salt and cayenne. Bring to a boil; reduce heat, cover and simmer for 10 minutes, stirring occasionally. Return to a rolling boil and add pectin, stirring until dissolved. Add sugar and return to a full rolling boil, stirring; boil hard for 1 minute, stirring constantly. Remove from the heat and stir for 5 minutes, skimming off any foam that rises.

3. Pour into hot, sterilized, 1-cup (250 mL) jars, leaving 1/4 inch (5 mm) headspace. Seal with 2-piece metal lids. Process in a boiling water canner for 5 minutes. Remove jars to a folded towel on the counter and let cool for 24 hours. Check seals, label and store in a cool, dark place.

spiced pear butter

MAKES 3 JARS

In farm kitchens like ours, nothing was wasted, a habit I probably can't break. I can never resist buying a whole basket of perfectly shaped pears when I see them at our local farmers' market. Pears are interesting creatures, however, since they ripen from the inside out. I will bring home the basket, set it down in the cellar and after a few days the pears may still look firm, but perhaps they get just a little too ripe for eating out of hand. I sometimes use them to make pear sauce, like applesauce, and this dark, flavourful spread is a terrific way to use up that basket of very ripe pears.

10	large, very ripe pears	10
1/2 cup	liquid honey	125 mL
1/2 tsp	grated orange zest	2 mL
1/4 cup	fresh orange juice	50 mL
2 cups	granulated sugar	500 mL
1 tsp	cinnamon	5 mL
1/2 tsp	ground ginger	2 mL
1/4 tsp	each nutmeg and ground cloves	1 mL

1. Wash pears and remove stems and cores. Chop coarsely. Place in a large heavy-bottomed saucepan over low heat. Bring to a simmer, cover and cook for 30 minutes or until tender, stirring often. Press pulp through a sieve or food mill. You should have about 5 cups (1.25 L) of purée.

2. Return the purée to the saucepan with the honey, orange zest and juice, sugar, cinnamon, ginger, nutmeg and cloves. Bring to a boil, then reduce heat to medium-low and cook, uncovered, for 45 to 60 minutes or until reduced by half and very thick. Stir often. To test for doneness, place a spoonful on a chilled saucer and, holding over the sink, turn it over. If pear butter is done, it won't fall off.

3. Pour into hot 1-cup (250 mL) jars, leaving 1/4 inch (5 mm) headspace. Seal with 2-piece metal lids. Process in a boiling water canner for 10 minutes. Remove jars to a folded towel on the counter and let cool for 24 hours. Check seals, label and store in a cool, dark place up to 1 year.

down-home desserts

Ask a food lover what stand out as favourite recipes from his or her childhood and you'll probably hear about desserts. Often, we remember that Sunday dinner was a golden roast chicken or, as one of my friends recalls, a piece of roast beef that was cooked until quite grey. Main courses seldom had recipes attached, but somewhere in the kitchens of our mothers and grandmothers there would be a sketchy outline for a cake or cookies.

My own mother could make a cake simply by stirring together what seemed like a handful of this and that, and she was a master at pies, putting them together in a flash. Granted, she did have all of the lovely fruit on the farm available for those pies, and it was the fact that she made so many that contributed to her speed and the wonderfully flaky crusts. In those days, it was an everyday sort of dessert. There were countless kinds of pies that were all delicious, but everyone remembers one that was not, and of course, for years, this is the one she heard about most. Mom was great at trying new things; if a recipe in a newspaper appealed to her, she would try it. Well, there was an unfortunate recipe for Shoo-Fly Pie (a Mennonite pie that is rather like a cake baked in a pie shell) that was so strong with molasses no one could manage to eat a whole piece. This kind of pie can be quite delicious if the recipe is right, but this recipe was far from accurate. Needless to say, she went back to making her own creations.

On the farm, the noon meal was what we now normally prepare for our evening dinner and was called "dinner," while the evening meal, which was also of generous proportions, was called "supper." My mother made desserts for both meals, and I well remember coming home from school to find a helping of dinner's dessert awaiting me as a snack: a bowl of apple crisp or pudding, a piece of one of those pies and, of course, often cookies or a square.

Today, in our own house, we seldom indulge in dessert except for fresh fruit, but if the children are coming or other company is expected, I'll make a sweet offering, perhaps even a pie. If it's a fancy dinner party, I'll make something more elaborate, but something that can be made a day or two ahead.

In this chapter, there are a couple of these company desserts, such as Black Forest Trifle, but for the most part I've taken us all back to those wonderful desserts we remember from childhood: Runny Gooey Butter Tarts, Date Squares, puddings and cobblers and, of course, a good number of pies.

birthday cakes

I must have had a reputation as a mean mother because when each of my children reached the age of seven, I said, "No more birthday parties; seven is the age limit." I did, however, say that they could pick a restaurant and invite one friend as a guest.

No fast food joints for these kids! Sometimes, we would even journey to upscale or ethnic restaurants in Toronto, then a two-hour trip each way. I guess I should have set a limit on restaurants as well as age, but I really didn't mind introducing them to the interesting food such places offered.

To give them a touch of a homegrown birthday party as well, I would make a cake, often a kind they requested. This part of birthdays always reminded me of my childhood because such celebrations called out for cake that was often just a "stir cake" (an easy one-bowl affair for which my mother never seemed to measure anything). It was so important that we each had a birthday cake, I remember my young brother making my cake when my mother was ill one year.

My father tried for two cakes at one point. For many years, we celebrated his birthday on May 15 and thought he was a certain age, but when he contacted the government for his birth certificate, we discovered my father had actually been born on May 1 and was a year younger than he thought. This confusion was understandable when you considered the fact that he was one of the youngest in a family of thirteen and, in fact, had only one name, George; I guess his parents had run out of names by then. He really did try to take advantage of this new bit of information by wanting to celebrate on both May 1 and May 15!

My son, Allen, asked me to make a variety of cakes over the years—Doboschtorte (a many-layered sponge cake filled with chocolate cream and glazed with caramel sugar), a real Black Forest Cake or his favourite, a simple Angel Food Cake (see page 167). My daughter, Anne, didn't seem to care, as long as it was chocolate.

one-bowl birthday cake

MAKES 10 SERVINGS

This is like my mother's "stir cake," but I did measure everything exactly.

2 cups	all-purpose flour	500 mL
1-1/4 cups	granulated sugar	300 mL
4 tsp	baking powder	20 mL
1/2 tsp	salt	2 mL
1 cup	milk	250 mL
1/2 cup	shortening	125 mL
1 tsp	almond extract	5 mL
3	eggs	3
1 cup	sweetened flaked coconut	250 mL
	Easy Chocolate Icing (recipe follows)	
	Coconut (optional)	

1. Grease and flour two 9-inch (1.5 L) round cake pans. Set aside.
2. In a large bowl, stir together the flour, sugar, baking powder and salt. Add 3/4 cup (175 mL) of the milk, shortening and almond extract; beat for 1 minute. Add remaining milk and eggs; beat for 1 minute or until smooth. Stir in flaked coconut.
3. Pour into prepared pans; bake in a 350°F (180°C) oven for 30 to 40 minutes or until cake tester inserted in the centre comes out clean. Let cool in pans for 5 minutes; turn out onto racks and let cool completely. Spread Easy Chocolate Icing between the cake layers and over top and sides. Garnish with coconut if desired.

easy chocolate icing

MAKES ABOUT 2 CUPS (500 ML)

2 cups	real chocolate chips	500 mL
1/2 cup	milk	125 mL
1/3 cup	butter, in bits	75 mL

1. In a small saucepan, heat chocolate chips with milk over low heat, stirring, until melted and smooth. Remove from heat; stir in butter, a little at a time, until smooth. Pour into a bowl and refrigerate until firm enough to spread, about 2 hours.

VARIATION

COFFEE HAZELNUT CAKE
Add 4 tsp (20 mL) instant coffee granules dissolved in 1 tbsp (15 mL) water to milk. Add 1/2 cup (125 mL) chopped toasted hazelnuts instead of flaked coconut to batter. Use vanilla instead of almond extract.

---

rhubarb stir cake

MAKES ABOUT 12 SERVINGS

My mother used to make cakes in a flash, just stirring everything together without seeming to expend any effort at all. This is that kind of cake—incredibly easy to make and even better the day after it's baked. Moist with a crunchy sweet topping, it makes a great spring brunch dessert.

1/4 cup	butter, softened 50 mL
1-1/2 cups	packed brown sugar 375 mL
1	egg 1
1 tbsp	vanilla 15 mL
2-1/3 cups	all-purpose flour 575 mL
1 tsp	baking soda 5 mL
1/2 tsp	salt 2 mL
1 cup	sour cream (light or regular) 250 mL
4 cups	rhubarb (1/2-inch/ 1 cm pieces) 1 L
1/2 cup	granulated sugar 125 mL
1/2 tsp	nutmeg 2 mL

1. In a large bowl, cream together butter and brown sugar. Beat in egg and vanilla.
2. Sift or stir together flour, baking soda and salt; gradually stir into butter mixture. Fold in sour cream and rhubarb. Spoon into a greased 13- x 9-inch (3.5 L) glass baking dish. Stir together granulated sugar and nutmeg; sprinkle over batter. Bake in 350°F (180°C) oven for 40 minutes or until a tester comes out clean.

raspberry streusel coffee cake

MAKES 10 TO 12 SERVINGS

I've never tasted raspberries like those we grew on the farm when I was a child. They were big, red and fragrant, and the picking of them was left to my mother and me, but I didn't mind. It was a special time to be together, and we spent it chatting and laughing. Our henhouse was close by, and sometimes the hens would all cluck at once; Mom always said, "Oh, they've just told another joke." It truly sounded like it. As if picking our domestic raspberries wasn't enough work, we would occasionally go back to our maple bush (a mile from the house) with honey pails strapped around our waists and pick wild red raspberries, thimbleberries and what we called black caps. I can still taste those berries, and I wish I had some right now.

House guests will happily awake to the aroma of this moist cake ... just the kind of thing I like to stir up for a company breakfast. If using frozen raspberries, buy unsweetened, individually quick frozen (IQF) berries; do not thaw to use, and bake five to ten minutes longer.

1/2 cup	butter, softened 125 mL
1 cup	granulated sugar 250 mL
2	eggs 2
1 tsp	vanilla 5 mL
2 cups	all-purpose flour 500 mL
1 tsp	baking powder 5 mL
1 tsp	baking soda 5 mL
1/2 tsp	salt 2 mL
1 cup	sour cream 250 mL
3 cups	fresh or frozen raspberries 750 mL

STREUSEL TOPPING

1-1/2 cups	all-purpose flour 375 mL
1/2 cup	finely chopped pecans 125 mL
1/3 cup	packed brown sugar 75 mL
1/3 cup	granulated sugar 75 mL
1/2 cup	butter 125 mL

CREAM CHEESE FILLING

1	pkg (8 oz/250 g) cream cheese, softened 1
1/4 cup	granulated sugar 50 mL
1	egg 1
2 tsp	finely grated lemon zest 10 mL

1. Grease a 13- x 9-inch (2.5 L) metal cake pan; set aside.
2. Streusel Topping: In a bowl, combine flour, pecans and sugars. Using a pastry blender or 2 knives, cut in butter until crumbly. Set aside.
3. Cream Cheese Filling: In a bowl, beat cream cheese with granulated sugar until fluffy. Beat in the egg and lemon zest. Set aside.
4. In a large bowl, beat butter with granulated sugar until light and fluffy. Beat in eggs, 1 at a time, beating well after each; beat in vanilla. Whisk together flour, baking powder, baking soda and salt; stir into butter mixture alternately with sour cream, making 3 additions of dry ingredients and 2 of sour cream. Spread in prepared pan; sprinkle raspberries over top. Gently spread with cream cheese filling; sprinkle evenly with streusel topping.
5. Bake in the centre of a 350°F (180°C) oven until a tester inserted in the centre of the cake comes out clean, 45 to 50 minutes. Serve warm or at room temperature.

date and nut cake with broiled icing (queen elizabeth cake)

MAKES 16 SERVINGS

It is amazing how many of my friends remember their mothers making this moist treat with its chewy coconut topping. It is my husband's favourite family cake memory. This is how I remember my mother making it.

1 cup	chopped pitted dates	250 mL
1 tsp	baking soda	5 mL
1 cup	boiling water	250 mL
1/2 cup	butter, softened	125 mL
1 cup	granulated sugar	250 mL
1	egg	1
1 tsp	vanilla	5 mL
1-1/2 cups	all-purpose flour	375 mL
1 tsp	baking powder	5 mL
1/2 tsp	salt	2 mL
1/2 cup	chopped walnuts	125 mL

BROILED ICING

1/2 cup	packed brown sugar	125 mL
1/4 cup	butter, softened	50 mL
1 cup	shredded coconut, preferably unsweetened	250 mL
3 tbsp	10% cream	45 mL

1. Grease a 9-inch (2.5 L) square metal cake pan; set aside. In a small bowl, combine dates with baking soda; pour boiling water over top and set aside to let cool.

2. In a large bowl, beat butter with granulated sugar. Blend in the egg. Stir in vanilla, then date mixture. Whisk together flour, baking powder and salt; stir into date mixture. Stir in nuts. Spread in prepared pan; bake in the centre of a 325°F (160°C) oven until a tester inserted in the centre of the cake comes out clean, about 45 minutes.

3. Broiled Icing: Beat brown sugar with butter. Stir in coconut and cream. Gently spread over the hot cake. Place the cake on a rack 4 inches (10 cm) below preheated boiler; broil until icing is lightly browned and bubbly, about 3 minutes. Let cool in the pan on a rack before cutting.

peach upside-down cake

MAKES ABOUT 6 SERVINGS

My husband is not much of a cake fan, but this is one he adores, and he would be very disappointed indeed to see a peach season slip by without having it at least once. It is best served warm with sweetened whipped cream, to which I often add a splash of kirsch.

3 tbsp	butter	45 mL
1/2 cup	brown sugar	125 mL
6	ripe peaches	6
1/3 cup	butter, softened	75 mL
1/2 cup	granulated sugar	125 mL
1	egg	1
1/2 tsp	each vanilla and almond extract	2 mL
1-1/4 cups	cake and pastry flour*	300 mL
1-1/2 tsp	baking powder	7 mL
Pinch	salt	Pinch
1/2 cup	milk	125 mL
	Additional granulated sugar (optional)	

1. Place the 3 tbsp (45 mL) butter and the brown sugar in a deep 9-inch (1.5 L) round cake pan and set it in the oven while you are preheating it to 350°F (180°C). As soon as the butter melts, remove the pan and stir well, spreading the mixture evenly in the bottom.

2. Meanwhile, blanch the peaches, slip off the skins, halve, remove the pits, and cut into 1-inch (2.5 cm) slices. Arrange slices, rounded side down, very close together in circles in the prepared pan.

3. In a large bowl, cream together the remaining butter and the granulated sugar. Stir in egg, vanilla and almond extract, beating until well combined. Sift together twice the flour, baking powder and salt. Gradually stir one-third of the flour mixture, then half of the milk into butter mixture. Repeat, ending with remaining flour mixture. Spoon evenly over peaches and smooth the top.

4. Bake in 350°F (180°C) oven for 55 to 60 minutes or until well browned and cake springs back when lightly touched. Let cool in pan on a rack for 10 minutes. Run a knife around edges and invert onto a plate. Or, if you wish, rather than a plate, set a rack and a baking sheet over the cake and invert it onto them. Sprinkle peaches with granulated sugar and set under a preheated broiler for about 5 minutes or until the sugar is melted and the peaches are slightly browned.

* Sift flour before measuring.

old-fashioned fresh fruit shortcake

MAKES 6 TO 8 SERVINGS

Instead of layering the fruit with soft cake, my mother always used a sweetened biscuit base for fruit short-cake. I like this best, too. Enjoy the classic dessert with fragrant, bright red strawberries in June and July; then with dark, juicy raspberries, cherries, blueberries, blackberries and finally unpeeled sliced peaches and plums for a treat to take you right into fall. Just sweeten the fruit according to taste and let it sit for a time in the sugar so that wonderful juices form to drench the shortcake. I even coarsely slice strawberries to help this along.

2 cups	all-purpose flour	500 mL
1/2 cup	granulated sugar	125 mL
1 tbsp	baking powder	15 mL
1/4 tsp	salt	1 mL
1/2 cup	butter	125 mL
2/3 cup	10% cream	150 mL
1	egg	1
1 cup	whipping cream	250 mL
4 cups	prepared fresh fruit	1 L
1 tbsp	fresh lemon juice	15 mL
1 tbsp	icing sugar	15 mL
1 tsp	vanilla	5 mL

1. Stir together flour, 2 tbsp (25 mL) of the granulated sugar, baking powder and salt in a large bowl. Cut in the butter with a pastry blender or 2 knives until the mixture resembles coarse crumbs. In a 2-cup (500 mL) glass measure, beat together 10% cream and the egg. Add cream mixture all at once to the flour mixture, then stir just until dry ingredients are moistened and a soft, slightly sticky dough forms. Gather dough into a ball, then, with floured hands, pat into a greased 8-inch (1.2 L) round cake pan. Brush with 1 tsp (5 mL) of the whipping cream, then sprinkle with 2 tsp (10 mL) of the remaining granulated sugar. Bake in a 450°F (230°C) oven for 15 to 18 minutes or until golden brown on top. Run a metal spatula around the sides of the pan to loosen the shortcake. Turn out onto a wire rack.

2. In a bowl, stir together fruit, remaining granulated sugar and lemon juice. In a separate chilled bowl, beat remaining whipping cream with icing sugar and vanilla until soft peaks form.

3. With a serrated knife, slice warm shortcake in half horizontally. Place the bottom layer cut side up on a serving plate. Reserving 1 cup (250 mL) of the fruit for garnish, spoon remainder with juices over the bottom layer of shortcake. Top fruit with half of the whipped cream. Place the second shortcake layer cut side down on top, then spread with remaining whipped cream. Garnish with reserved fruit, then serve at once.

black forest trifle

MAKES 12 SERVINGS

Cherries are one of my favourite fruits, and every time they are in season, I yearn for the row of cherry trees that lined the lane of our family farm when I was a child. Even before home freezers were available, in our nearby town we had a freezer locker into which we would put our own fresh produce as it came into season. It meant going into town every time we wanted a package during the winter, but it was worth the effort to have that delicious fruit for pies, cakes, jams or whatever treat my mother decided to make. Now, I buy a pail of pitted, sugared sour cherries when they are in season, package them into pie amounts and freeze them at home—no picking or pitting. But occasionally I'll buy a basket of fresh sour cherries at our farmers' market just so I can pit them and make a pie ... for old times' sake!

All through the season, we buy lovely big sweet cherries for eating out of hand. They disappear like candy at our house. For this sensational dessert, choose red sour cherries—fresh, frozen or canned.

1	Chocolate Cake (recipe follows) 1
1/3 cup	chocolate liqueur, kirsch or cherry liqueur 75 mL
4 cups	pitted fresh cherries, drained canned cherries or drained thawed frozen cherries 1 L
1 cup	whipping cream 250 mL
2 tbsp	icing sugar 25 mL
1 tsp	vanilla 5 mL
	Chocolate curls*

CUSTARD

3 cups	milk 750 mL
5	egg yolks 5
1/2 cup	granulated sugar 125 mL
1/4 cup	cornstarch 50 mL
1 tsp	vanilla 5 mL

1. Custard: In a saucepan, heat milk just until bubbles form around the edge. In a heavy saucepan, beat egg yolks with sugar and cornstarch until smooth; gradually whisk in milk. Cook over medium heat, stirring constantly, for 3 to 5 minutes or until thickened. Reduce heat to low and simmer, stirring, for 1 minute. Strain into a bowl; stir in vanilla. Place plastic wrap directly on surface; refrigerate until cooled or up to 2 days.

2. Break chocolate cake into chunks; arrange in the bottom of a 14-cup (3.5 L) trifle bowl. Drizzle with chocolate liqueur. Set 1/4 cup (50 mL) cherries aside; spoon in remaining cherries, arranging attractively around the side of the bowl. Spoon in the custard. (Trifle can be prepared to this point, covered and refrigerated for up to 1 day.)

3. Whip cream with icing sugar; beat in vanilla. Spread over the trifle. Garnish with chocolate curls and reserved cherries.

* Hold a wrapped square of chocolate in your hand for about 1 minute or until softened but not melted. Slowly draw a vegetable peeler along the underside of the square for wide curls; for smaller curls, draw the peeler along the narrow side.

chocolate cake

MAKES 1 CAKE

1/2 cup	butter, softened 125 mL
1-1/3 cups	granulated sugar 325 mL
2	eggs 2
1 tsp	vanilla 5 mL
1-1/3 cups	all-purpose flour 325 mL
1/2 cup	sifted unsweetened cocoa powder 125 mL
1/2 tsp	baking powder 2 mL
1/2 tsp	baking soda 2 mL
1/4 tsp	salt 1 mL
3/4 cup	milk 175 mL

1. Line the bottom of a 9-inch (1.5 L) round cake pan with waxed paper. Grease the side.

2. In a large bowl, beat butter with sugar until fluffy; beat in eggs, 1 at a time. Beat in vanilla. Stir together flour, cocoa, baking powder, baking soda and salt. Stir into the creamed mixture alternately with milk, making 3 additions of flour mixture and 2 of milk. Pour into the pan.

3. Bake in a 350°F (180°C) oven for 30 to 35 minutes or until a cake tester inserted into the centre of the cake comes out clean. Let cool in the pan for 10 minutes; turn out onto a rack to let cool completely.

pecan-whisky cake

MAKES 10 TO 12 SERVINGS

A pecan topping and a glaze laced with rye whisky make this a very special Adults Only cake. It's wonderful with tea in front of the fire.

1 cup	chopped pecans	250 mL
1-1/2 cups	butter, softened	375 mL
1 cup	granulated sugar	250 mL
6	eggs	6
1/4 cup	rye whisky	50 mL
1-1/2 tsp	vanilla	7 mL
2-1/4 cups	all-purpose flour	550 mL
1-1/2 tsp	baking powder	7 mL
1/4 tsp	salt	1 mL

GLAZE

1/4 cup	butter	50 mL
1 cup	granulated sugar	250 mL
1/4 cup	water	50 mL
1/2 cup	rye whisky	125 mL
	Whipped cream	

1. Lightly butter and flour a 9- or 10-inch (3 or 4 L) tube or Bundt pan. Sprinkle nuts over the bottom. Set aside.
2. In a large bowl, cream butter thoroughly; gradually beat in sugar until light and fluffy. Add eggs, 1 at a time, beating well after each addition. Stir in rye and vanilla. Stir together flour, baking powder and salt; gradually add to butter mixture, stirring just until combined.
3. Spoon batter over pecans. Bake in a 325°F (160°C) oven for about 1 hour or until a tester inserted in the centre of the cake comes out clean. Let cool in the pan for 5 minutes; invert on a rack set over a baking sheet.
4. Glaze: Meanwhile, in a small saucepan, melt the butter; stir in sugar and water. Bring to a boil, stirring constantly. Reduce heat to low and simmer for 5 minutes, without stirring. Remove from the heat; stir in rye.
5. Using a long skewer, make several holes through the top of the cake, almost to its bottom. Drizzle some of the warm glaze over the hot cake and brush over the sides. Let cake absorb glaze; repeat drizzling until all of the glaze is used. Let cool. Garnish top with rosettes of whipped cream.

harvest pies

There would be a choice of apple, squash, plum, and maybe even an old-fashioned butterscotch pie with meringue topping. I can well remember those noon meals when a crowd of men would come in from the fields to gather around our big round kitchen table. Before my family bought a modern combine, harvest time meant a threshing machine that travelled from farm to farm, and every farmer helped his neighbour. Each farmer's wife would take her turn at providing meals for all of the hungry threshers.

There was always pie for dessert—with, I'm sure, much expert assessment among the men as to who made the best elderberry or peach pie.

The variety was infinite—raisin, pear, lemon meringue, grape, custard, maple syrup, even green tomato (if there was danger of early frost)—but it always depended on what was in season and what was at hand, abundant choices, indeed, at harvest time.

Although it may seem extraordinary to many young cooks, a pie was just about the easiest thing a busy farm wife could make. It was also an economical method of making a few ingredients go a long way around a table of hungry diners. Early cooks had already discovered that round pans could help them literally cut corners and stretch ingredients. The other advantage was that a pie didn't have to be eaten immediately. (Pies, however, are always best eaten on the same day as they are made.) Farm men came in for dinner—the name always given to the noon meal—when *they* were ready, not when dinner was ready.

Appetites have changed, and my immediate family hasn't seen as many pies as I remember from my own well-fed childhood, but no matter what sophisticated desserts I serve, a good old-fashioned pie is still a treat.

dutch apple pie

MAKES 6 TO 8 SERVINGS

I've asked many good friends what they remember as comfort food from their youth. My friend Diane Slimmon, an excellent cook, didn't hesitate for a minute in describing her favourite meal as a kid: "We had this every Saturday at noon—fresh frying [farmer's] sausage from the market, home fried potatoes, coleslaw, Dutch apple pie and Cheddar cheese." Diane remembered her mother using the cream from the top of the milk bottle to drizzle on top of the apple pie before it was baked. "Whether the cream was fresh or sour, Mom would pour it on top until she could see cream in between the clumps of apples."

In the Waterloo region, where Dutch apple pie reigns, everyone makes a slightly different version, but all agree it is a real treat. My friend Mary Lou Ruby Jonas, who has a Mennonite background, shared this recipe with me. She lends a slightly modern twist to it since she partially cooks the apples in the microwave before using them as pie filling. This technique gives them a lovely flavour and a slightly softer, melting texture, but you can omit this step if you like. The apple of choice for this old-fashioned treat is Spy, but if these are unavailable, choose any good cooking apple that will hold its shape. Formerly, the apple slices, or *apfel schnitz*, were dried for longer storage, but now fresh apples are used. Serve the pie warm or at room temperature with Cheddar cheese.

	Pastry for a 9-inch (23 cm) single-crust pie
4 cups	peeled, cored and thickly sliced Spy apples 1 L
2 tbsp	water 25 mL
1/4 cup	butter 50 mL
1/2 cup	packed brown sugar 125 mL
1/2 cup	granulated sugar 125 mL
1/4 cup	all-purpose flour 50 mL
1/2 tsp	cinnamon 2 mL
1/4 cup	whipping cream 50 mL

1. On a lightly floured surface, roll out the pastry and fit it into a 9-inch (23 cm) pie plate; trim and flute the edge.
2. Combine the apples with water in a microwaveable dish and cook at High for 2 minutes; stir and cook for 2 minutes longer. Let cool while preparing the rest of the ingredients.
3. Set aside 1 tbsp (15 mL) of the butter. In a food processor, combine sugars, flour, remaining butter and cinnamon; process with on/off pulse until like crumbs. (Alternatively, combine sugars and flour in a bowl; cut in remaining butter with a pastry blender or 2 knives until like coarse oatmeal. Stir in cinnamon.) Sprinkle half of this crumb mixture evenly in the bottom of the pie shell. Pour apples and juice on top and sprinkle them with the remaining crumb mixture. Pour cream over top and dot with reserved butter. Bake in a 425°F (220°C) oven for 10 minutes. Reduce temperature to 375°F (190°C); bake for 40 minutes longer or until crust is golden brown and apples are tender and bubbly.

apples

The heady fragrance of freshly picked apples on a sunny September day. The comforting aroma of an apple pie just out of the oven. It's no wonder this homegrown fruit has been such a favourite over the years and across the country: in the Okanagan Valley in British Columbia, along the Lower Great Lakes in southern Ontario, in Quebec's St. Lawrence Valley, in the St. John River Valley of New Brunswick and in Nova Scotia's Annapolis Valley, where French settlers planted orchards in 1632.

Since the Collingwood and Meaford areas near our farm in Ontario are such huge apple-growing ones, it was not surprising that we grew several varieties for our own use. Without today's sophisticated storage facilities, my mother would extend the life of our apples by peeling and slicing, then drying them for use during the winter. I can still taste her pie made with dried apple slices. It was sweet with the concentration of natural sugars through drying, and it had an inviting texture unlike any found in fresh apple pie.

The tree I remember most was an old Snow apple tree that sat in a field north of our house. It was gnarled and misshapen, but yielded fruit that I have never been able to find again. Snow apples are not very common, and when I do see them at the farmers' market, I buy a basket just to see if I can recreate that taste of the past.

Although we find only a handful of varieties in the supermarket (those that are appealing to the eye and hearty enough to withstand the hardships of travel and display), our ancestors probably enjoyed more than six hundred types of apples.

Apple picking in Ontario starts in late July or early August with the first non-storing varieties such as Yellow Transparent, Paula Red, Melba, Wealthy, St. Lawrence and Tydeman Red. These are often soft, not as sweet as later apples, but very good for something like applesauce. Many of these older varieties you may not find in a supermarket, but these apples were very welcome to early farmers long after their winter supply of fruit had vanished.

Of the apples you might find in a supermarket, one of the most popular is the McIntosh, a truly Ontario variety named for John McIntosh, who discovered it as a seedling on a farm in Dundas County around 1811. This bright red apple that is usually picked in September has white, juicy, crisp flesh and is excellent for eating out of hand or mashed smoothly into applesauce. People who don't mind the apples losing their shape will use it for pies as well. Spartans and Gravensteins also cook smoothly into sauce, with Spartans a choice for pies, too.

The Northern Spy (my favourite cooking apple), Idared, Golden Delicious, Red Rome and Newton apples all hold their shape when cooked and are excellent for pies and baked apples.

On the other hand, Red Delicious, with showy, dark red skin and sweet flavour, is an eating rather than cooking apple. Good for fresh eating, too, are the Empire and Mutsu (Crispin), which is also good for baking. If you need an apple for a salad, the best choice is the Cortland, known as "The Caterer's Apple" because it stays white longer after being cut and is also good for fresh eating, baking, pies and sauces.

And, of course, the best place to look for any of these is the local farmers' market, especially if you are looking for a taste of the past.

blueberry peach pie

MAKES 8 SERVINGS

When I first started to haunt the Cambridge Farmers' Market here in Galt, Ontario, peach season always found Philip and Mary Tufford at the same corner of the market each Wednesday and Saturday. Beside their white van were shelves piled high with baskets of the biggest ripe peaches you would probably ever find anywhere in the country. Because Philip used to cull them in their early stages on the trees, they were not only huge but also juicy and full of flavour. I've seen none like them since Philip died years ago and Mary could no longer carry on the business. Mary still calls me every Christmas, and I still miss Philip's peaches.

For best results, use fresh fruit for this juicy pie; it's a great way to use up the last of the late-summer harvest. There's no need to peel the peaches.

	Pastry for a 9-inch (23 cm) double-crust pie
2 cups	each blueberries and sliced pitted peaches 500 mL
2/3 cup	granulated sugar 150 mL
2 tbsp	cornstarch 25 mL
2 tbsp	fresh lemon juice 25 mL
1/2 tsp	cinnamon 2 mL
2 tbsp	butter, cubed 25 mL
1 tsp	cream or milk 5 mL
2 tsp	granulated sugar 10 mL

1. On a lightly floured surface, roll out half of the pastry to 1/4-inch (5 mm) thickness. Use pastry to line a 9-inch (23 cm) pie plate.
2. In a large bowl, toss blueberries and peaches with 2/3 cup (150 mL) sugar, cornstarch, lemon juice and cinnamon. Spoon blueberry mixture into the pie shell; dot with butter.
3. Roll out the remaining pastry to 1/4-inch (5 mm) thickness. Moisten the edge of the pastry shell with water; cover with second round of pastry. Trim pastry edges to within 1/2 inch (1 cm) of the rim of plate; tuck pastry under and crimp the edge. If you wish, cut out decorative shapes from the pastry trimming. Brush top of the pie with cream; arrange pastry decorations on top. Brush decorations with cream; sprinkle top of pie evenly with 2 tsp (10 mL) sugar. Cut slits in pie for steam to escape.
4. Bake in a 425°F (220°C) oven for 15 minutes. Reduce temperature to 350°F (180°C); bake 35 minutes or until crust is golden brown and filling is bubbly.

almond-plum tart

MAKES 8 SERVINGS

On the farm where I grew up, I remember the most marvellous plum tree beside our lane. Its trunk was very dark and gnarled, its branches erratic and the fruit big, dark purple and deliciously warm and sweet.

Except for knowing that almost every farm harbours at least one old knotted tree, I didn't realize, until I started doing extensive research on the fruit, that the plum is one of the world's most widely distributed fruit, growing on almost every continent and encompassing more than two thousand varieties.

Plums are always a favourite eaten out of hand, but few people realize how delicious they are in so many other ways: in pies, tarts, cakes, sauce, jams, salads, chutneys, soups, sorbets, shortcakes and crisps, or sautéed with meat or poultry. Reine Claude (Greengage), Valor, Burbank (for canning) and the prune varieties are all good for cooking.

This elegant company dessert needs a sturdier crust than most, so substitute butter for 1/2 cup (125 mL) of the shortening or lard in your favourite recipe for pie crust, use all-purpose flour and add 2 tablespoons (25 mL) of granulated sugar.

	Pastry for a 9-inch (23 cm) tart shell (see pastry recipe with Runny Gooey Butter Tarts, page 135)
2/3 cup	ground almonds 150 mL
2/3 cup	granulated sugar 150 mL
1	egg 1
2 tbsp	butter, softened 25 mL
1 tsp	each vanilla and grated lemon zest 5 mL
1/4 tsp	almond extract 1 mL
15	prune plums, pitted and quartered 15
1/4 cup	currant jelly 50 mL
1 tbsp	port or grape juice 15 mL

1. On a lightly floured surface, roll out the pastry to 1/4-inch (5 mm) thickness. Use pastry to line the base and sides of a 9-inch (23 cm) round tart pan with removable bottom, building pastry up sides of pan so it extends 1/4 inch (5 mm) above the rim of the pan. Chill at least 15 minutes.

2. Line the pastry shell with foil; weigh down with dried beans, rice or other pie weights. Bake in a 400°F (200°C) oven for 8 minutes. Remove beans and foil. With a fork, prick pastry base at 1/2-inch (1 cm) intervals; bake for 2 to 3 minutes or until pastry looks dry. Let cool.

3. In a medium bowl, combine the almonds, 1/3 cup (75 mL) of the sugar, egg, butter, vanilla, lemon zest and almond extract. Spread mixture evenly over base of tart shell.

4. In a large bowl, toss plums with remaining sugar; arrange over almond mixture. Bake in a 350°F (180°C) oven for 40 minutes or until filling is set and pastry is browned. Let cool in pan on a wire rack.

5. In a small saucepan, combine jelly and port; heat over medium-low heat until melted and smooth. Spoon jelly mixture over tart; let cool to room temperature. Remove tart from pan before serving.

mom's butterscotch meringue pie

MAKES 6 SERVINGS

When the supply of fruit started to dwindle, my mother's pie repertoire didn't because she could still make lemon meringue, custard, chocolate and this wonderful silky smooth butterscotch pie.

Pastry for 9-inch (23 cm)
   single-crust pie

FILLING

2 tbsp	butter	25 mL
3/4 cup	packed brown sugar	175 mL
2 cups	whole milk	500 mL
1/4 cup	cornstarch	50 mL
Pinch	salt	Pinch
2	egg yolks	2
1 tsp	vanilla	5 mL

MERINGUE TOPPING

2	egg whites	2
1/4 tsp	cream of tartar	1 mL
1/4 cup	granulated sugar	50 mL
2 tbsp	cold water	25 mL
1/2 tsp	vanilla	2 mL
Pinch	salt	Pinch

1. On a lightly floured surface, roll out pastry and line a 9-inch (23 cm) pie plate. Line pastry with a piece of foil or parchment paper; fill with pie weights or dried beans. Bake in a 400°F (200°C) oven for 15 minutes. Remove weights and foil. Prick shell all over with a fork; bake for 5 to 10 minutes longer or until evenly golden. Let cool on a rack.

2. Filling: In a medium saucepan, melt butter over medium heat; stir in brown sugar. Cook, stirring, for 2 to 3 minutes until the mixture is smooth, thick and starts to sizzle. Watch carefully; it burns easily. Remove saucepan from the heat.

3. In a medium bowl, combine 1/4 cup (50 mL) milk, cornstarch and salt until smooth; whisk in remaining milk. Gradually whisk milk mixture into sugar mixture (mixture will be lumpy). Cook over medium heat, whisking constantly, for 2 to 3 minutes, until smooth and starting to thicken.

4. In a small bowl, beat egg yolks lightly. Stir a little of the hot milk mixture into the egg yolks until well combined. Add egg yolk mixture to saucepan. Cook, whisking constantly, for 2 to 3 minutes until thickened and bubbly. Remove from the heat; stir in vanilla. Let cool completely, stirring occasionally to prevent a skin from forming. Pour into the baked pie shell, spreading evenly.

5. Meringue Topping: In a medium bowl, using an electric beater, beat egg whites and cream of tartar until soft peaks form. Gradually beat in granulated sugar until all is combined and mixture no longer feels gritty when a little is rubbed between a finger and thumb. Add water, vanilla and salt; beat until stiff, shiny peaks form.

6. Spoon meringue evenly over filling, spreading right to the edges so there are no gaps between meringue and pastry. With the flat side of a knife, make decorative peaks in the meringue. Place pie on a baking sheet and bake in a 375°F (190°C) oven for 12 to 15 minutes, until the tips of meringue are golden brown. Let cool before serving, but do not refrigerate.

acadian sugar pie

MAKES 6 TO 8 SERVINGS

This old-fashioned treat is rich and sweet and best served in very small wedges topped with whipped cream.

	Pastry for 9-inch (23 cm) single-crust pie
2 cups	packed brown sugar 500 mL
2 tbsp	all-purpose flour 25 mL
Pinch	salt Pinch
2	eggs 2
1	egg yolk 1
1 cup	milk 250 mL
1 tsp	vanilla 5 mL

1. On a lightly floured surface, roll out the pastry and fit it into a 9-inch (23 cm) pie plate; trim and flute the edge.
2. In a bowl, blend sugar, flour and salt. In a separate bowl, beat eggs and yolk until frothy; beat in milk and vanilla. Stir into sugar mixture until smooth.
3. Pour into the pie shell and bake in a 400°F (200°C) oven for 10 minutes; reduce the heat to 350°F (180°C) and bake for about 35 minutes longer or until the crust is golden brown and filling is set.

fresh grape pie

MAKES 8 SERVINGS

Winter baking in decades like the thirties often meant making use of dried fruit such as raisins and dates, and raisin pie remains a favourite despite the availability of good frozen fruit one could use for pies today. If you like raisin pie, you will absolutely love this fresh grape version. Use red, green or black seedless grapes.

5 cups	stemmed seedless grapes (about 2 lb/1 kg) 1.25 L
1/2 cup	granulated sugar 125 mL
1/3 cup	orange juice 75 mL
2 tbsp	quick-cooking tapioca 25 mL
1 tbsp	grated orange zest 15 mL
1/4 tsp	nutmeg 1 mL
Pinch	salt Pinch
	Pastry for a 9-inch (23 cm) double-crust pie
2 tbsp	butter, cubed 25 mL
1 tsp	cream or milk 5 mL
2 tsp	granulated sugar 10 mL

1. With a large sharp knife, coarsely chop 1-1/2 cups (375 mL) of the grapes. In a deep saucepan, combine chopped grapes, 1/2 cup (125 mL) sugar, orange juice, tapioca, orange zest, nutmeg and salt. Cook over medium heat for 3 to 5 minutes until bubbly, stirring often. Reduce heat to low; cook for 2 minutes. Remove from the heat; stir in remaining grapes. Let cool slightly.

2. On a lightly floured surface, roll out half of the pastry to a 1/4-inch (5 mm) thickness. Use pastry to line a 9-inch (23 cm) pie plate, letting edges of pastry overhang edge of plate.

3. Pour grape mixture into pie shell; dot with butter. Roll out remaining pastry to 1/4-inch (5 mm) thickness; cut into 1/2-inch (1 cm) strips. Arrange strips on top of pie to form a lattice, trimming ends of strips to fit plate. Fold edge of bottom crust over latticed edges; crimp to seal. Brush pastry with cream; sprinkle evenly with 2 tsp (10 mL) sugar. Bake in a 425°F (220°C) oven for 12 minutes. Reduce temperature to 350°F (180°C); bake for 25 minutes longer or until crust is golden brown. Serve warm or at room temperature.

spicy dried fruit pie

MAKES 8 SERVINGS

My mother was never out of ideas for dessert pies. Here is one of her easy and aromatic alternatives to fresh fruit pie fillings. In the fall, she would slice and dry apples and often make a pie with just the dried apples, an amazing difference in flavour from using fresh. If you don't have one of the dried fruits called for, substitute an equal amount of one of the others. Serve with thin custard, whipped cream or Cheddar cheese.

1 cup	dried apple slices	250 mL
3/4 cup	raisins	175 mL
1/2 cup	each chopped dried figs (remove stems), pitted prunes and dried apricots	125 mL
2-1/2 cups	apple juice	625 mL
1/4 cup	packed brown sugar	50 mL
2 tbsp	fresh lemon juice	25 mL
1 tsp	grated lemon zest	5 mL
1/2 tsp	cinnamon	2 mL
1/4 tsp	each ground cloves and nutmeg	1 mL
1 tsp	vanilla (or 2 tbsp/25 mL brandy)	5 mL
1 cup	toasted, coarsely chopped walnuts*	250 mL
	Pastry for a 9-inch (23 cm) double-crust pie	
	Cream or milk	
	Granulated sugar	

1. In a medium saucepan, combine the apple slices, raisins, figs, prunes, apricots and apple juice; bring to a boil. Reduce heat to medium-low; simmer, uncovered, for 15 minutes. Remove from heat.
2. Stir in brown sugar, lemon juice, lemon zest, cinnamon, cloves, nutmeg, vanilla and walnuts. Let cool for 15 minutes.
3. Meanwhile, roll out half of the pastry on a lightly floured surface; use to line a 9-inch (23 cm) pie plate. Spread fruit mixture in pie shell; dampen edges of pastry. Roll out remaining pastry; place over filling, pressing edges together to seal. Trim edges, then flute by making decorative indentations around the edge of the pie. Cut 4 or 5 slits in the top for steam to escape. Brush top of pie with cream; sprinkle with granulated sugar. Bake in a 425°F (220°C) oven for 10 minutes; reduce heat to 350°F (180°C) and bake for 45 to 50 minutes longer or until golden brown.

* To toast walnuts, spread out on a baking sheet and bake in a 350°F (180°C) oven for 7 to 10 minutes or until golden brown and fragrant.

apple cranberry pandowdy

MAKES 6 TO 8 SERVINGS

When Elizabeth Baird and I were working on an heirloom dessert article for *Canadian Living* magazine, we couldn't resist doing a pandowdy, which is an old-fashioned pie-like dessert that everyone loves. And I couldn't resist using my favourite combination of apples and cranberries. Since cranberries freeze so well for up to a year, I always buy many extra bags to throw into my freezer so I can make desserts like this year-round.

Serve warm with whipped cream or Cheddar cheese.

5	large apples, peeled and sliced 1/2-inch (1 cm) thick 5
1-1/2 cups	fresh or frozen (unthawed) cranberries 375 mL
2 tbsp	fresh lemon juice 25 mL
1/2 cup	granulated sugar 125 mL
1/2 cup	maple syrup 125 mL
1/4 cup	all-purpose flour 50 mL
1/2 tsp	cinnamon 2 mL
1 tbsp	butter, cut in bits 15 mL
	Pastry for 9-inch (23 cm) single-crust pie
1 tbsp	10% cream or milk 15 mL
2 tsp	granulated sugar 10 mL

1. Grease an 11- x 7-inch (2 L) glass baking dish; set aside. In a bowl, toss apples, cranberries and lemon juice together; stir in sugar, maple syrup, flour and cinnamon. Spread in prepared dish. Dot with butter. Roll out the pastry; fit over filling, tucking in edges.

2. Brush pastry with cream. Sprinkle with sugar. Bake on a baking sheet in the centre of a 400°F (200°C) oven for 30 minutes. Remove from the oven. Cut pastry into 2-inch (5 cm) squares, pulling apart slightly and pushing some edges down to allow juices to flow over top. Reduce heat to 350°F (180°C); bake until pastry is golden and filling is bubbly, about 30 minutes. Serve warm.

runny gooey butter tarts

MAKES 24 TARTS

Uniquely Canadian, butter tarts were probably adapted from old-fashioned sugar or maple syrup pies. There is constant controversy as to how runny they should be, or whether they should include currants, raisins or nuts. My husband, Kent, has always talked about how delicious his mother's butter tarts were, saying, "They were so runny you had to double up the pastry to hold them together at the first bite." When I asked his sister, Alene, if she still had the recipe, the request set her off too: "Mom's were THE BEST ... always went first at the First Baptist bake sales." Alene wasn't sure she could duplicate her mother's, but this recipe she sent certainly seems to fit the description. I've added a bit of lemon juice to cut the sweetness somewhat, but it isn't necessary; they are still super-sweet but amazing. Use very fresh walnuts, cracking them from the shell if possible.

PASTRY

3 cups	all-purpose flour	750 mL
1 tsp	salt	5 mL
1/4 tsp	baking powder	1 mL
3/4 cup	chilled lard or shortening, cubed	175 mL
1/4 cup	chilled butter, cubed	50 mL
1	egg	1
2 tsp	white vinegar	10 mL
	Cold water	

FILLING

2	eggs	2
1 cup	packed brown sugar	250 mL
1 cup	corn syrup	250 mL
1/4 cup	butter, melted	50 mL
2 tsp	vanilla	10 mL
2 tsp	fresh lemon juice (optional)	10 mL
2/3 cup	coarsely chopped walnuts	150 mL

1. Pastry: In a large bowl, stir together flour, salt and baking powder. Cut in lard and butter with a pastry blender or 2 knives, until mixture resembles coarse crumbs. In a glass measure, whisk together egg, vinegar and enough cold water to measure 2/3 cup (150 mL). With a fork, gradually stir egg mixture into flour mixture until the dough begins to clump together; gather dough into a ball. Divide into 2 even pieces and form each into a disc. Wrap in plastic wrap and refrigerate for at least 1 hour or overnight.

2. Filling: In a bowl, beat eggs well with a whisk, then whisk in sugar, corn syrup, butter, vanilla and lemon juice, if using. Stir in nuts. (Some people prefer to distribute the nuts among the pastry shells, then spoon the filling on top.)

3. On a lightly floured surface, roll out the pastry (half at a time) to 1/8-inch (3 mm) thickness. Using a 4-inch (10 cm) round cookie cutter (or the top of a clean can), cut out 24 circles, rerolling scraps if necessary. Fit pastry circles into 2-3/4- x 1-1/4-inch (7 x 3 cm) muffin cups. Spoon in filling until three-quarters full, trying not to get filling on edges of the pastry.

4. Bake in the bottom third of a 400°F (200°C) oven for 17 to 19 minutes or until filling is puffed and bubbly and the pastry is golden. Let stand on a rack for 1 minute, then run a dinner knife around the outside of each tart to loosen it. Carefully transfer tarts to a rack to cool.

never-fail big batch pastry

MAKES THREE 9-INCH (23 CM) DOUBLE-CRUST PIES OR SIX 9-INCH (23 CM) PIE SHELLS

This easy pastry is great if you are making a number of pies, as I know many people do when apples are at their best. Or, with a batch of it stored in the freezer, a homemade pie will take just minutes to make after the pastry thaws.

For best results, work the pastry gently and quickly, and keep everything cold as you do. Every time I give that last piece of advice I think of one of my pastry students running back and forth from her workstation to the freezer. When I asked what she was doing, she explained she had hot hands and went to cool them off occasionally. A pair of thin latex gloves is an easier solution.

4 cups	cake-and-pastry flour 1 L	
2 cups	all-purpose flour 500 mL	
1-1/2 tsp	salt 7 mL	
1 lb	cold lard or shortening 500 g	
1	egg 1	
1 tsp	white vinegar 5 mL	
	Ice water	

1. In a large bowl, combine the flours and salt. In a food processor, process one-third of the flour mixture with one-third of the lard until the mixture resembles coarse rolled oats; transfer to another large bowl. Repeat in 2 batches with remaining flour and lard.
2. Alternatively, in a large bowl, with a pastry blender or 2 knives, cut lard into flour mixture until mixture resembles coarse rolled oats.
3. In a 1-cup (250 mL) measure, beat egg and vinegar together. Fill measure with ice water; stir well. Gradually add liquid to flour/lard mixture, blending lightly with a fork until the dough just holds together (you may have to add a little more water). Finish by combining the mixture gently with your hands. The dough may crumble slightly at this point. Form dough into 6 rounds. Wrap each round in waxed paper, then seal in plastic bags. Refrigerate for up to 1 day or freeze for up to 2 months. If frozen, thaw in the refrigerator.

> **NOTE**
> See also the pastry recipe on page 135 used for Runny Gooey Butter Tarts; it makes enough for two 9-inch (23 cm) pie crusts or one 9-inch (23 cm) double-crust pie and is sturdy enough for a tart shell.

rhubarb-pineapple cobbler

MAKES 8 SERVINGS

You can use any fresh, seasonal or sliced fruit under this light-as-a-feather cobbler topping. My spring favourite is a combination of fresh rhubarb and canned pineapple.

FRUIT FILLING

4 cups	chopped rhubarb 1 L
1	can (19 oz/540 mL) unsweetened pineapple tidbits, drained 1
3/4 cup	packed brown sugar 175 mL
2 tbsp	all-purpose flour 25 mL

TOPPING

1-1/2 cups	all-purpose flour 375 mL
1 tbsp	each granulated sugar and baking powder 15 mL
Pinch	salt Pinch
1/2 cup	cold butter, cubed 125 mL
3/4 cup	buttermilk or whipping cream 175 mL
	Additional granulated sugar

1. Fruit Filling: In an 8-inch (2 L) square baking dish, combine rhubarb, pineapple, brown sugar and 2 tbsp (25 mL) flour; set aside.

2. Topping: In a food processor, combine flour, granulated sugar, baking powder and salt; process until combined. Add butter; process until mixture resembles coarse oatmeal. Add buttermilk; process using on/off pulses, just until a thick, sticky dough forms. (Alternatively, combine flour, sugar, baking powder and salt in a large bowl. With a pastry cutter or 2 knives, cut in butter until mixture resembles coarse oatmeal. Stir in buttermilk until thick, sticky dough forms.)

3. Using a large spoon, scoop 8 rounds of topping onto the fruit to cover it. Sprinkle with a little additional granulated sugar. Bake in a 375°F (190°C) oven for 45 minutes or until top is golden brown and cooked through and fruit juices bubble up.

simply splendid rice pudding

MAKES 4 TO 6 SERVINGS

My landlady while I was at university was a lovely English woman who provided me with all my meals. On Thursdays, no matter how badly my day had gone, I took much solace in anticipating her wonderful home-made fish and chips as I travelled home on the streetcar. The same could be said for those cold days when I just knew we would have her warm, creamy rice pudding.

Risottos seem to have replaced the old-fashioned rice pudding as modern comfort food, but I think that the traditional baked rice pudding should be revived since it is so easy to make and provides the same wonderfully creamy texture as an upscale risotto. It takes just minutes to prepare, then can sit happily in the oven for a couple of hours ... no constant stirring here. Buy short-grain rice for puddings; I've used arborio rice with good success.

4 cups	milk (not skim) 1 L
1/3 cup	uncooked short-grain rice 75 mL
1/4 cup	packed brown sugar 50 mL
1 tbsp	butter 15 mL
1 tsp	vanilla 5 mL
Pinch	salt Pinch

1. In a large saucepan, heat the milk over medium-high heat until bubbles appear around the edge; remove from heat.
2. In a greased 8-cup (2 L) baking dish (preferably glass), combine the milk, rice, sugar, butter, vanilla and salt. Bake in a 300°F (150°C) oven about 2 hours or until rice is just tender and most of the milk is absorbed, stirring twice during the first hour.

bread and butter pudding

MAKES 8 TO 10 SERVINGS

Bread puddings were the invention of thrifty cooks to make good use of stale bread. This one gives us a tasty reminder of the past. If using fresh bread, place the slices in a single layer on a tray and let them dry at room temperature for one hour. We encountered a very interesting version once at a breakfast buffet in a Montreal hotel. They had made a bread pudding with leftover Chelsea buns ... a great idea that I've been meaning to use, but I never seem to have any Chelsea buns left over!

8	large slices firm white stale bread 8
2 tbsp	butter 25 mL
1/2 cup	raisins 125 mL
1/4 cup	currants 50 mL
4	eggs 4
2/3 cup	lightly packed brown sugar 150 mL
4 cups	hot milk 1 L
1 tsp	vanilla 5 mL
1/2 tsp	nutmeg 2 mL
1/4 tsp	salt 1 mL
1/4 cup	red currant jelly 50 mL
	Cream (optional)

1. Trim crusts from bread; spread slices with butter and cut into quarters. Place half the bread, buttered side up, in a buttered 11- x 7-inch (2 L) baking dish. Sprinkle with raisins and currants.
2. Beat eggs well; beat in sugar and blend well. Slowly whisk in hot milk, vanilla, nutmeg and salt. Pour half the mixture over bread in the dish. Top with remaining bread and pour remaining egg mixture over it.
3. Place baking dish in a large shallow pan. Pour 1 inch (2.5 cm) boiling water into the pan and bake in a 325°F (160°C) oven for about 45 minutes or until almost set. Remove baking dish to a rack.
4. In a small saucepan, melt jelly over medium heat and brush over top of the pudding. Serve hot or warm with cream (if using).

hot chocolate fudge pudding

MAKES 4 TO 6 SERVINGS

Also called Batter Pudding or Hasty Pudding and dating back to the thirties, this homey dessert was probably in your grandmother's favourite cookbook. It's still very welcome on a cold winter night when you want a super-easy dessert. When baked, the pudding forms a rich chocolate sauce beneath a cake topping. Serve warm with whipped cream.

1-1/4 cups	packed brown sugar	300 mL
3 tbsp	butter, softened	45 mL
1 tsp	vanilla	5 mL
1 cup	all-purpose flour	250 mL
1/3 cup	unsweetened cocoa powder, sifted	75 mL
2 tsp	baking powder	10 mL
1/4 tsp	salt	1 mL
1/2 cup	milk	125 mL
1/2 cup	chopped pecans or walnuts	125 mL
1-2/3 cups	boiling water	400 mL

1. In a large bowl, cream together 3/4 cup (175 mL) of the sugar, 2 tbsp (25 mL) of the butter, and vanilla; set aside.
2. In a separate bowl, stir together flour, 2 tbsp (25 mL) of the cocoa, baking powder and salt. Add flour mixture to sugar mixture alternately with milk until well blended. Stir in nuts.
3. Spoon mixture into a greased 8-inch (2 L) square baking dish. In a medium bowl, combine remaining sugar, cocoa and butter. Stir in boiling water until smooth. Carefully pour cocoa mixture over batter in baking dish. Do not stir. Bake in a 350°F (180°C) oven for 30 to 40 minutes or until a skewer inserted in the cake comes out clean. (The sauce thickens as the cake cools.)

smooth and creamy butterscotch pudding

MAKES 4 SERVINGS

You can't beat the flavour and comforting texture of homemade pudding, whether you make it in the microwave oven or on top of the stove.

3/4 cup	packed light brown sugar 175 mL	
2 tbsp	cornstarch 25 mL	
2 cups	milk 500 mL	
1	egg 1	
1 tbsp	butter 15 mL	
1 tsp	vanilla 5 mL	

Microwave Method:

1. In an 8-cup (2 L) glass measure, stir together sugar and cornstarch; whisk in milk until well combined. Cook at High (100%) for 3 minutes. Whisk briskly; cook at High for 2 minutes.
2. In a small bowl, beat egg lightly; whisk in 1/2 cup (125 mL) of the sugar mixture. Stir egg mixture back into glass measure. Cook at High for 2 to 3 minutes, until thickened and bubbly. Stir in butter and vanilla until butter is melted and mixture is smooth. Pour into 4 individual dishes; chill before serving.

Stove-Top Method:

1. In a medium saucepan, stir together sugar and cornstarch; whisk in milk until well combined. Bring to a boil over medium heat, stirring constantly; remove from heat.
2. In a small bowl, beat egg lightly; whisk in 1/2 cup (125 mL) of the sugar mixture. Stir egg mixture back into saucepan. Cook over medium heat for 2 to 3 minutes, until thickened and bubbly. Remove from heat; stir in butter and vanilla until butter is melted and mixture is smooth. Pour into 4 individual dishes; chill before serving.

daiene's bodacious chocolate chip cookies

MAKES ABOUT 4 DOZEN COOKIES

Cookie-making seems to be the first foray most children make into the world of cooking. Kids love cookies, and the size of these miniature confections makes this a reasonable achievement for a little one. Our kids were standing on chairs, barely able to see over the kitchen counter, when they first started to mix, roll and form the dough. When they were older and still at home, they were the official cookie-makers in the house. I do enjoy seeing young mothers carrying on this tradition with their children. Daiene Vernile, who was my host for many years on Kitchener's CKCO-CTV *Noon News*, makes these old favourites with her three children. The recipe is much the same as others, but Daiene's method is a bit different, and the result delicious. What could be more comforting with a glass of milk and a book?

1 cup	butter, softened 250 mL
1 cup	packed brown sugar 250 mL
1/2 cup	granulated sugar 125 mL
2	eggs 2
2 tsp	vanilla 10 mL
2-1/4 cups	all-purpose flour (approx.) 550 mL
2 tsp	baking soda 10 mL
1	pkg (10-1/2 oz/300 g) chocolate chips 1

1. In a large bowl, cream the butter with sugars until fluffy. Beat in eggs, 1 at a time; stir in vanilla until well mixed.

2. Stir or sift flour and baking soda together; gradually stir into the creamed mixture, adding up to 1/4 cup (50 mL) more flour if necessary until the batter loses its wet look but isn't too stiff. Stir in the chocolate chips and stick the bowl in the freezer for 8 minutes.

3. Drop by rounded tablespoonfuls (15 mL), about 2 inches (5 cm) apart, onto parchment paper–lined or greased baking sheets. With a fork, flatten to 1/2 inch (1 cm) thickness. Bake in a 375°F (190°C) oven for 8 to 10 minutes or until golden. Let cool on the pan on a rack for a couple of minutes, then transfer to a rack to cool.

hazelnut shortbread

MAKES 4 DOZEN

There is a certain air of richness to these nut-filled shortbread rounds. If you wish, you can decorate them with a sprinkle of icing sugar and a whole hazelnut in the centre, or you can spread them with the hazelnut glaze in this recipe. They are even good without any topping. Be sure to taste the hazelnuts first to make sure they are perfectly fresh.

1 cup	hazelnuts (filberts)	250 mL
1 cup	butter, softened	250 mL
1/2 cup	packed brown sugar	125 mL
3 tbsp	hazelnut liqueur, such as Frangelico	45 mL
1 tsp	vanilla	5 mL
1/4 cup	cornstarch	50 mL
Pinch	salt	Pinch
1-3/4 cups	all-purpose flour	425 mL

HAZELNUT GLAZE

1-1/2 cups	icing sugar, sifted	375 mL
2 tbsp	hazelnut liqueur	25 mL
2 tbsp	water (approx.)	25 mL

1. Spread hazelnuts out on cookie sheet and toast in 350°F (180°C) oven for about 15 minutes or until fragrant. Wrap hot nuts in a clean tea towel and rub to remove most of the skins. Cool, then finely chop in a food processor or by hand with a sharp knife.

2. In large bowl, beat butter and brown sugar until fluffy. Stir in liqueur and vanilla.

3. Stir in cornstarch and salt, then flour, about a third at a time to make smooth dough. Add nuts and mix gently until well blended. Divide dough in half. Refrigerate for 30 minutes to 1 hour or until firm but not hard.

4. Roll each half between 2 sheets of waxed paper to 1/4-inch (5 mm) thickness; refrigerate until chilled, about 30 minutes. Using a 2-inch (5 cm) floured cookie cutter, cut out rounds, rerolling scraps. Transfer cookies to parchment paper-lined cookie sheets, leaving 1 inch (2.5 cm) between cookies. Chill until firm, about 2 hours.

5. Bake in the centre of a 325°F (160°C) oven until golden, 15 to 20 minutes. Let cool on pans on racks for 2 minutes. Transfer to racks; let cool.

6. Hazelnut Glaze: In a bowl, whisk together icing sugar, liqueur and water until smooth, adding up to 1 tbsp (15 mL) more water, if necessary, to make spreadable. Spread over cookies. (Cookies can be layered with waxed paper in airtight container and stored at room temperature for up to 1 week or frozen for up to 1 month.)

squares and bars

What could be a quicker way of filling the cookie jar than making an easy batch of squares or bars? They are so satisfying to enjoy with an afternoon cup of tea, and wonderful to have on hand if someone drops in to have a cup with you.

As the story goes, at the beginning of the twentieth century, a rural Canadian homemaker (who could very well have been my own mother, who was always entertaining our minister and his family) invited her minister and his wife to tea. She had baked a cake for the occasion but, as sometimes happens, it didn't rise. With no time to make anything else, the undaunted hostess iced it, cut it into little pieces and had an instant hit on her hands—squares.

Since then, squares have appeared at potluck suppers, bazaars, teas, receptions and showers. Easier to make than cookies, as there's no rolling, slicing or shaping, these sweet finger foods are infinitely versatile. With fruit or ice cream, they make an easy family dessert. Served with a cup of coffee or tea when friends drop by, they spell hospitality.

date squares

MAKES 24 SQUARES

Called Matrimonial Cake in the West, these oatmeal and date squares seemed to be in everyone's recipe collection years ago. Both my mother and my sister, Muriel, made very good versions of this old-time favourite, but I'm afraid I have neither of those recipes (if, in fact, they were ever written down). My husband, Kent, remembered his mother's date squares as particularly delicious too, and fortunately his sister, Alene, did write that recipe down. Since they are quite sweet, I tend to cut them into tiny squares.

1 cup	all-purpose flour	250 mL
1/2 tsp	baking soda	2 mL
Pinch	salt	Pinch
1 cup	butter	250 mL
1 cup	packed brown sugar	250 mL
2 cups	rolled oats	500 mL

FILLING

1/2 lb	pitted dates (about 2 cups/ 500 mL)	250 g
3/4 cup	water	175 mL
1 tbsp	brown sugar	15 mL

1. Filling: There's no need to chop the dates. In a small saucepan, combine dates, water and sugar. Bring to a boil; reduce heat to medium and cook until dates can be mashed, about 10 minutes, stirring often. Mash well and let cool.

2. Sift flour, baking soda and salt into a large bowl. With a pastry blender or 2 knives, cut in butter until like coarse crumbs. Push 1 cup brown sugar through a coarse sieve to remove any lumps. Stir sugar and oats into butter mixture until well combined. Press half of the mixture evenly in a greased 8-inch (2 L) square metal cake pan; spread evenly with the date mixture. Top with remaining oat mixture, patting down smoothly and evenly. Bake in a 325°F (160°C) oven for 30 to 35 minutes or until light golden. Do not overbake. Let cool in the pan on a rack before cutting into squares.

> **TIP**
> Use old-fashioned or quick oats, not instant oatmeal, for this recipe.

walnut date chews

MAKES 20 BARS

With today's trend toward cutting down on fat, this old favourite finds new appeal because it contains no butter. It is such a simple way to fill your cookie jar, and you can easily double the recipe; just be sure to write the doubled amounts of ingredients down before you start. Use a 13- x 9-inch (3.5 L) pan instead of the 8-inch (2 L) square pan and bake for 5 to 10 minutes longer, shielding the edges with foil if necessary to prevent browning.

2	eggs	2
1 cup	packed brown sugar	250 mL
1 cup	chopped dates	250 mL
1 tsp	vanilla	5 mL
1/2 cup	all-purpose flour	125 mL
1/4 tsp	each baking soda and salt	1 mL
1 cup	toasted chopped walnuts or pecans	250 mL
1 tsp	icing sugar	5 mL

1. Grease an 8-inch (2 L) square cake pan; set aside. In a large bowl, beat eggs with brown sugar until doubled in volume. Stir in dates and vanilla. Stir together flour, baking soda and salt; stir into sugar mixture. Stir in nuts. Spread in prepared pan. Bake in the centre of a 350°F (180°C) oven for 20 to 30 minutes or until golden, crusty, edges are puffed and centre underneath is still soft. Let cool in the pan on a rack. Cut into bars. (Bars can be stored in an airtight container or wrapped in plastic wrap and frozen in a rigid airtight container for up to 2 weeks.) Sift icing sugar over top.

almond orange shortbread bars

MAKES 2 DOZEN BARS

A tender shortbread base and sweet, slightly chewy topping of nuts and orange make an easy and delicious cookie bar. Use a zester, if you have one, to make longer strips of zest for a prettier bar.

3/4 cup	butter, softened	175 mL
1/2 cup	icing sugar	125 mL
1 cup	all-purpose flour	250 mL
Pinch	salt	Pinch
1/2 cup	packed brown sugar	125 mL
1 tbsp	grated orange zest	15 mL
2 tbsp	fresh orange juice	25 mL
3/4 cup	sliced almonds	175 mL
1/4 tsp	almond extract	1 mL

1. Line a 9-inch (2.5 L) square metal cake pan with parchment paper; set aside.
2. In large bowl, cream together 1/2 cup (125 mL) of the butter and icing sugar. Gradually stir in flour and salt. With floured hands, pat into prepared pan. Bake in 350°F (180°C) oven for 12 to 15 minutes or until lightly coloured.
3. Meanwhile, in small saucepan, melt remaining 1/4 cup (50 mL) butter. Stir in brown sugar, zest and juice; bring to boil, stirring constantly. Remove from heat; stir in almonds and almond extract.
4. Spread over base; bake for 12 to 15 minutes or until golden brown. Let cool slightly; cut into bars while still warm.

classic chocolate brownies

MAKES 32 BROWNIES

I am so happy that my Turtle Brownies, which appeared first in *Canadian Living* and then in *A Year in My Kitchen*, have become a classic in many other kitchens. Since I develop recipes so others can use them, it is good indeed to know that they do. I've had more than one reader say, "I freeze them so that I won't eat them all at once; my, they're good frozen." These fudge-like brownies, without the caramel topping of the Turtle Brownies, are just plain, but are still just plain addictive.

1 cup	butter	250 mL
4 oz	unsweetened chocolate	125 g
2 cups	granulated sugar	500 mL
4	eggs	4
1 tsp	vanilla	5 mL
1 cup	all-purpose flour	250 mL
1/2 tsp	salt	2 mL
1 cup	coarsely chopped nuts (pecans or walnuts)	250 mL

1. In the top of a double boiler over barely simmering water, melt butter with chocolate. Remove from heat and stir in sugar until well combined. Beat in eggs, 1 at a time, stirring after each addition until eggs are fully incorporated and chocolate mixture is shiny. Stir in vanilla. Gradually add flour and salt; mix until well blended. Stir in nuts. Pour into a greased 13- x 9-inch (3.5 L) cake pan and bake in a 400°F (200°C) oven for about 18 minutes or until brownies feel slightly firm and a tester inserted in the centre shows that brownies are moist but doesn't show raw batter. Cool in the pan on a rack. Cut into bars.

> **VARIATION**
>
> **DOUBLE CHOCOLATE BROWNIES**
> For something even more decadent, stir 1 cup (250 mL) chocolate chips into the batter.

glazed apricot blondies

MAKES 20 SQUARES

Blondies are the golden version of traditional brownies, and these are loaded with lovely sweet-sour apricots and pecans. The hint of lemon in the glaze cuts the sweetness of the icing sugar.

1/2 cup	butter, softened	125 mL
1-1/4 cups	packed brown sugar	300 mL
2	eggs	2
2 tsp	vanilla	10 mL
1-1/4 cups	all-purpose flour	300 mL
1 cup	chopped dried apricots	250 mL
1/2 cup	chopped pecans	125 mL
1/4 tsp	salt	1 mL

GLAZE

1/2 cup	icing sugar	125 mL
2 tbsp	butter, softened	25 mL
2 tsp	fresh lemon juice	10 mL

1. Grease an 8-inch (2 L) square cake pan; set aside. In a large bowl, beat butter with brown sugar until fluffy; beat in eggs, 1 at a time. Beat in vanilla. Stir together flour, apricots, pecans and salt; stir into butter mixture in 2 additions until combined. Scrape into prepared pan. Bake in the centre of a 325°F (160°C) oven for 40 to 50 minutes or until cake tester inserted in the centre of the cake comes out clean. Let cool in the pan on a rack until just slightly warm.

2. Glaze: Stir together icing sugar, butter and lemon juice; spread over base. Let cool; cut into squares. (Squares can be stored in an airtight container for up to 5 days.)

TIP

This recipe is easily doubled; just be sure to write out the double amounts of the ingredients before starting so you won't get confused. Use a 13- x 9-inch (3.5 L) pan instead of the 8-inch (2 L) square cake pan and allow 10 to 15 minutes more baking time.

---

lemon meringue slices

MAKES 54 SLICES (OR MORE IF CUT INTO TINY SQUARES)

I've never been a great lover of lemon meringue pie, probably because along the way I've had to taste some nasty pies made with artificial lemon filling. I do love real lemon, however, and these easy squares are my choice over pie. They are slightly chewy with a melt-in-your-mouth shortbread base.

BASE

1/2 cup	butter, softened	125 mL
1/2 cup	icing sugar	125 mL
1 cup	all-purpose flour	250 mL

FILLING

2	egg whites	2
Pinch	salt	Pinch
1/2 cup	granulated sugar	125 mL
1 tsp	grated lemon zest	5 mL
2 tbsp	fresh lemon juice	25 mL

1. Base: In a bowl, cream butter; gradually beat in icing sugar and beat until light and fluffy. Stir in flour (mixture will be crumbly). With floured fingers, pat evenly into an ungreased 13- x 9-inch (3.5 L) pan and bake in a 350°F (180°C) oven for about 10 minutes or until light golden around the edges. Let cool while preparing filling.

2. Filling: Beat egg whites with salt until stiff. Gradually beat in granulated sugar. Add zest and juice; beat until meringue stands in peaks. Spread over base and bake in a 350°F (180°C) oven for 20 to 25 minutes or until golden brown. Let cool completely in pan on a wire rack before cutting.

white chocolate pecan rum balls

MAKES ABOUT 36 RUM BALLS

This quick and easy treat was one I developed for a *Canadian Living* article called "It's Never Too Late ... There's Still Time to Whip Up Holiday Treats," and this one really is fast and delicious. These rum balls keep for at least one week in the refrigerator—if you can resist eating them!

8 oz	white chocolate, chopped 250 g
2 cups	ground pecans (about 7 oz/ 200 g) 500 mL
1/4 cup	white rum 50 mL
1/4 cup	granulated sugar 50 mL

1. In a large heatproof bowl over hot (not boiling) water, melt chocolate, stirring often. Stir in pecans and rum. Cover and refrigerate for 20 minutes or until firm. Using 2 spoons, shape into 1-inch (2.5 cm) balls. Place sugar in a bag; add rum balls and shake to coat evenly. Serve chilled.

> **TIP**
> Store nuts in the freezer and always sample nuts before adding them to a recipe to make sure they aren't rancid.

MENUS

the pleasures
of entertaining

It gives me great pleasure to prepare food and share it with good friends and family.

As I grew up, it seemed that our house was always full of people. At Christmas, my much older sisters, who were married when I was very young, would come home for the holidays. Throughout the year, aunts and uncles would often visit from various provinces across Canada. And there would be a constant stream of friends on planned or spontaneous visits. For whoever came and for whatever length of time, there was always good food in abundance. I just naturally inherited this "entertaining gene," which to my joy I seem to have passed on to my children, who enjoy cooking for others. I was absolutely delighted, too, that they both chose to have their weddings in our garden with a homemade feast.

In a world that is becoming more and more restless, there is something peaceful and gratifying about entertaining at home, whether it is a party of one hundred or one other special person.

a company
breakfast

As I was growing up, I remember our farmhouse filled often with weekend guests, especially in the summers when the garden gave forth its bounty of fresh fruit and vegetables. Or, it might have been my mother's great baking skills that caused no hesitation in people we invited to stay overnight. I remember her saying that the worst thing about house guests was not knowing when everyone would get up in the morning, but that didn't stop her from having a wonderful breakfast awaiting even the latest risers.

Who could go wrong, however, with fresh homemade bread, butter made from our own cream, eggs gathered just that morning and enticing preserves from the garden?

Over the years, my husband and I have had our share of overnight guests as well, and although I don't have those resources we had on the farm, I've tried to make breakfast and brunches a little bit special if we have company. Sometimes I make a strata the day before just to pop into the oven in the morning (see Savoury Prosciutto and Cheese Bread Pudding, page 80). Or, I prepare a casserole of cheese and tomatoes, a frittata, a baked pancake or some kind of waffles. If I am very short on time, good scrambled eggs (not the cardboard, stiff kind) and peameal bacon from the farmers' market fill the bill very nicely. I'll add an easy muffin or scone and open a jar of whatever jam I have made.

This easy menu will get any company out of bed in a hurry.

make-ahead fruit salad

MAKES 6 SERVINGS

I love starting a company brunch or breakfast with a colourful and refreshing fruit salad, but I would rather do the peeling and dicing (with the inevitable juice running down my arms) the day before and have it ready to set on the table. Some fruit salads don't stand up well for twenty-four hours, but this one is really better if made ahead. The raw cranberries add a festive touch that makes this a good choice for a holiday breakfast too.

1	large pineapple 1
2	kiwi fruits 2
1/4 cup	fresh cranberries, coarsely chopped 50 mL
2 tbsp	liquid honey 25 mL
2 tbsp	fresh orange juice 25 mL
1/4 cup	water 50 mL
2 tbsp	orange liqueur or Grand Marnier (or additional orange juice) 25 mL

1. Peel and core pineapple; cut into bite-sized cubes and place in a large serving bowl. Peel and slice kiwi fruits; add to pineapple with cranberries.
2. In a small saucepan, stir together honey, orange juice and water. Bring to a boil, reduce heat and simmer for 5 minutes. Cool, stir in liqueur, toss with the fruit, cover and refrigerate for at least 2 hours or overnight.

creamy scrambled eggs

MAKES 4 TO 6 SERVINGS

My daughter, Anne Loxton, is a pro at making these eggs from *Canadian Christmas Cooking*; it's a treat to have her make them when she visits. With the addition of cream cheese, these scrambled eggs will hold longer—even in a chafing dish for a company brunch, but have the serving dish hot so the eggs can be transferred to it as soon as they are done.

6	eggs 6
1/4 cup	cream (18% or whipping) 50 mL
1/4 cup	dry white wine 50 mL
1/2 tsp	salt 2 mL
	Freshly ground black pepper
2 tbsp	butter 25 mL
4 oz	cubed cream cheese 125 g

1. Beat the eggs lightly. Add the cream, wine, salt and pepper. Melt the butter in a chafing dish or double boiler. Pour in the egg mixture. Stir occasionally over medium-low heat until the eggs are almost firm, but still very moist. Stir in the cream cheese until it melts and blends. Serve hot.

glazed canadian back bacon

MAKES 6 TO 8 SERVINGS

Our back bacon (also known as peameal) is internationally famous for its leanness and good flavour. Since the meat vendors at our local Cambridge Farmers' Market always have lovely back bacon, I quite often buy a few slices to fry for a weekend treat. It is also delicious for breakfast or even supper when roasted in a whole piece as in this easy glazed version.

1	centre-cut peameal back bacon roast (2 to 3 lb/1 to 1.5 kg) 1	
1/3 cup	maple syrup 75 mL	
2 tbsp	all-purpose flour 25 mL	
1 tbsp	Dijon mustard 15 mL	
1 tbsp	fresh lemon juice 15 mL	
Pinch	ground cloves Pinch	

1. Place the bacon on a rack in a shallow baking pan. Roast, uncovered, in a 325°F (160°C) oven for 1 hour.
2. In a measuring cup, stir together maple syrup, flour, mustard, lemon juice and cloves. Spread half of the mixture over the roast, increase oven temperature to 425°F (220°C) and roast until a meat thermometer inserted in the centre registers 130°F (55°C), about 20 to 30 minutes longer, basting with the remaining maple syrup mixture after 10 minutes.
3. Transfer to a cutting board; tent with foil and let stand for 10 minutes before thinly slicing.

the very best home fries

MAKES 4 SERVINGS

When Elizabeth Baird and I were testing this recipe for an article we wrote together for *Canadian Living*, we used my well-seasoned cast-iron frying pan, but a nonstick skillet will still get you the golden crusty bits and steaming chunky potatoes that are so wonderful with eggs and peameal bacon. For quick preparation, cook four extra potatoes when you are making dinner the night before.

4	large potatoes 4	
2 tbsp	vegetable oil 25 mL	
1 tbsp	butter 15 mL	
1	green onion, sliced 1	
1	clove garlic, minced 1	
1/4 tsp	salt 1 mL	
Pinch	each pepper and paprika Pinch	

1. Scrub potatoes. In a pot of boiling salted water, cook potatoes for 15 minutes or until tender but firm; drain well. Refrigerate until cold. Cut into 1/2-inch (1 cm) cubes.
2. In a nonstick skillet, heat oil and butter over high heat; cook potatoes, turning to coat all over, for 3 to 4 minutes.
3. Cook for about 8 minutes longer, turning often, or until crisp and golden. Remove from the heat; stir in onion, garlic, salt, pepper and paprika.

cranberry oat muffins

MAKES 10 LARGE MUFFINS

One of my favourite fruits helps make these muffins moist and delicious. I always keep bags of cranberries in the freezer so I can prepare treats like this year-round. Served warm from the oven, these colourful muffins have a crunchy cinnamon-sprinkle topping.

If you wish, you can mix the dry ingredients with the oats and flour and make the sugar-cinnamon topping the night before so you are ready to put the muffin batter together in the morning.

3/4 cup	rolled oats (not instant)	175 mL
1-1/2 cups	all-purpose flour	375 mL
1 cup	granulated sugar	250 mL
2 tsp	baking powder	10 mL
1/2 tsp	salt	2 mL
1/2 cup	butter	125 mL
2/3 cup	milk	150 mL
1	egg	1
2 cups	coarsely chopped cranberries*	500 mL
4 tsp	grated lemon zest	20 mL

TOPPING

4 tsp	granulated sugar	20 mL
1 tsp	cinnamon	5 mL

1. In a food processor or blender, grind rolled oats until powdered; transfer to a large bowl. Stir in flour, 1 cup (250 mL) sugar, baking powder and salt; cut in butter until crumbly.
2. Whisk together milk and egg; pour over dry ingredients. Sprinkle with cranberries and lemon zest; stir just until dry ingredients are moistened. Spoon into large greased or paper-lined muffin cups, filling three-quarters full.
3. Topping: Combine 4 tsp (20 mL) sugar and cinnamon; sprinkle over batter. Bake in a 400°F (200°C) oven for 25 to 30 minutes or until tops are firm to the touch.

* If using frozen cranberries, do not thaw.

baked apple pancake

MAKES 4 SERVINGS

This is one of our most-loved family breakfast pancakes, along with maple syrup and tiny pork sausages. The puffy giant pancake is also perfect for a company breakfast.

Use a cast-iron skillet if you have one, or sauté the apples in a regular skillet and transfer them to an 8-inch (1.2 L) nonstick round cake pan before adding the batter.

2/3 cup	granulated sugar	150 mL
1/2 tsp	cinnamon	2 mL
1/4 cup	butter	50 mL
2	apples, peeled, cored and thinly sliced	2
1/2 cup	all-purpose flour	125 mL
1/2 cup	milk	125 mL
2	eggs	2
1/2 tsp	vanilla	2 mL
1/4 tsp	salt	1 mL
Pinch	nutmeg	Pinch
	Maple syrup	

1. In a small bowl, stir together 1 tbsp (15 mL) of the sugar and the cinnamon; set aside.
2. In a heavy 8-inch (20 cm) ovenproof skillet, melt butter over medium-high heat. Add apples; cook for 5 minutes, stirring often, until apples are translucent.
3. Meanwhile, in a large bowl, whisk together remaining sugar, flour, milk, eggs, vanilla, salt and nutmeg just until blended; do not overmix.
4. Remove skillet from heat; pour batter evenly over apples (there will be only a thin layer of batter). Bake in a 425°F (220°C) oven for 15 minutes, until batter is set.
5. Remove skillet from the oven; run a thin metal spatula around the edge of the skillet to loosen the pancake. Invert pancake onto a large plate; carefully slide it back into the skillet. Sprinkle evenly with reserved cinnamon sugar. Bake for 10 minutes or until puffy and golden brown and a toothpick inserted into the centre comes out clean. Loosen edges of the pancake as before; slide pancake onto a warmed serving plate. Serve at once, cut into wedges. Pass maple syrup for drizzling on top.

VARIATION

BAKED PEAR PANCAKE
Substitute pears for the apples, cardamom for the cinnamon and omit the nutmeg.

a portable feast
for a mother's day reunion

Mother's Day is always a good time for families to get together, especially fun if little ones are involved. I do remember those early days when we lived in a big house in Owen Sound, Ontario, and our bedroom was on the third floor at the front of the house with the kitchen on the first floor at the back. Our kids, Allen and Anne, were very young at the time, but would make me breakfast and carry the tray all the way up two sets of stairs so I could have breakfast in bed. Of course, I would declare the soggy cereal and cold toast delicious.

Although I haven't seen my daughter lately on Mother's Day because she has been living too far away, my son will still cook something as a treat for me, and now, it truly is delicious.

In this menu, I have concentrated on make-ahead and portable dishes that will appeal to all generations. The preparation can be divided easily among members of the clan, even giving kids a chance to help. This menu would also make an excellent family birthday party for any time of the year.

* Set out mini pitas, pizza sauce, a choice of toppings (pepper slivers, cherry tomato slices, sliced mushrooms, pepperoni, ham, small shrimp, etc.) and some shredded cheese. Have the kids in the crowd design their own pizzas. Just before serving, bake them in a 425°F (220°C) oven for about 5 minutes or until the cheese is melted.

old-fashioned real lemonade

MAKES 5 CUPS (1.25 L) CONCENTRATE SYRUP, ENOUGH FOR 20 TALL GLASSES

During the hot summer months, I remember my mother making all kinds of cool, refreshing drinks such as homemade sodas and real lemonade. This lemon concentrate syrup makes the drink that brings back memories of sitting on our farmhouse veranda; perhaps it will take you back to your own grandmother's porch. Easy to make, it has none of the bitter aftertaste you often get with store-bought lemonade, and the syrup keeps for weeks.

Get the maximum juice from lemons by having them at room temperature and rolling them between your palms before cutting.

6 to 9	large lemons	6 to 9
2 cups	granulated sugar	500 mL
2 cups	water	500 mL
Pinch	salt	Pinch

1. Finely grate the zest from 2 of the lemons and stir together in a small saucepan with the sugar, water and salt. Bring to a boil, stirring constantly; boil for 5 minutes, stirring. Remove from the heat and let cool.
2. Meanwhile, cut enough lemons in half to squeeze out 2 cups (500 mL) juice. When syrup is cool, stir in lemon juice; transfer to a large clean jar, cover and refrigerate for up to 3 weeks.
3. For each tall glass, use 1/4 cup (50 mL) syrup and 3/4 cup (175 mL) cold water or cold soda water. For a 4-cup (1 L) pitcher, combine 1 cup (250 mL) syrup with cold water to fill the pitcher. Add ice and, if you wish, thin lemon slices to the glass or pitcher.

VARIATIONS

PINK LEMONADE
Stir 1 tbsp (15 mL) grenadine syrup into 1 glass lemonade made as above.

PINK LEMONADE GIN
Add 1-1/2 oz (45 mL) gin to Pink Lemonade.

LEMON ICED TEA
Stir 1/4 cup (50 mL) of lemon concentrate syrup into 3/4 cup (175 mL) iced tea.

---

flowerpot vegetables with caesar dip

MAKES ABOUT 3 CUPS (750 ML)

When you want an appealing and quick appetizer for a spring party, serve a colourful bouquet of asparagus spears, green onions, sweet pepper strips and carrot sticks, arranged in a pretty ceramic flowerpot. The flavours of a popular salad dressing take their turn as the dip.

8 oz	light cream cheese	250 g
6 oz	feta cheese, rinsed	175 g
1 cup	freshly grated Parmesan cheese	250 mL
1/2 cup	light sour cream	125 mL
1	green onion, chopped	1
2 tbsp	fresh lemon juice	25 mL
2 tsp	each Dijon mustard, anchovy paste and Worcestershire sauce	10 mL
Dash	hot pepper sauce	Dash
2	cloves garlic	2
	Milk (optional)	

1. In a food processor or blender, combine cream cheese, feta, Parmesan, sour cream, onion, lemon juice, mustard, anchovy paste, Worcestershire sauce and hot pepper sauce. Process until very smooth and creamy, dropping garlic through the feed tube while the machine is running. If too thick, add a bit of milk. Transfer to a serving dish. (Dip can be made up to 1 day ahead, covered and refrigerated.)

roast chicken dinner pot pie

MAKES 8 SERVINGS

This updated version of pot pie combines the ingredients of a delicious roast chicken dinner in one portable dish. Roasting the chicken and vegetables together gives wonderful flavour, and the pie is easy to assemble; it can be refrigerated and baked just before serving.

1	roasting chicken (5 to 6 lb/ 2.2 to 2.7 kg) 1
3 tbsp	olive oil 45 mL
	Salt and pepper
4	unpeeled red potatoes, cut into 1-inch (2.5 cm) cubes 4
1/2 lb	small mushrooms 250 g
1/2 lb	mini carrots 250 g
1	pkg (about 10 oz/284 g) pearl onions, peeled 1
2-1/2 cups	chicken stock 625 mL
1 tsp	each dried sage, marjoram and thyme 5 mL
2 tbsp	cornstarch 25 mL
1/4 cup	whipping cream 50 mL
2 cups	frozen peas 500 mL
Half	pkg (14 oz/397 g) frozen puff pastry, thawed Half
1	egg 1
1 tsp	cold water 5 mL

1. Remove any fat from the inside of the chicken and wipe with a damp paper towel. Place chicken in a large shallow roasting pan. Drizzle 1 tbsp (15 mL) of the oil over it and sprinkle with salt and pepper. Roast, uncovered, in a 400°F (200°C) oven for 40 minutes.

2. Add potatoes, mushrooms, carrots and onions to the pan in a single layer. Drizzle vegetables with remaining oil, sprinkle with salt and pepper, and stir to coat well. Roast for 30 to 40 minutes or until the vegetables are tender and the chicken juices run clear when the thickest part of the thigh is pierced.

3. Remove chicken and set aside; with a slotted spoon, remove vegetables to a large bowl, leaving pan juices in the roasting pan. When cool enough to handle, remove chicken meat from the bones and cut meat into bite-sized pieces, discarding skin and bones. Add chicken meat to vegetables in the bowl.

4. Skim off any excess fat from pan drippings. Add to drippings 2 cups (500 mL) of the stock, sage, marjoram and thyme; bring to a boil, scraping up any brown bits from the bottom of the pan. Dissolve cornstarch in remaining stock; add to pan and cook, stirring, until thickened. Remove from heat, stir in cream and peas, and combine with chicken mixture. Taste and adjust seasoning. Spoon into a greased 13- x 9-inch (3.5 L) baking dish. Let cool.

5. Roll out pastry to fit the top of the dish. For a glaze, lightly beat together egg and cold water. Brush onto the rim of the dish and place pastry on top. Make a small hole in the middle. Brush pastry all over with the glaze. (Pie can be prepared to this point and refrigerated for up to 6 hours.)

6. Bake in a 400°F (200°C) oven for about 30 minutes or until pastry is golden brown and filling is bubbly.

TIP

If you don't have homemade stock, 1 can (10 oz/284 mL) chicken broth plus 1 can water will give you 2-1/2 cups (625 mL) chicken stock.

salad of spring greens with mango

MAKES 8 SERVINGS

An attractive mix of fresh greens and exotic fruit, enhanced with a sweetish dressing, is appealing to all ages.

DRESSING

2 tbsp	white wine vinegar	25 mL
2 tbsp	granulated sugar	25 mL
1/2 tsp	each paprika and dry mustard	2 mL
1/4 tsp	salt	1 mL
1 tsp	minced onion or shallot	5 mL
1/2 cup	vegetable oil	125 mL

SALAD

1	bunch each leaf spinach and watercress	1
1	head leaf or Boston lettuce	1
1	head Belgian endive	1
1	mango, peeled and diced	1

1. Dressing: In a microwaveable bowl or a small saucepan, combine vinegar and sugar; in a microwave or on top of the stove, heat until sugar is dissolved. Stir in paprika, dry mustard and salt. Transfer to a blender, add the onion and blend until smooth. With the motor running, add the oil in a thin stream until blended and smooth. Transfer to a jar with a lid. (Dressing can be made and refrigerated up to 1 day ahead.) Shake well before using.

2. Salad: Wash and dry spinach, watercress and lettuce, removing thick stems from spinach and watercress. Separate endive into leaves. Tear greens into bite-sized pieces and toss together in a large bowl. (Salad can be prepared to this point, covered and refrigerated for up to 2 hours.)

3. Just before serving, toss with mango and dressing.

chocolate angel food cake

MAKES ABOUT 12 SERVINGS

One of my son's favourite desserts, angel food cake is easy to transform into a chocolate version that is still virtually fat free. Serve with ice cream, if desired.

1/3 cup	unsweetened cocoa powder 75 mL
1/4 cup	boiling water 50 mL
1-1/2 tsp	vanilla 7 mL
1-1/4 cups	sifted cake and pastry flour 300 mL
1-3/4 cups	granulated sugar 425 mL
12	egg whites, at room temperature 12
1 tsp	cream of tartar 5 mL
1/4 tsp	salt 1 mL

1. In a small bowl, mix together cocoa and water; add vanilla, stirring until smooth. Set aside.
2. Sift flour with 1 cup (250 mL) of the sugar into a bowl; set aside.
3. Put egg whites in a very large bowl. With an electric mixer, beat until foamy. Add cream of tartar and salt; beat to soft peaks. Very gradually add 3/4 cup (175 mL) sugar, beating until mixture holds stiff, shiny peaks. Stir about 1 cup (250 mL) of the egg whites into the cocoa mixture; set aside.
4. Sift flour mixture, a quarter at a time, over remaining whites, folding in each addition with a rubber spatula. Gently but thoroughly fold in cocoa mixture. Pour batter into an ungreased 10-inch (4 L) tube pan; run a knife through the batter to remove any air bubbles; smooth the top with a spatula.
5. Bake in a 325°F (160°C) oven for 55 to 60 minutes or until the top of the cake springs back when touched.
6. Remove from the oven and immediately turn pan upside down (invert over neck of a bottle if pan has no feet). Let stand inverted until completely cooled. Run a knife around the inside edge and tube of pan and remove cake. To serve, cut into slices with a serrated knife.

VARIATION

PLAIN WHITE ANGEL FOOD CAKE
Omit the cocoa and boiling water. Proceed as above, keeping all of the beaten egg whites together and gently folding in the vanilla after the flour mixture at the end with the addition of 1/2 tsp (2 mL) almond extract and 1 tsp (5 mL) fresh lemon juice, also folded in at the end.

an easy oriental menu

Around about February, everyone is ready for a break from day-to-day life. Why not celebrate the Chinese New Year—whether you are Chinese or not? Nowhere is the celebration bigger than in Hong Kong. Two memorable visits to its food festival have inspired these dishes, which will bring a little taste of the Orient to your table. If you lack the time or energy to make the whole menu, any part of it will give you an excuse for a party or just a break from everyday fare.

Typically, a Chinese meal for family or casual entertaining consists of about one different dish per person at the table, with everything shared; if more people come along, more dishes are added. Serve the soup first, then bring everything else (except dessert) to the table at the same time. I always try to do one oven dish and invite family or guests to help with the last-minute stir-frying.

hot and sour soup

MAKES 6 SERVINGS

The Cantonese think of soup not only as a delicious food but also as essential therapy for rehydrating the body and skin. Many wonderful soups were offered for sampling at the Magnificent Soup Carnival I attended as part of the Hong Kong Food Festival one year. This version of the popular hot and sour soup is thick and full flavoured. Different brands of chili oil vary in hotness, so adjust it to taste.

12 oz	tofu (extra-firm or firm) 375 g	
1 cup	Chinese dried mushrooms 250 mL	
3/4 cup	warm water 175 mL	
8 cups	chicken broth 2 L	
1/2 lb	lean pork butt, slivered 250 g	
1-1/2 cups	matchstick-cut bamboo shoots (fresh or canned, rinsed) 375 mL	
2 tbsp	rice vinegar 25 mL	
1 tbsp	Chinese black vinegar or Worcestershire sauce 15 mL	
1 tbsp	rice wine or sherry 15 mL	
1 tbsp	minced fresh ginger 15 mL	
1/2 tsp	each salt and pepper 2 mL	
2 tbsp	cornstarch 25 mL	
1/4 cup	cold water 50 mL	
1 cup	frozen peas 250 mL	
1	egg, lightly beaten 1	
2 tsp	sesame oil 10 mL	
1 tsp	chili oil (or to taste) 5 mL	
1	green onion, finely chopped 1	

1. If using firm rather than extra-firm tofu, wrap it in a paper towel and place on a plate with a heavy weight on top. Let stand for 30 minutes, then press out excess water. Cut tofu into thin julienne strips.
2. In a small bowl, cover mushrooms with warm water and let soak for 30 minutes. Drain and discard water. Trim off any tough stems; slice caps into thin julienne strips.
3. In a large pot, bring chicken broth to a boil. Add mushrooms, pork and bamboo shoots; return to a boil, reduce heat, cover and simmer for 3 minutes.
4. Add tofu, rice vinegar, black vinegar, rice wine, ginger, salt and pepper. (Soup can be prepared ahead to this point, cooled, covered and refrigerated.)
5. Heat to boiling; taste and adjust seasoning. Dissolve cornstarch in cold water. Slowly add cornstarch mixture to hot soup, stirring constantly; simmer until thickened. Stir in peas and heat through.
6. Remove from heat and slowly add egg, pouring it in a thin stream around the edge and carefully stirring once or twice to have egg form streamers. Transfer to a heated tureen or serving bowl. Carefully stir in sesame oil and chili oil. Sprinkle with green onion and serve immediately.

szechwan chicken and peanuts with chili peppers

MAKES 4 TO 6 SERVINGS

Szechwan vies with Hunan province for the spiciest of Chinese regional cuisines. One of the special events I attended during the 1997 Hong Kong Food Festival was a Dual Spicy Banquet composed of Hunan and Szechwan dishes. This simple stir-fry is similar to one of the chicken dishes served that night.

2	whole chicken breasts*	2
1 tbsp	minced fresh ginger	15 mL
2 tsp	light soy sauce	10 mL
1 tsp	cornstarch	5 mL
1/4 tsp	salt	1 mL
2 tbsp	peanut or vegetable oil	25 mL
1 cup	unsalted skinless peanuts	250 mL
4	small dried red chili peppers	4
1 tsp	rice vinegar	5 mL
1/2 tsp	granulated sugar	2 mL
	Boston or leaf lettuce leaves	

1. Cut chicken into 1/2-inch (1 cm) dice. In a bowl, combine the chicken, ginger, soy sauce, cornstarch and salt; set aside.

2. In a wok, heat the oil and stir-fry peanuts for 2 minutes. Remove with a slotted spoon and set aside. Add chili peppers and stir-fry for 1 minute. Remove with a slotted spoon and set aside. Add chicken mixture and stir-fry for 2 minutes. Add vinegar, sugar, peanuts and chilies; heat through. Serve immediately on a lettuce-lined platter.

* Chinese chefs usually bone chicken breasts but leave the skin on before dicing them. You can do the same, or use 4 skinless boneless chicken breast halves.

shrimp and mixed vegetable stir-fry

MAKES 4 TO 6 SERVINGS

Have everything cut, measured and sitting at the side of the stove before you start cooking this colourful stir-fry. If you wish, you can omit the shrimp, making this strictly a vegetable dish. In that case, add salt to taste and the sesame oil at the end.

1 lb	large shrimp	500 g
1 tsp	each salt and sesame oil	5 mL
1	sweet red pepper	1
Half	bunch broccoli	Half
2 cups	snow peas, trimmed	500 mL
2 cups	sliced mushrooms	500 mL
2 tbsp	vegetable oil (approx.)	25 mL
2	cloves garlic, minced	2
1 tbsp	minced fresh ginger	15 mL
1/2 cup	water	125 mL
2 tbsp	soy sauce	25 mL
1 tbsp	cornstarch	15 mL
	Black pepper	

1. Peel and devein the shrimp. Place in a small bowl and stir in salt and sesame oil. Let sit for 10 minutes.
2. Cut pepper into strips. Trim end from broccoli stem; cut broccoli into small florets and then cut stem into 1/4-inch (5 mm) slices. Combine in a bowl with snow peas and mushrooms; set aside.
3. In a wok or large skillet, heat oil over high heat. Gently stir-fry shrimp until pink, about 1 minute. Remove with a slotted spoon and keep warm.
4. Add more oil to the wok if necessary. Add garlic and ginger; stir-fry for 30 seconds. Add vegetables; stir-fry for 1 minute. Stir in water, cover and cook until vegetables are tender-crisp, about 5 minutes.
5. Meanwhile, stir together soy sauce and cornstarch. Add to vegetables and stir well. Cook, stirring, until thickened and shiny. Stir in shrimp and heat through. Season with pepper to taste and serve immediately.

cantonese barbecued spareribs

MAKES 4 TO 6 SERVINGS

Not really barbecued at all, but roasted in the oven, providing an oven dish that doesn't need last-minute attention.

4 lb	lean pork spareribs 1.8 kg	
1/3 cup	hoisin sauce 75 mL	
1/4 cup	packed brown sugar 50 mL	
1 tbsp	rice wine or dry sherry 15 mL	
1 tbsp	oyster sauce 15 mL	
2	cloves garlic, crushed 2	
1/2 tsp	five-spice powder* 2 mL	
	Salt	

1. Trim any fat from the ribs; cut between the bones into serving-sized pieces. Place in a sturdy plastic bag or glass bowl. Stir together the hoisin sauce, brown sugar, wine, oyster sauce, garlic and five-spice powder. Pour over the ribs and rub to coat well. Cover and marinate in the refrigerator for at least 4 hours or up to 1 day.

2. Line a large shallow roasting pan with foil and place a rack on top of the foil. Arrange the ribs, meaty side up, on the rack. Roast in a 400°F (200°C) oven for 10 minutes. Reduce heat to 375°F (190°C) and roast, turning occasionally and basting, for 1 to 1-1/4 hours or until tender. Sprinkle with salt to taste, if needed.

* A mixture of such spices as star anise, licorice root, cinnamon, cloves and Szechwan peppercorns, available in Oriental grocery stores. Ingredients such as hoisin sauce and oyster sauce usually can be found in the international section of the supermarket.

chinese steamed rice

MAKES 4 TO 6 SERVINGS

Steamed rice is an essential part of any Chinese menu.

1-1/2 cups	long-grain white rice (not parboiled) 375 mL
2-1/4 cups	cold water 550 mL

1. Place rice in a medium saucepan. Add enough cold water to cover. Stir well. Pour off water by pouring the contents of the saucepan into a big fine sieve.
2. Return rice to the pan. Add measured cold water. Bring to a boil, uncovered, over high heat. Boil for 2 to 3 minutes until holes appear on the surface. Cover and reduce heat to low; cook for 20 minutes. Remove pan from heat and, without lifting the lid, let rest for 10 minutes. (Rice will stay warm for up to 30 minutes in the pan.)
3. Fluff with chopsticks or a fork to serve.

chinese fruit salad

MAKES 4 TO 6 SERVINGS

This is a very pretty but simple dessert that everyone will love. Cut each type of melon in two, remove seeds and form balls by pushing the baller right down into the top surface of the melon. A helpful hint when making the balls is to slice off the top of the melon half once you have shaped all of the melon on the top surface so you have another flat exposed surface on which to work. If you are serving the salad to adults only, you might like to add 1/2 cup (125 mL) ginger or plum wine.

3 cups	each watermelon and cantaloupe balls 750 mL
1	can (19 oz/540 mL) lychees (litchis) in syrup 1
3 tbsp	minced candied ginger 45 mL

1. Gently combine melon balls in a large bowl. Drain off syrup from lychees into a measuring cup. Gently combine lychees with melon and ginger. Carefully stir in about 1/2 cup (125 mL) of the syrup, reserving the remainder. Cover and refrigerate for several hours or overnight. Add more of the syrup, if desired, and spoon into serving bowls.

almond cookies

MAKES ABOUT 4 DOZEN COOKIES

These tender cookies make a great ending to any meal, especially with a fruit dessert.

1 cup	shortening	250 mL
1/2 cup	each granulated and packed brown sugar	125 mL
1	egg, beaten	1
1/2 cup	ground almonds	125 mL
2 tsp	almond extract	10 mL
2-1/2 cups	all-purpose flour	625 mL
1-1/2 tsp	baking powder	7 mL
1/2 tsp	baking soda	2 mL
1/4 tsp	salt	1 mL
1/3 cup	blanched whole almonds	75 mL
1	egg yolk	1
1 tbsp	cold water	15 mL

1. In a large bowl, cream together shortening and sugars until fluffy. Blend in egg, ground almonds and almond extract.
2. Sift or stir together flour, baking powder, baking soda and salt. Gradually blend into the creamed mixture. Shape dough into 1-1/4-inch (3 cm) balls. Place 2 inches (5 cm) apart on greased baking sheets. Press an almond into the centre of each cookie. With a fork, lightly beat egg yolk with water. Brush lightly over cookies to glaze. Bake in a 350°F (180°C) oven for about 15 minutes or until golden brown. Let cool on baking sheets for 5 minutes, then remove to a rack to cool completely.

friday night
pizza party

Herb-Crusted Pizza with Prosciutto 178

Chorizo, Artichoke and Roasted Pepper Pizza 179

Blue Cheese, Pear and Radicchio Pizza 180

Cappuccino Ice Cream Sundaes 182

When Friday night comes along, most people are happy just to stay in, have a simple supper and watch a movie or two. Perhaps you want only the family around after a hard week at work, or maybe there are a couple of close friends who have the same taste in movies as you do.

On such a night, a formal sit-down dinner is just not appropriate. You might order in or have the makings all ready for these easy pizzas.

When I spent some time in Bermuda helping to care for my newborn granddaughter, I needed to test some recipes and suggested a Friday night pizza party one week. It was interesting how excited my son-in-law, the CEO of a company there, got when he knew he could leave his management problems at work and come home to these three pizzas. I hope they are as soothing to everyone else who makes and enjoys them. All three pizzas serve six; choose only two of them to serve four.

In a totally Italian bistro mode, abandon your elegant, long-stemmed wineglasses and use the kitchen tumblers for your favourite wine to go along with the pizzas.

Grown-up sundaes make a fun and yummy dessert with which to finish the evening. You can make the ice cream, or cheat and buy a good-quality coffee and chocolate flake ice cream.

herb-crusted pizza with prosciutto

MAKES 4 SERVINGS

Make this easy and fresh-tasting pizza when fresh herbs are available in your garden or in the market. Homemade pizza dough is very easy to make, but if you are short on time, store-bought dough is quite acceptable. Look for it in the freezer section or sometimes at the deli counter. I have even gone into a pizza parlour to buy dough, although the pizza maker on hand will often think this strange.

1/4 cup	chopped fresh parsley	50 mL
2 tbsp	chopped fresh oregano	25 mL
1-1/2 lb	pizza dough	750 g
	Cornmeal	
2 tbsp	olive oil	25 mL
2-1/2 cups	shredded Fontina cheese (1/2 lb/250 g)	625 mL
2/3 cup	tomato sauce	150 mL
1/4 cup	chopped fresh basil	50 mL
6	thin slices prosciutto, coarsely chopped	6

1. On a lightly floured surface, knead parsley and oregano into dough until evenly distributed. Cut in half and form into 2 balls; cover and let rest for 15 minutes. Roll out each ball thinly to make a 12-inch (30 cm) round.

2. Place each pizza round on a cornmeal-dusted pizza pan; brush with some of the oil. Scatter cheese evenly over top; spoon tomato sauce over cheese. Drizzle with remaining oil.

3. Bake in a 500°F (260°C) oven for about 12 minutes or until the crust is crisp and the cheese is melted and bubbly. Scatter basil and prosciutto over the top.

chorizo, artichoke and roasted pepper pizza

MAKES 2 TO 3 MAIN-COURSE SERVINGS

This simple pizza gets much interest from flavourful ingredients such as a strong Portuguese cheese and spicy chorizo (or chourico), that pork sausage seasoned with sweet or hot paprika or red pepper pulp. In our city of Cambridge, Ontario, where there is a large Portuguese population, I am very lucky to have good Portuguese ingredients available in many stores. Cooked Italian sausage or slices of kielbasa sausage can be substituted for the chorizo, and if the Portuguese cheese is not available, use a provolone. If you don't have your own roasted peppers, look for a jar of them at the supermarket, usually where the pickles and such are displayed.

3/4 lb	pizza dough 375 g
	Cornmeal
1	jar (6 oz/170 mL) marinated artichoke hearts 1
3 cups	shredded Portuguese São Jorge cheese or provolone (about 3/4 lb/375 g) 750 mL
1/2 cup	sliced roasted red peppers 125 mL
1/4 lb	chorizo, thinly sliced 125 g
1/4 cup	sliced black olives 50 mL

1. Roll out dough to make a 12-inch (30 cm) round and press into a cornmeal-dusted pizza pan. Drain artichoke hearts in a sieve set over a small bowl. Brush pizza base lightly with some of the artichoke marinade. Sprinkle with two-thirds of the cheese. Arrange artichokes, peppers, chorizo and olives on top. Sprinkle with remaining cheese and drizzle with 1 tbsp (15 mL) of the marinade. Bake in a 500°F (260°C) oven for 12 to 15 minutes or until crust is golden brown.

blue cheese, pear and radicchio pizza

MAKES 2 TO 3 MAIN-COURSE SERVINGS

This easy pizza has the flavours one sometimes combines in an interesting salad—pears, nuts and blue cheese. Adding sliced radicchio after the pizza is baked is a refreshing touch.

1	pear, unpeeled 1
1 tbsp	butter 15 mL
1/4 tsp	each black pepper and dried thyme 1 mL
3/4 lb	pizza dough 375 g
1/4 cup	finely chopped pecans or walnuts 50 mL
	Cornmeal
	Vegetable oil
1/4 lb	blue cheese 125 g
1 cup	slivered radicchio 250 mL

1. Core and slice the pear. In a small skillet, melt butter over medium heat; cook the pear for 5 minutes. Sprinkle with pepper and thyme; set aside.
2. Meanwhile, punch down dough and knead in pecans. Cover with a bowl and let stand for 10 minutes. Form into a 12-inch (30 cm) pizza base and press into a pizza pan that's lightly sprinkled with cornmeal. Brush lightly with oil. Scatter with pear mixture.
3. Cut cheese into 1/2-inch (1 cm) cubes. Scatter over pizza. Drizzle lightly with oil. Bake in a 500°F (260°C) oven for 12 to 15 minutes or until crust is golden brown. Scatter with radicchio.

pizza dough

MAKES 12 OZ (375 G) DOUGH, ENOUGH FOR ONE 12-INCH PIZZA BASE

Pizza dough is available in more and more supermarkets, sometimes fresh but usually in the freezer compartment. It is perfectly fine to use, although you might have an urge to make a pizza when it's not convenient to shop. Just keep a bit of yeast on hand and this easy, versatile recipe will come in handy indeed. It takes just minutes to make and can sit and do its rising for up to 3 hours. The dough can also be rolled out, wrapped and refrigerated on the pan for up to 8 hours. Or, wrap the risen dough in plastic wrap, then in a plastic bag to freeze. Thaw in the refrigerator before rolling out. The recipe itself can be doubled easily.

Pinch	granulated sugar	Pinch
2/3 cup	warm water	150 mL
2 tsp	active dry yeast	10 mL
2 tbsp	vegetable oil	25 mL
1-1/2 cups	all-purpose flour (approx.)	375 mL
1/2 tsp	salt	2 mL

1. In a measuring cup, combine sugar and water; sprinkle with yeast and let stand in a warm place until bubbly, about 5 minutes. Stir in oil.
2. In a large bowl, mix together flour and salt. Make a well in the centre and pour in yeast mixture. With a fork, gradually blend together flour and yeast mixtures to form dough. With floured hands gather it into a ball.
3. Turn the dough out onto a lightly floured surface; knead for about 5 minutes, adding just enough extra flour to make a soft, slightly sticky dough. Place in a greased bowl, turning once to grease all over. Cover the bowl with greased waxed paper and a tea towel. Let stand in a warm, draft-free place until tripled in size, 1-1/2 to 3 hours.
4. Punch down the dough and form into a ball. Turn out onto a lightly floured surface and cover with a bowl; let stand for 10 minutes. Roll out the dough into a 12-inch (30 cm) circle.

cappuccino ice cream sundaes

I shall never forget the strawberry ice cream of my childhood. But then, its thick, fresh cream came straight from our Jersey cows, and the intense red berries from our garden.

Nothing could beat the sodas of those days, either, so tall and cold on hot evenings. Our local ice cream parlour offered fabulous sundaes, too, heaped with banks of whipped cream and lava flows of the darkest melted chocolate, blanketing dense, rich ice cream. If you have a yearning for some of those old-fashioned flavours, you might like to make your own ice cream for these simple sundaes. Or, make the French Vanilla or Butter Pecan Ice Cream (page 183) and top with your favourite sauce.

For Cappuccino Ice Cream Sundaes, layer Brandied Cappuccino Ice Cream with Chocolate Flake Ice Cream and toasted hazelnuts in tall dessert glasses; drizzle each serving with brandy or coffee liqueur.

brandied cappuccino ice cream
MAKES ABOUT 3 CUPS (750 ML)

1/2 cup	granulated sugar 125 mL (approx.)
2 tbsp	ground espresso coffee beans 25 mL
1 tsp	cinnamon 5 mL
1/2 tsp	ground cardamom 2 mL
2 cups	18% cream 500 mL
1/2 cup	milk 125 mL
2 tbsp	brandy or coffee liqueur 25 mL

1. In a small heavy-based saucepan, whisk together the sugar, coffee, cinnamon and cardamom, then whisk in cream and milk. Over medium heat, bring almost to a boil (mixture should be foaming), stirring to dissolve sugar. Remove saucepan from heat, cover and let stand for about 1-1/2 hours or until cool.

2. Line a small sieve with several layers of rinsed cheesecloth, then set the sieve over a bowl. Strain the cream mixture, pressing down on the solids and scraping the bottom of the sieve to extract as much liquid as possible. Stir in brandy. Taste and add more sugar if necessary, keeping in mind that freezing diminishes the sweetness of the mixture. Refrigerate, covered, for about 1 hour or until cold. Pour cream mixture into an ice cream maker, then process according to the manufacturer's instructions.

3. Alternatively, pour into a shallow non-aluminum metal pan, cover and freeze for about 4 hours, until partially firm. Break ice cream into chunks, then purée in a food processor until smooth. Pour ice cream into a chilled plastic airtight container and freeze for about 2 hours or until firm enough to serve.

french vanilla ice cream

MAKES ABOUT 2-1/2 CUPS (625 ML)

This velvety-smooth classic goes well with almost any sauce or fruit and makes absolutely the best accompaniment to a fresh fruit pie.

2 cups	whipping cream	500 mL
1/3 cup	granulated sugar	75 mL
Half	vanilla bean	Half
3	egg yolks	3
1 tsp	all-purpose flour	5 mL
1	egg white, beaten just enough to break it up	1

1. In a heavy-based saucepan, stir together the cream and sugar. Split the vanilla bean in half lengthwise and scrape the seeds into the cream, adding the bean as well. Bring just to a boil over medium-high heat, stirring to dissolve the sugar. Remove from the heat, cover and let stand for 15 minutes.
2. Lightly whisk the egg yolks in a large bowl, then whisk in flour until smooth. Gradually pour in the warm cream, whisking constantly. Pour back into the saucepan, then cook over medium-low heat for 6 to 8 minutes, stirring constantly, until the mixture thickens slightly and lightly coats the back of a spoon. Remove from the heat and let cool to room temperature, stirring occasionally. Strain through a fine sieve into a clean bowl, then refrigerate for at least 1 hour until cold, stirring occasionally. Stir in egg white until well combined.
3. Pour the custard into an ice cream maker, then process according to the manufacturer's instructions.
4. Alternatively, pour into a shallow non-aluminum metal pan, cover and freeze for about 1-1/2 hours, until partially firm. Spoon the mixture into a bowl; beat well until smooth. Pour ice cream into a chilled plastic airtight container, then freeze for about 2 hours or until firm enough to serve.

VARIATIONS

CHOCOLATE FLAKE ICE CREAM
Stir 2 oz (50 g) shaved bittersweet chocolate into the cold custard before freezing. (Shave a piece of room-temperature chocolate with a vegetable peeler.)

BUTTER PECAN ICE CREAM
In a small skillet, over medium heat, melt 2 tbsp (25 mL) unsalted butter. Add 1/2 cup (125 mL) coarsely chopped pecans; cook for 3 minutes, stirring constantly, until pecans are golden and fragrant. Let cool completely, then stir into the cold custard before freezing.

---

a farmers' market supper

On my parents' farm near Collingwood, Ontario, the garden had a bit of everything in it ... even a couple of peach trees that produced a small taste of that sweet, juicy treat. So my mother could fill her many preserving jars with fruit, however, we would drive each year to the Niagara area and bring home a couple of bushels of peaches and often other tender fruit we did not produce in abundance.

We did grow enough of most other fruits and vegetables—pink stalks of rhubarb in the spring; bright red strawberries hidden under their protective green leaves from the June sun; baskets of big raspberries; currants in red, white and black; gooseberries; tart red cherries in a long line of trees by our lane; then later a few melons with pears, plums and apples stretching into the frosty fall days. The vegetable garden yielded a similar abundance—Swiss chard, onions, lettuce, radishes, beans and peas for freezing, and a lot of tomatoes ripening for chili sauce. Our potatoes saw us through the winter; other root vegetables like carrots were stored in sand in the cellar while parsnips were left to freeze in the ground, which made them sweeter, for early spring digging.

After I was married, we lived in apartments and townhouses for the first few years, without any hope of a garden. However, while we lived in Owen Sound, Ontario, our friends on a nearby farm loaned us a huge plot of land on which we planted a garden. Our kids, who were quite young then, would go with me to help weed and pick the produce. Each Easter, we would give them a few seeds of their own to plant and nurture.

Since moving to Cambridge, Ontario, however, we have not had the chance to have a garden. Fortunately, there is a wonderful farmers' market that I haunt every week, coming home from each trip loaded down with every good thing each season gives forth.

This easy early fall menu showcases local produce you might find at a farmers' market.

roasted eggplant soup with mascarpone swirl

MAKES 6 SERVINGS

For best texture, use a blender, not a food processor, to purée this silken soup.

4	baby eggplants (or 1 large)	4
1	large baking potato	1
1	onion, chopped	1
4	cloves garlic, chopped	4
1/4 cup	olive oil	50 mL
2 tsp	chopped fresh oregano	10 mL
	Salt and pepper	
5 cups	chicken broth	1.25 L
1/4 tsp	saffron threads	1 mL

MASCARPONE SWIRL

1 cup	mascarpone cheese	250 mL
1	small clove garlic, minced	1
2 tbsp	chopped fresh parsley	25 mL
1 tbsp	chopped fresh oregano	15 mL
	Salt and pepper	

1. Cut unpeeled eggplants and potato into 1-inch (2.5 cm) cubes. Toss with onion, garlic, olive oil and oregano in a large greased shallow roasting pan. Spread out in a single layer and sprinkle with salt and pepper. Roast in 500°F (260°C) oven for 20 to 30 minutes, until soft, stirring occasionally.

2. Transfer vegetables to a blender in batches, add a little broth and purée until smooth. Transfer to a medium saucepan, stir in remaining broth and saffron and bring to a simmer. Season to taste.

3. Mascarpone Swirl: In a small bowl, blend together mascarpone, garlic, parsley, oregano, and salt and pepper to taste. Ladle soup into warm soup bowls and swirl in some mascarpone mixture.

grilled farmer's sausage with polenta

MAKES 6 SERVINGS

Farmers' markets usually have an assortment of rustic sausages and good chili sauce for sale. Or, if you have already made your own chili sauce, serve some of it on the sausage. Make the polenta a day ahead.

6 cups	water 1.5 L
1/4 cup	butter 50 mL
1 tsp	each salt and pepper 5 mL
2-1/2 cups	cornmeal 625 mL
1/4 cup	whipping cream 50 mL
2 cups	shredded Fontina cheese (about 1/2 lb/250 g) 500 mL
1	egg, beaten 1
2 lb	farmer's sausage 1 kg
	Olive oil
	Chili sauce

1. Line the base and sides of a 9- x 5-inch (2 L) loaf pan with plastic wrap. In a medium saucepan, bring water, butter, salt and pepper to a full rolling boil. Very gradually, whisk in cornmeal in a slow, steady stream, continuing to whisk until slightly thickened. Reduce heat to medium-low and cook, stirring often, for 15 to 20 minutes or until the mixture comes away from side of saucepan. Stir in cream, then cheese. Remove from heat and stir in egg. Pour evenly into loaf pan. Refrigerate, covered, overnight.

2. Place sausage in a large skillet with enough water to cover it. Bring to a boil over high heat. Reduce heat to medium-low, then simmer, covered, for 10 minutes. Drain well and cut into pieces.

3. Preheat the barbecue to medium-high. Place sausage on the greased grill; cook, turning often, for 12 to 15 minutes or until the sausage is browned on the outside and cooked through.

4. Using the plastic wrap to lift polenta, remove it from the pan. Peel off plastic wrap. With a serrated knife, carefully cut polenta into 1/2-inch (1 cm) slices. Brush slices with olive oil, then place them on the greased grill. Cook for 10 minutes, turning carefully once, until the slices are golden brown on both sides. Arrange polenta slices on a warm platter, arrange sausage alongside and serve with chili sauce.

rainbow pepper salad

MAKES 6 SERVINGS

Don't overcook the peppers since they should still have a touch of crunch to them.

2 tbsp	olive oil 25 mL
1	each red, yellow, orange and green sweet pepper, seeded and cut into strips 1
3	cloves garlic, minced 3
1 to 2 tsp	seeded and minced hot pepper 5 to 10 mL
1 tbsp	balsamic vinegar 15 mL
	Salt and pepper

1. Heat oil in a very large skillet over medium-high heat, then cook sweet peppers for 6 to 8 minutes, tossing constantly, until tender-crisp. Sprinkle with garlic and hot pepper. Cook, stirring, for 2 minutes. Toss with vinegar and salt and pepper to taste. Serve hot or at room temperature.

tarragon-dressed corn and bean salad

MAKES 6 SERVINGS

The dressing on this pretty salad may become runnier if left to stand overnight, but will still taste very good.

3	ears of corn, shucked 3
3/4 lb	green beans, trimmed and sliced 375 g
1	stalk celery, sliced diagonally 1
1/2 cup	mayonnaise 125 mL
1	small clove garlic, minced 1
2 tsp	fresh tarragon leaves 10 mL
1/2 tsp	Worcestershire sauce 2 mL
	Salt and pepper
1 tbsp	capers, drained 15 mL
1/4 cup	toasted pine nuts 50 mL

1. Cook corn and beans in a large pot of boiling salted water for 3 to 4 minutes, until just tender. Drain and cool under running water. Cut kernels from corn and add to beans and celery in a large bowl.

2. In a small bowl, whisk together mayonnaise, garlic, tarragon, Worcestershire sauce, and salt and pepper to taste. Stir in capers. Pour dressing over vegetables and toss to coat well. Refrigerate, covered, for at least 30 minutes or up to 24 hours. Stir in pine nuts just before serving.

mustardy beet-carrot salad

MAKES 6 SERVINGS

Two ordinary root vegetables team up to make this stunning jewel-toned salad.

1 lb	beets (about 6) 500 g
1 lb	carrots (about 4), peeled 500 g
3 tbsp	olive oil 45 mL
1 tbsp	each balsamic vinegar and
	Dijon mustard 15 mL
1/2 tsp	granulated sugar 2 mL
	Salt and pepper
2 tbsp	chopped fresh parsley 25 mL

1. Wash and trim beets, leaving on roots and 1 inch (2.5 cm) of the stems. Place beets in a shallow roasting pan with 1/4 inch (5 mm) water. Cover with foil and bake in a 375°F (190°C) oven for 35 minutes to 1 hour (depending on age and size of beets), until beets are tender. Let cool, then remove skins and cut beets into 2- x 1/4-inch (5 cm x 5 mm) julienne strips. Set aside in a large bowl.
2. Cut carrots into strips the same size as beets. Steam carrot strips for 5 to 8 minutes, until tender-crisp. Add to beets.
3. Whisk together oil, vinegar, mustard, sugar, and salt and pepper to taste. Add dressing to vegetables and toss gently. Stir in parsley and let cool.

peach tarte tatin

MAKES 8 SERVINGS

Peaches make an interesting version of a tart usually made with apples in this final flourish in our market dinner. This recipe makes two batches of pastry; freeze the remainder for future use.

PASTRY

3 cups	all-purpose flour	750 mL
1 tsp	salt	5 mL
1/4 tsp	baking powder	1 mL
3/4 cup	chilled lard or shortening, cubed	175 mL
1/4 cup	chilled butter, cubed	50 mL
1	egg	1
2 tsp	white vinegar	10 mL
	Cold water	

FILLING

1/3 cup	granulated sugar	75 mL
1/4 cup	water	50 mL
4 cups	peeled sliced peaches	1 L
1 tbsp	fresh lemon juice	15 mL
1/4 cup	granulated sugar	50 mL
2 tbsp	cornstarch	25 mL
1	egg, beaten	1
	Whipped cream	

1. Pastry: Stir together flour, salt and baking powder in a large bowl. Cut in lard and butter with a pastry blender or 2 knives, until mixture resembles coarse crumbs. In a glass measure, whisk together egg, vinegar and enough cold water to measure 2/3 cup (150 mL). Stir egg mixture into flour mixture until dough begins to clump together, then gather dough into a ball. Divide dough into 2 even-sized pieces and form each into a disc. Wrap each in plastic wrap. Freeze 1 disc for future use; refrigerate the other for 30 minutes.

2. Filling: Bring 1/3 cup (75 mL) sugar and water to a boil in a small saucepan over high heat. Boil for 5 minutes, without stirring, until syrup is a light caramel colour. Working quickly (before it hardens), pour syrup into a 9-inch (23 cm) pie plate, tilting to cover bottom and halfway up the sides.

3. Toss peach slices with lemon juice in a large bowl and arrange the best-looking slices on the plate, radiating out from the middle and overlapping the slices. Stir 1/4 cup (50 mL) sugar and cornstarch into remaining peach slices, then spoon mixture over peaches in pie plate.

4. Roll out pastry on a lightly floured surface to 1/8 inch (3 mm) thickness. Place pastry on top of the peaches. Trim and flute the edge, then brush with beaten egg. Prick in several places with a fork and set pie on a large baking sheet. Bake in 450°F (230°C) oven for 15 minutes. Reduce heat to 350°F (180°C), then bake for 30 to 35 minutes or until crust is golden brown. Remove from the oven, run a knife around the edge of pie to loosen crust, then let stand for 10 minutes.

5. Invert pie onto a large serving plate. If some peach slices stick to the pie plate, remove them and arrange them on top of the pie where they belong. Serve, barely warm, with whipped cream.

> **TIP**
> If you want to make this tart out of season, use thoroughly thawed, well drained frozen peach slices rather than canned peaches since the latter are too soft.

a casual
laptop supper with good friends

We have a large formal dining room that we use often. I do enjoy presiding over the table when it's set with all of my best china and silver. Occasionally, however, when good friends are with us on a cold winter night and we are basking in front of the wood fire in the living room, I don't like to leave its warmth, and we stay right there to enjoy the fire while we eat.

Or, perhaps it's a warmer time of the year, and we just want everyone to see the great movie we have just discovered. The fireplace will be replaced by the television set, but this menu is perfect for either setting with its easy, make-ahead dishes that everyone can enjoy without sitting at a table.

quick chunky chicken liver pâté

MAKES 6 SERVINGS

Spread this tasty, coarse-textured pâté on crackers or toasted slices of baguette and serve with cornichons or other pickles.

2 tbsp	olive oil 25 mL
3/4 lb	chicken livers, trimmed and halved 375 g
1/3 cup	brandy or apple cider 75 mL
1/4 cup	minced shallots 50 mL
1/2 tsp	salt 2 mL
1/4 tsp	each black pepper and dried thyme 1 mL
1/4 cup	whipping cream 50 mL
2 tbsp	snipped fresh chives 25 mL

1. In a large skillet, over high heat, heat the olive oil. Add livers; cook for about 4 minutes, turning once, until browned and crisp but still slightly pink inside. Remove livers to a plate.
2. Add brandy, shallots, salt, pepper and thyme to the skillet; cook, stirring, for 2 minutes, until almost all of the liquid has evaporated. Stir in whipping cream; boil for about 1 minute, until thickened.
3. Remove skillet from the heat. Return livers to the skillet, along with any juices that have accumulated on the plate; stir well. With a fork, mash the livers until coarsely broken up but not smooth. Stir in chives. Taste and add more salt and pepper if necessary. Spoon pâté into a serving bowl. Let cool; refrigerate, covered, until slightly chilled. (Pâté can be refrigerated for up to 3 days; let stand at room temperature for 30 minutes before serving.)

herbed penne with roasted vegetables

MAKES 6 SERVINGS

Roasted vegetables and fresh herbs combine in this easy baked pasta dish that's hearty and rich-tasting. It's meatless, but no one will notice.

3	zucchini, sliced (about 1 lb/ 500 g total) 3
3	baby eggplants, halved lengthwise, then sliced (or 1 small eggplant, quartered lengthwise, then sliced), about 1 lb (500 g) 3
1	onion, coarsely chopped 1
3	cloves garlic, minced 3

1. On a large rimmed baking sheet, toss zucchini, eggplants, onion and garlic with oil. Spread vegetables out on sheet; sprinkle with rosemary, salt and pepper. Roast in a 400°F (200°C) oven for about 30 minutes, stirring once or twice, until tender and just beginning to colour.
2. Meanwhile, in a large pot of boiling salted water, cook penne for about 8 minutes or until tender but still firm. Drain pasta well, reserving 1/2 cup (125 mL) of the cooking water. Return pasta to the pot. Add roasted vegetables; toss well. Gently stir in 1/4 cup (50 mL) parsley and the basil. Gently stir in sauce, reserved pasta water, ricotta cheese, Fontina and 1/2 cup (125 mL) of the Parmesan cheese.

1/4 cup	olive oil 50 mL
1 tbsp	chopped fresh rosemary (or 1 tsp/5 mL dried) 15 mL
1/2 tsp	each salt and pepper 2 mL
4 cups	penne (1 lb/500 g) 1 L
1/2 cup	chopped fresh parsley 125 mL
1/4 cup	torn fresh basil leaves 50 mL
3 cups	homemade or good-quality store-bought meatless pasta sauce 750 mL
1 cup	ricotta cheese 250 mL
1/2 lb	Fontina or mozzarella cheese, cubed 250 g
1 cup	freshly grated Parmesan cheese 250 mL

3. Spoon pasta mixture into a greased 13- x 9-inch (3 L) baking dish. Sprinkle with remaining parsley and Parmesan cheese. (Casserole can be refrigerated, covered, for up to 6 hours; let stand at room temperature for 1 hour before baking.)

4. Bake, uncovered, in a 400°F (200°C) oven for about 20 minutes, until cheese has melted, top is lightly golden around the edges and the sauce is bubbling. (Casserole can take 10 to 15 minutes longer to bake if it has been refrigerated.)

> **NOTE**
> The sizes of commercial jars or cans of pasta sauce vary and keep changing. Right now, the usual size is 25 oz (700 mL), and if that is all you can find, make up the extra liquid by reserving and using 1/4 cup (50 mL) more pasta cooking water.

mixed greens with roasted mushrooms

MAKES 6 TO 8 SERVINGS

A garlicky mushroom mixture tops crisp greens in this interesting salad. Put the mushrooms in the oven to roast alongside the vegetables for the pasta dish. You can wash and dry the greens the day before; just intersperse them with paper towels and store them in a plastic bag in the refrigerator.

1/4 cup	white wine vinegar 50 mL
1 tbsp	Dijon mustard 15 mL
2	cloves garlic, minced 2
1/4 tsp	each dried oregano and black pepper 1 mL
1/2 cup	olive oil 125 mL
1 lb	large mushrooms, quartered 500 g
16 cups	washed, dried and torn mixed greens 4 L
4	green onions, thickly sliced 4
1/2 tsp	salt 2 mL

1. In a glass measure, whisk together vinegar, mustard, garlic, oregano and pepper. Gradually whisk in oil. (Dressing can be covered and refrigerated for up to 24 hours; let stand at room temperature for 30 minutes, then whisk well before proceeding with the recipe.)

2. In a medium non-metallic bowl, toss mushrooms with 1/3 cup (75 mL) of the dressing; let stand at room temperature for 30 minutes.

3. Spread mushrooms out on a baking sheet; roast in a 400°F (200°C) oven for 25 to 30 minutes, stirring once or twice, until browned. Let cool completely.

4. In a large salad bowl, toss greens with green onions and mushrooms. Add salt to remaining dressing; whisk well. Add dressing to greens; toss to coat well. Serve at once.

lemon cheesecake with spiced plum sauce

MAKES 10 SERVINGS

Beaten egg whites folded into the mix make this pretty cheesecake fluffy and light, while the rosy-red plum sauce adds colour and a delicious fruit flavour. Any leftovers will keep well for a day or so.

CRUST

1-1/2 cups	graham wafer crumbs	375 mL
1/3 cup	granulated sugar	75 mL
1/4 cup	butter, melted	50 mL

CHEESECAKE

4	eggs, separated	4
1 cup	granulated sugar	250 mL
2	pkgs (8 oz/250 g each) cream cheese, softened	2
1 cup	sour cream	250 mL
1 tbsp	grated lemon zest	15 mL
2 tbsp	fresh lemon juice	25 mL
1 tsp	vanilla	5 mL
	Spiced Plum Sauce (see recipe on page 197)	

1. Crust: In a medium bowl, stir together crumbs, sugar and butter until well combined. Press the crumb mixture over the base and 1 inch (2.5 cm) up the sides of a greased 9-inch (2.5 L) springform pan. Centre pan on a large square of foil; press foil up sides of pan. Set aside.

2. Cheesecake: In a medium bowl, beat egg whites until soft peaks form. Gradually beat in 1/4 cup (50 mL) sugar just until incorporated. Set aside.

3. In a large bowl, beat cream cheese until fluffy; beat in egg yolks 1 at a time. On low speed, gradually beat in remaining sugar, sour cream, lemon zest, lemon juice and vanilla. Carefully fold in egg whites, until well combined.

4. Pour cheesecake mixture into prepared pan. Put pan in a roasting pan. Pour boiling water into the roasting pan to come halfway up the sides of the springform pan. Bake in a 325°F (160°C) oven for 1 hour and 15 minutes, until cheesecake is set around the edges but still wobbly in the middle. It will be quite puffy and cracked, but don't worry, it will settle down as it cools.

5. Immediately run a knife all around the inside edge of the pan to loosen the cheesecake. Turn off the oven and leave its door ajar. Let cheesecake cool in the oven for 1 hour. Remove cheesecake from the oven; let cool completely in the pan on a wire rack. Refrigerate, loosely covered, for 6 hours.

6. Remove sides of the pan and transfer cake to a plate. (Cheesecake can be refrigerated on the plate, loosely covered, for up to 2 days. Leaving it in the pan for longer storage may discolour the cheesecake.) Let cheesecake stand at room temperature for 30 minutes before serving. Use a knife dipped in hot water to slice cheesecake into wedges, wiping knife dry before cutting each piece. Serve drizzled with Spiced Plum Sauce.

spiced plum sauce
MAKES 3-1/2 CUPS (875 ML)

This dazzling sauce is also good spooned over pound cake or French toast.

1-1/2 lb	plums (about 7 large)	750 g
1/2 cup	granulated sugar	125 mL
1/2 cup	port or apple juice	125 mL
1	3-inch (8 cm) cinnamon stick	1
4	whole cloves	4
2 tsp	cornstarch	10 mL
2 tbsp	cold water	25 mL

1. Halve plums and remove pits; slice plums thickly. In a medium saucepan, stir together sugar, port, cinnamon stick and cloves. Bring to a boil over medium heat, stirring until sugar has dissolved. Boil for 5 minutes. Add plums; return to a simmer. Cook, covered, for 5 to 8 minutes, stirring occasionally, until plums are tender but not mushy.
2. In a small bowl, stir together cornstarch and cold water until smooth. Add cornstarch mixture to plum mixture. Cook for about 2 minutes, stirring gently, until thickened. Let cool completely before serving. (Sauce can be refrigerated, covered, for up to 5 days.)

a fall supper for
friends or family

When the maple leaves start to take on their gold and red hues, and the air has a certain crisp edge to it, the farmers' markets and roadside stands will be overflowing with the fall harvest. Sweet peppers will have had a chance to turn a bright red; apples and pears will be at their best; root vegetables will be more than abundant; cranberries will be gathered; and there will be whole fields magically dotted with bright orange pumpkins. This is the time of year we know how lucky we are to have such wonderful food at our disposal throughout the country.

It is no wonder our ancestors chose this time of year to give thanks. Throughout the country, there will be fall suppers held in church or community halls. I have had the good fortune to take part in many of these meals in various provinces, including in northern Saskatchewan. It usually means that the whole community gets together, either in the making or the eating, and the menu is fairly simple ... perhaps roast beef, ham and very often turkey with all the trimmings.

This menu is a traditional fall supper, but some of it with a twist, using turkey and all the trimmings in new and different ways. It could be a fresh new Thanksgiving feast for you or just a nice easy dinner party menu to make when ingredients are good and abundant. Most of it can be made ahead, adding to the cook's comfort level.

This menu appeared a few years ago in *Homemakers* magazine. That fall, we were invited to a dinner party in Toronto; the hostess had made most of the menu before she looked at the byline to see who had created the recipes. When she discovered I was the writer, she was very embarrassed, but I was flattered and happy to have the chance to taste someone else's interpretation of my recipes.

red pepper soup

MAKES 8 SERVINGS

If you wish, garnish small bowls of this pretty and intensely flavoured soup with garlic croutons or a little sour cream.

4	large sweet red peppers (2 lb/1 kg) 4
1 tbsp	butter 15 mL
2	onions, chopped 2
2	cloves garlic, minced 2
1 cup	water 250 mL
5 cups	chicken broth 1.25 L
2 tsp	paprika 10 mL
1 tsp	granulated sugar 5 mL
2 tbsp	fresh lemon juice 25 mL
1/4 tsp	cayenne 1 mL
	Salt and pepper

1. Place peppers on a baking sheet; roast in a 500°F (260°C) oven for about 20 minutes, turning occasionally, until evenly charred. Invert a large bowl over top of the peppers; let stand for 10 minutes.

2. Working over a bowl, remove as much skin as possible from the peppers, reserving any juice but discarding stems and seeds. Cut peppers into 1-inch (2.5 cm) strips.

3. In a large saucepan, melt butter over medium-low heat; cook onions for 10 minutes, stirring often, until softened but not browned. Add peppers and their juice, garlic and water; cook, uncovered, for 10 minutes. Stir in broth, paprika and sugar. Bring to a boil over medium-high heat. Reduce heat to medium-low; simmer, uncovered, for 20 minutes.

4. In a blender or food processor, process soup in batches, until smooth. Strain soup through a sieve if you wish, or leave it unstrained for more texture. Pour into a clean saucepan. Stir in lemon juice and cayenne; season with salt and pepper to taste. (Soup can be prepared ahead. Refrigerate, covered, for up to 24 hours.) Reheat gently; taste and adjust seasoning if necessary before serving.

pear salad with rosemary vinaigrette

MAKES 8 SERVINGS

Serve this simple salad as a starter, or enjoy it after the main course and before dessert. Rosemary is one of my favourite herbs, and when I see it growing all year round in a country with a Mediterranean climate, I always wish I had a hedge of it from which I could gather bunches in the middle of the winter. I do, however, make good use of rosemary when it is available.

1/4 cup	olive oil	50 mL
2 tbsp	chopped fresh rosemary	25 mL
3 tbsp	fresh lemon juice	45 mL
	Salt and pepper	
3	ripe Bartlett pears	3
1	small head red leaf lettuce, washed and torn	1
1/2 cup	toasted walnut pieces	125 mL

1. Dressing: In a small saucepan, combine oil and 1 tbsp (15 mL) of the rosemary. Stir over low heat for about 10 minutes, just until warm; let cool. Let stand, covered, at room temperature overnight.
2. The next day, strain oil into a small bowl. Whisk in remaining rosemary, 2 tbsp (25 mL) of the lemon juice, and salt and pepper to taste.
3. Cut pears into quarters lengthwise; remove cores but do not peel. Cut pears into thin slices. In a medium bowl, toss pear slices gently with the remaining lemon juice.
4. Place lettuce in a salad bowl; arrange pear slices on top. Whisk dressing to combine; drizzle over pears. Sprinkle with walnuts. Serve at once.

roast turkey breast with prosciutto stuffing

MAKES 8 SERVINGS (WITH SOME LEFTOVERS)

Since the cooking time is much shorter for a turkey breast than for a whole bird, the meat remains moister.

1	whole boneless turkey breast (3 lb/1.5 kg), skin on	1
1/2 tsp	each salt and pepper	2 mL
1 cup	coarsely shredded Emmenthal or Gruyère cheese (1/4 lb/ 125 g)	250 mL
1/4 lb	prosciutto, coarsely chopped	125 g

1. Place turkey, skin side down, on a board. Cut a pocket in each side of the breast meat by slicing from the long thin side to the thicker side. Sprinkle with 1/4 tsp (1 mL) each salt and pepper.
2. In a small bowl, combine cheese, prosciutto and sage. Spread cheese mixture in each pocket and down the centre of the turkey breast. Roll breast up to enclose stuffing; tie securely in several places with string. Place breast, seam side down, on an oiled rack in a shallow roasting pan. Rub with olive oil; sprinkle with lemon juice, thyme, and remaining salt and pepper. Cover loosely with foil.

2 tsp	chopped fresh sage (or 1/2 tsp/2 mL dried) 10 mL
1 tbsp	each olive oil and fresh lemon juice 15 mL
1/2 tsp	dried thyme 2 mL
2 cups	chicken stock 500 mL
1 tbsp	cornstarch 15 mL
2 tbsp	cold water 25 mL

3. Roast in a 350°F (180°C) oven for about 2 hours or until a meat thermometer inserted in the thickest part of the meat registers 170°F (75°C) and the juices run clear when meat is pierced with the tip of a sharp knife; remove foil for the last 30 minutes of cooking time to allow breast to brown.

4. Remove breast from pan; place on a warm platter. Let stand in a warm place, loosely covered with foil, while you make the gravy.

5. Skim off any excess fat from the juices in roasting pan. Add stock to the pan; place over high heat and bring to a boil, scraping up any brown bits from the bottom of the pan. In a small bowl, combine cornstarch with cold water. Add cornstarch mixture to pan; simmer, stirring constantly, until gravy is thickened and smooth. Strain (if you wish) into a heated sauceboat. Cut turkey breast into thin slices; serve with the gravy.

oven-roasted parsnips

MAKES 8 SERVINGS

Although we always left parsnips in the ground over the winter so they would become even sweeter by the time we dug them up in the spring, there are always plenty of these roots available in markets in the fall, especially with new varieties. If you wish, add 1/2 cup (125 mL) grated Parmesan cheese to the crumbs.

8	large parsnips (about 2 lb/1 kg total) 8
1	egg 1
2 tbsp	milk 25 mL
1/2 cup	dry bread crumbs 125 mL
2 tbsp	chopped fresh parsley 25 mL
1/2 tsp	each salt, pepper and dried basil 2 mL
1 tbsp	each vegetable oil and butter 15 mL

1. Peel parsnips; cut into 2-1/2-inch (6 cm) long pieces, cutting thicker pieces in half lengthwise. Cook in a saucepan of boiling salted water for 10 minutes or until almost tender. Drain well.

2. In a small bowl, beat together egg and milk. In a shallow dish, combine bread crumbs, parsley, salt, pepper and basil. Grease a baking sheet. Dip each piece of parsnip into the milk mixture, then coat in crumb mixture. Arrange in a single layer on the baking sheet. (Recipe can be prepared ahead up to this point. Refrigerate, covered, up to 24 hours.)

3. With a pastry brush, brush parsnips with oil; dot with butter. Roast in a 350°F (180°C) oven for 20 to 30 minutes, turning occasionally, until crisp and golden.

creamy mashed potatoes

MAKES 8 SERVINGS

When there is lovely rich gravy to puddle on top of them, nothing beats soft, creamy mashed potatoes. I often make them ahead by omitting the cream and beating in 4 ounces (125 g) cream cheese and 1/2 cup (125 mL) sour cream with an electric hand mixer. Then I pop the whole mixture into a greased casserole, top with buttered crumbs and refrigerate for a day or two; to serve, heat in a 350°F (180°C) oven for 20 to 30 minutes.

6	potatoes, peeled	6
1 cup	whipping cream	250 mL
1 tbsp	butter	15 mL
	Salt and pepper	

1. In a saucepan of boiling salted water, cook potatoes for about 20 minutes or until fork-tender. Drain; return to low heat for 3 minutes to dry. Mash, rice or pass potatoes through a food mill to remove all lumps.
2. Meanwhile, in a separate saucepan, heat cream to steaming; using a fork, gradually beat cream into potatoes. Beat in butter. Season with salt and pepper. (Potatoes can be refrigerated for up to 1 day and reheated in the microwave at High for 5 minutes.)

VARIATION

BUTTERMILK MASHED POTATOES
Substitute 1-1/4 cups (300 mL) buttermilk for the whipping cream, but do not heat.

---

balsamic-glazed onions

MAKES 8 SERVINGS

Onions are too often confined to a supporting role of flavouring soups and stews, but here they star in their own way. Balsamic vinegar, which is now easy to find in most grocery stores, adds a rich flavour to this simple side dish.

2	pkgs (10 oz/284 g each) pearl onions (about 4-1/2 cups/ 1.12 L) 2
1/4 cup	balsamic vinegar 50 mL
1 tbsp	each butter and vegetable oil 15 mL
1 tbsp	chopped fresh thyme (or 1 tsp/ 5 mL dried) 15 mL
1 tsp	black pepper 5 mL
1/2 tsp	each salt and granulated sugar 2 mL
2 tbsp	chopped fresh parsley 25 mL

1. In a large saucepan of boiling salted water, blanch onions for 2 minutes. Drain well; place onions in a bowl of cold water. Drain well; peel.
2. In a shallow 8-cup (2 L) baking dish, combine vinegar, butter, oil, thyme, pepper, salt and sugar. Place dish in a 400°F (200°C) oven for 3 to 5 minutes, until butter melts; stir well. Add onions; toss to coat with vinegar mixture. Spread out onions in a single layer in the dish; cook, uncovered, 35 to 40 minutes, stirring occasionally, until golden brown and tender. Sprinkle with parsley to serve. (Recipe can be prepared ahead without the parsley. Refrigerate, covered, up to 24 hours. Remove from refrigerator 30 minutes before reheating. Reheat, covered, in a 350°F/180°C oven for about 20 minutes or until heated through, then sprinkle with parsley to serve.)

pumpkin brûlées

MAKES 8 SERVINGS

The finale to many fall suppers is often a smooth, rich pumpkin pie. Here, I've used all of the same flavours, but in easy brûlées. Serve them on dessert plates alongside small bunches of grapes or a crisp cookie. Be sure to start the recipe at least 8 hours before serving.

2 cups	whipping cream	500 mL
5	egg yolks	5
1/3 cup	granulated sugar	75 mL
3/4 cup	canned pumpkin purée*	175 mL
1/2 tsp	cinnamon	2 mL
Pinch	salt	Pinch
2 tsp	vanilla	10 mL
1/2 cup	packed brown sugar	125 mL

1. In a small heavy saucepan, heat cream over medium-high heat just until tiny bubbles appear around the edge of the saucepan. Remove from the heat.

2. In a large bowl, whisk together egg yolks and granulated sugar just until combined. Stir in pumpkin, cinnamon and salt. Slowly whisk in hot cream; stir in vanilla. Pour mixture into eight 1/2-cup (125 mL) ramekins or custard cups. Place ramekins in a metal baking pan just large enough to hold them; pour hot water into the pan to come two-thirds of the way up the sides of ramekins. Cover pan with foil.

3. Bake in a 325°F (160°C) oven for 25 to 30 minutes or until custards are just set but centres still jiggle (do not overcook). Remove ramekins to a rack; let cool. Refrigerate, covered, at least 6 hours or up to 2 days, until very cold.

4. One to 2 hours before serving, place ramekins on a baking sheet. Sieve brown sugar to remove any lumps; sprinkle evenly over custards. Broil as close as possible to the element of a preheated broiler for 2 to 3 minutes, until the sugar caramelizes. Let cool; serve within 2 hours. (Alternatively, you can caramelize the sugar with a small blowtorch made for kitchen use.)

* Spoon the remaining pumpkin purée into an airtight container and freeze for up to 3 months.

> TIP
> The egg whites can be frozen for up to 3 months in an airtight container. Thaw in the refrigerator and use in any recipe calling for egg whites.

a canadian thanksgiving

When our children were growing up, we made an effort to have them know Canada and all the wonderful things it has to offer. For each vacation, we would pick a different province and either drive or fly to it and rent a car, then spend the whole time exploring that particular part of the country. As a result, they got to know their own territory before venturing out into the rest of the world.

I loved those trips and the many times I've gone across the country on a book tour or explored a province as research for a magazine article. Each area has not only wonderful vistas and culture to offer but also exciting food. What better time than Thanksgiving to celebrate this good food from across the country?

potted pork

MAKES ABOUT 3 CUPS (750 ML)

Quebec's favourite pâté is called *cretons* and is most often made with ground pork. This simple make-ahead version uses chunks of lean pork. Serve accompanied with cornichons, pickled pearl onions and slices of baguette ... the wheat for which would have come from the Prairies, of course.

2	whole cloves 2
1	small onion, halved 1
12	sprigs fresh parsley 12
1	bay leaf 1
1 tsp	dried thyme 5 mL
1-1/2 lb	pork shoulder, cut into 1-inch (2.5 cm) cubes 750 g
1/2 lb	pork fatback, cut into 1-inch (2.5 cm) cubes 250 g
3	cloves garlic, halved 3
3/4 tsp	salt 4 mL
1/2 tsp	black pepper 2 mL
1/8 tsp	each cinnamon and ground allspice 0.5 mL
4 cups	cold water 1 L

1. Stick 1 clove into each onion half. Tie parsley, bay leaf and thyme in a small square of rinsed cheesecloth to make a bouquet garni.

2. In a large heavy saucepan, combine pork shoulder, pork fatback, onion halves, bouquet garni, garlic, salt, pepper, cinnamon and allspice. Add cold water. Bring to a boil over high heat. Reduce heat to medium; simmer, covered, for 2 to 2-1/2 hours or until meat is falling apart.

3. Discard onion and bouquet garni. With a slotted spoon, transfer meat to a food processor, reserving liquid and fat. Process meat just until shredded. Do not purée. Set aside.

4. Simmer cooking liquid, uncovered, stirring often, over medium-low heat for 20 to 30 minutes or until liquid is reduced and fat is slightly transparent. Let cool slightly, then stir in shredded meat. Adjust seasoning to taste. Pack into a 3-cup (750 mL) terrine or other serving dish. Refrigerate, covered, at least 24 hours or up to 3 days. Serve at room temperature.

roast ducks with wild rice-apple stuffing

MAKES 8 SERVINGS

A favourite in the Yukon and the Northwest Territories, roast duck with a stuffing of two other Canadian harvest treats makes a perfect centrepiece for our cross-country Thanksgiving.

STUFFING

2 tbsp	butter	25 mL
2	onions, chopped	2
1 cup	diced celery	250 mL
1 cup	wild rice, rinsed	250 mL
3-3/4 cups	hot chicken stock	925 mL
1/2 tsp	each dried sage and thyme	2 mL
4 cups	diced unpeeled apples	1 L
1/2 cup	chopped fresh parsley	125 mL

ROAST DUCKS

2	ducks (5 lb/2.2 kg each)	2
1	lemon	1
	Salt and pepper	
1 cup	apple juice	250 mL
1 tbsp	cornstarch	15 mL
2 tbsp	cold water	25 mL

1. Stuffing: In a large saucepan, melt butter over medium heat. Cook onions and celery, stirring, for 3 minutes. Stir in rice; cook for 3 minutes. Stir in 2-3/4 cups (675 mL) of the stock, sage and thyme. Bring to a boil; reduce heat to medium-low. Cook, covered, for 45 to 60 minutes or until rice is tender but not mushy and the stock is absorbed. If necessary, simmer, uncovered, for the last 10 to 15 minutes so any excess stock evaporates. Let cool completely. Stir in apples and parsley; set aside.

2. Roast Ducks: Rinse ducks in cold water and wipe well; dry thoroughly. Remove any excess fat; prick skin all over with a needle.

3. Grate the zest from the lemon; set aside. Cut lemon in half; rub cut sides all over ducks, inside and out. Sprinkle cavities with salt and pepper.

4. Squeeze any juice remaining in the lemon halves into the cooled stuffing; stir in lemon zest. Stuff ducks with stuffing; sew or skewer shut. Skewer neck skins to bodies.

5. Place ducks on their sides on a rack in a large shallow roasting pan. Roast in a 450°F (230°C) oven for 15 minutes.

6. Discard fat from the pan. Pour in remaining stock; reduce temperature to 350°F (180°C). Lay ducks on their breasts; roast for 15 minutes. Turn ducks breast side up; roast for 1-1/4 hours or until juices run clear when thickest part of thighs are pierced with a skewer.

7. Remove ducks to a heated platter and cover loosely with foil; keep warm. Skim fat from the pan juices; add apple juice to pan juices and bring to a boil, scraping up any bits from the bottom of the pan. Dissolve cornstarch in cold water and add to pan. Cook, stirring, until gravy is smooth and thickened. Carve ducks and pass gravy in a heated sauceboat.

garlic-herbed potatoes
MAKES 8 SERVINGS

Much of Atlantic Canada's harvest comes from the sea, but the East Coast is also famous for its potatoes. These creamy mashed potatoes taste just right when splashed with a spoonful or two of dark gravy from the roast ducks.

3 lb	potatoes (7 to 10) 1.5 kg	
8	cloves garlic, peeled 8	
Pinch	salt Pinch	
3/4 cup	sour cream, at room temperature 175 mL	
2 tbsp	butter 25 mL	
1/3 cup	chopped fresh parsley 75 mL	
	Black pepper	

1. Peel and quarter potatoes. Place in a large pot with garlic and salt. Add enough cold water to cover potatoes by 1 inch (2.5 cm). Bring to a boil; reduce heat to medium. Cook, covered, 20 to 30 minutes or until fork-tender. Drain well. (Cooking liquid freezes well and can be reserved for use in another recipe such as soup or to thin gravy.)

2. Return potatoes to the saucepan; heat for 1 minute to dry out. Mash potatoes; add sour cream and butter. Beat with a whisk or electric mixer until smooth and fluffy. Stir in parsley and pepper to taste. Serve immediately.

salad of greens and toasted hazelnuts with raspberry vinaigrette
MAKES 8 SERVINGS

Many good things grow in British Columbia's temperate climate, but the province seems to lead the way in growing unusual salad ingredients. Choose a good variety of greens for this refreshing salad.

1/2 cup	coarsely chopped hazelnuts (filberts) 125 mL
3 tbsp	each hazelnut oil and vegetable oil 45 mL
2 tbsp	raspberry vinegar 25 mL
1-1/2 tsp	each liquid honey and Dijon mustard 7 mL
1/4 tsp	dried basil 1 mL

1. Spread hazelnuts on a baking sheet and toast in a 350°F (180°C) oven for 5 to 7 minutes or until fragrant. Let cool.

2. In a small bowl, whisk together oils, vinegar, honey, mustard, basil, salt and pepper. (Dressing can be made ahead and stored at room temperature for up to 2 hours or refrigerated, covered, for up to 3 days. Whisk again before tossing with salad greens.)

3. In a large salad bowl, combine greens and hazelnuts. Add dressing; toss well and serve immediately.

1/4 tsp	salt 1 mL
Pinch	black pepper Pinch
12 cups	assorted greens* 3 L

* Arugula, romaine lettuce, radicchio, lamb's lettuce, red leaf lettuce, Boston lettuce and kale would be lovely together, or buy the equivalent amount of mesclun.

> **TIP**
> Look for hazelnut oil in the specialty foods section of the supermarket or in your local deli.

lattice-top cranberry pie

MAKES 8 SERVINGS

In Ontario, there are two big cranberry-producing areas—the Johnston Cranberry Marsh near Bala and the Mohawks of Gibson reserve, south of MacTier. And if you have ever flown over Richmond, British Columbia, in October, you will remember the crimson carpet below. Cranberries are harvested in October, so pop a few bags into the freezer to use throughout the year.

Serve the pie warm or at room temperature with vanilla ice cream.

	Pastry for a 9-inch (23 cm) double-crust pie
4 cups	coarsely chopped cranberries 1 L
1/2 cup	seedless raisins 125 mL
1 cup	packed brown sugar 250 mL
1/4 cup	granulated sugar 50 mL
2 tbsp	quick-cooking tapioca 25 mL
1 tsp	grated lemon zest 5 mL
2 tbsp	fresh lemon juice 25 mL
1/4 tsp	almond extract 1 mL
2 tbsp	butter 25 mL

1. On a piece of waxed paper, invert a 9-inch (23 cm) pie plate; draw around the plate to make a circle. Roll out half of the pastry to 1/8-inch (3 mm) thickness; cut into sixteen 1/2-inch (1 cm) wide strips.
2. On waxed paper, weave the strips together, 8 crosswise, 8 lengthwise, trimming to fit the circle. Place the paper with the pastry flat in the freezer while preparing the rest of the pie.
3. Roll out the remaining pastry; line pie plate, pressing rim of pastry onto the edge of the pie plate and trimming edge. Set aside.
4. In a large bowl, combine cranberries, raisins, sugars, tapioca, lemon zest, lemon juice and almond extract. Spoon into pie shell; dot with butter. Moisten rim of pie shell with water; slide lattice pastry on top of pie, pressing lattice onto the rim of bottom pastry shell to seal edges. Bake in a 425°F (220°C) oven for 10 minutes. Reduce heat to 375°F (190°C) and bake 30 to 40 minutes or until filling is bubbly and pastry is golden brown. Let cool on a wire rack.

a halloween bash

Since we live close to the edge of town, Halloween night usually finds us answering the door non-stop. I think a few kids are driven into town from the country ... something my parents never did. We lived a mile and a half from the nearest village, and even driving us there would not have given us much of a haul since there were only about 50 inhabitants, if that. I remember dressing up in whatever old clothes I could find (with a few layers underneath for protection from the cold) and walking down to the village. I called on all the farms along the way, making the trek even longer because some of the lanes were a fair length. A few people would have candies, but more often than not a few coins would come my way; when I finally got down through the village of Duntroon and onto the road to Stayner, I remember Mrs. Bell having me come in and sit down at her table for a huge piece of chocolate cake. I wonder what our present-day Halloween visitors would do if we offered them this kind of treat.

I have fond memories of how our own children celebrated Halloween. We would buy just one big pumpkin and allow each of them to carve a face on either side of it. (No spoiling these kids with a pumpkin each!) Year after year, they took turns having his or her face to the window side when we lit the candle, and they would always remember who had the face looking out the last year.

When we lived in Owen Sound, Ontario, our street got truly into the Halloween spirit. There was a lovely lady next door who lived in a huge mansion of a house all on her own. She greeted our kids at her door with a mountain of candies served on a sterling silver tray. The doctor across the street always put out the jangling bones of a skeleton while his next-door neighbour played blood-curdling music on his porch.

As the kids grew, they created their own traditions around the night ... and their own costumes. Allen still creates costumes with flair. One year he dressed all in black with empty pop tins, cartons, popcorn and the like pasted on himself and went as a movie theatre floor; another year, he was a giant Rice Krispies square. Gluing on all of those little pieces of cereal took true devotion to the Halloween spirit.

If Halloween inspires you to throw a little party, this is a fun menu I created for *Confidante* magazine, and one you can easily recreate. Just carve the pumpkins, set out the candles and invite everyone to wear silly costumes. Even the kids will dig this "creepy cuisine."

howling hot seeds

MAKES 2 CUPS (500 ML)

Don't throw away those seeds after you carve your pumpkin; they make terrific munchies. These spicy seeds are not really that hot, but you can make them as howling as you want by adding more hot pepper sauce. They can also be prepared with squash seeds.

2 cups	pumpkin seeds	500 mL
2 tbsp	vegetable oil	25 mL
1 tbsp	Worcestershire sauce	15 mL
1/2 tsp	salt	2 mL
1/4 tsp	hot pepper sauce	1 mL

1. Don't wash the seeds, but discard any pulp and stringy matter attached to them. Spread out seeds on a baking sheet; set aside to dry for about 2 hours.

2. In a large bowl, toss seeds with oil, Worcestershire sauce, salt and hot pepper sauce. Spread out seeds on baking sheet; toast in a 325°F (160°C) oven for 15 to 20 minutes, stirring once, until crisp. Let cool completely before serving.

jangling bones with devilish dip

MAKES ABOUT 48 PIECES AND 1-1/4 CUPS (300 ML) SAUCE

Provide a lot of paper napkins when serving these spicy chicken wings; they're the ultimate in finger food and very messy. Look for oyster sauce in the Oriental section of your supermarket.

4 lb	chicken wings, separated at joints, tips discarded 1.8 kg	
5	cloves garlic, minced 5	
1/4 cup	each soy sauce, fresh lime juice and oyster sauce 50 mL	
2 tbsp	vegetable oil 25 mL	
1 tbsp	each dry mustard, paprika and minced fresh ginger 15 mL	
1 tsp	cayenne 5 mL	
1/2 tsp	salt and pepper 2 mL	

DEVILISH DIP

1 cup	jalapeño jelly* 250 mL
1/4 cup	Dijon mustard 50 mL

1. Put wings in a large sturdy plastic bag or in a large bowl. In a small bowl, stir together garlic, soy sauce, lime juice, oyster sauce, vegetable oil, dry mustard, paprika, ginger and cayenne. Pour garlic mixture over wings; shake bag or toss wings to coat well. Close bag or cover and refrigerate for at least 6 hours or overnight, turning occasionally. Let stand at room temperature for 30 minutes before cooking.

2. Line 2 baking sheets with well-greased foil. Drain wings, discarding marinade. Spread wings out, meaty side down, in a single layer on baking sheets. Sprinkle with salt and pepper. Cook, uncovered, in a 475°F (240°C) oven for 25 to 30 minutes or until brown and crisp, turning after 15 minutes. Arrange on a warm serving platter with a bowl of Devilish Dip in the centre.

3. Devilish Dip: In a small saucepan, stir together jelly and mustard; heat over medium heat, stirring often, until jelly melts. Let cool, stirring occasionally; spoon into a 1-1/2-cup (375 mL) serving bowl.

* Look for jalapeño jelly in the condiment or specialty food section of your supermarket. If unavailable, use another jelly—sweet red pepper, apple or red currant—and add hot pepper flakes or diced fresh jalapeño peppers to taste before heating jelly with mustard.

ghoulish goulash

MAKES 8 TO 10 SERVINGS

Bearing little resemblance to real goulash, this delicious chili (with the interesting addition of macaroni) looks great served in a pumpkin. After hollowing it out, heat the pumpkin for 20 minutes in a 350°F (180°C) oven before adding the hot stew. You could accompany it with some crusty bread and a green salad, if you wish.

2 lb	lean ground beef 1 kg	
2	large cloves garlic, minced 2	
1 tbsp	chili powder 15 mL	
2 tsp	each dried basil, dried oregano, paprika and brown sugar 10 mL	
1 tsp	salt 5 mL	
1/2 tsp	black pepper 2 mL	
1/4 tsp	hot pepper flakes (or more to taste) 1 mL	
2	cans (28 oz/796 mL each) diced tomatoes, undrained* 2	
2	cans (19 oz/540 mL each) red kidney beans, drained and rinsed 2	
2 cups	water 500 mL	
2	sweet green peppers, seeded and chopped 2	
2 cups	raw macaroni 500 mL	

1. In a large pot or Dutch oven, brown beef over high heat for about 5 minutes, breaking it up with a spoon. Drain off any fat. Reduce heat to medium. Add garlic, chili powder, basil, oregano, paprika, sugar, salt, black pepper and hot pepper flakes; cook, stirring, for 1 minute.

2. Stir in tomatoes, beans and water. Bring to a boil over high heat. Reduce heat to medium-low; simmer, covered, for 45 minutes. (Recipe can be prepared ahead, covered and refrigerated for up to 24 hours. Bring to a simmer before proceeding.)

3. Stir in peppers and macaroni. Return to a simmer; cook, covered, for about 10 minutes, stirring occasionally, until peppers are tender and macaroni is tender but firm. Taste and add more salt and pepper if necessary. Serve in warm pasta bowls.

* If diced tomatoes are unavailable, use regular tomatoes and chop them coarsely in the can with kitchen scissors.

black magic squares

MAKES 24 SQUARES

Even adults have to admit they can't resist an old-fashioned treat like Rice Krispies squares. This interesting version skips the marshmallows and adds cocoa and peanut butter. Work quickly when blending the ingredients because they will start to harden when the saucepan is removed from the heat.

3/4 cup	unsweetened cocoa powder, sifted 175 mL
3/4 cup	liquid honey 175 mL
3/4 cup	peanut butter 175 mL
1 tbsp	butter 15 mL
3-1/2 cups	crispy rice cereal 875 mL
1/2 cup	chopped pecans 125 mL

1. In a large saucepan, combine cocoa and honey; cook over medium heat for about 2 minutes, stirring constantly, until cocoa has dissolved. Remove the saucepan from the heat; quickly stir in peanut butter and butter, until well combined. Stir in cereal and pecans. Press into a greased 13- x 9-inch (3.5 L) baking pan, using the moistened base of a measuring cup to flatten the surface. Let cool completely for about 1 hour before cutting into squares with a sharp knife.

a make-ahead buffet for
friends or family

This would make a great buffet supper for the holidays or any time of the year when you want to entertain a gang without last-minute fuss ... a boon for me because I hate to miss anything that goes on at my own parties. There is something to please everyone (even the vegetarian in the crowd) here. Although our dining room table is large enough to seat twelve easily, I've designed the menu so you can simply arrange all of the dishes on the table and let guests help themselves to a "forks-only" buffet—simple to eat if you have to balance a plate on your lap.

* Simply cut fruit such as melons, oranges, mangoes, papayas, kiwi and whatever else looks good in the supermarket into large slices and wedges and arrange on a large platter. Intersperse with bunches of red and green grapes.

cornmeal olive bites

MAKES 30 MINI MUFFINS

Pass around these little bites for guests to enjoy with wine when they arrive.

3/4 cup	all-purpose flour	175 mL
1/2 cup	cornmeal	125 mL
1 tbsp	granulated sugar	15 mL
1 tsp	baking powder	5 mL
1/2 tsp	each chili powder and salt	2 mL
3/4 cup	milk	175 mL
3 tbsp	butter, melted	45 mL
1	egg, lightly beaten	1
30	pimiento-stuffed olives	30

1. Grease or line with paper mini muffin cups with a 1-1/4-inch (3 cm) base; set aside.
2. In a large bowl, whisk together flour, cornmeal, sugar, baking powder, chili powder and salt. In a separate bowl, whisk together milk, butter and egg; pour over dry ingredients and stir together just until blended.
3. Spoon into prepared pans, filling each about three-quarters full. Push 1 olive, pimiento side up, into each, so top of olive is showing. Bake in top and bottom thirds of a 400°F (200°C) oven, rotating and switching pans halfway through, for 8 to 10 minutes or until light golden. Let cool on racks. (Bites can be stored in an airtight container for up to 2 days.)

> **TIP**
> If you don't have enough mini muffin pans to bake batter all at once, it will hold so you can bake in batches.

prosciutto fruit rolls

MAKES 24 PIECES

During the summer, prosciutto wrapped around fresh melon or figs will always be my answer to a quick and delicious appetizer. This variation takes advantage of the wonderful dried fruit available year-round.

1/4 cup	light cream cheese	50 mL
2 tsp	grated lemon zest	10 mL
Pinch	black pepper	Pinch
12	small dried figs, pitted dates or a combination	12
24	fresh basil leaves	24
12	thin slices prosciutto, halved lengthwise	12

1. In a small bowl, mash together cheese, lemon zest and pepper.
2. Cut figs or dates in half. Spread 1/4 tsp (1 mL) of the cheese mixture on each cut side; top with 1 basil leaf. Place on narrow end of prosciutto; roll up with tip of basil sticking out. (Rolls can be made, covered loosely and refrigerated for up to 2 hours.)

chicken artichoke casserole with orange gremolata

MAKES 12 SERVINGS

Gremolata is traditionally made with lemon rind (the outer yellow zest). In this variation, fresh orange zest accentuates the sunny Mediterranean flavours of an easy chicken casserole.

12	boneless skinless chicken breast halves 12
1/4 cup	olive oil (approx.) 50 mL
2	pkgs (10 oz/284 g each) pearl onions (about 4 cups/1 L), peeled 2
2	sweet yellow peppers, diced 2
1/4 cup	all-purpose flour 50 mL
2	cans (28 oz/796 mL each) diced tomatoes 2
1 cup	slivered dry-packed sun-dried tomatoes 250 mL
4 tsp	dried Italian herb seasoning 20 mL
1 tbsp	anchovy paste 15 mL
3	cans (14 oz/398 mL each) artichoke hearts, drained and cut in thirds 3
Pinch	granulated sugar Pinch

ORANGE GREMOLATA

4	cloves garlic, minced 4
1 cup	coarsely chopped fresh parsley 250 mL
2 tbsp	coarsely grated orange zest 25 mL

1. Cut chicken into 1-inch (2.5 cm) cubes. In a Dutch oven or heavy saucepan, heat half the oil over medium-high heat; brown chicken in batches, adding a bit more oil if necessary and transferring browned pieces to a large bowl.

2. Add remaining oil to the pan; cook onions and peppers, stirring occasionally, for about 5 minutes or until beginning to brown. Stir in flour; cook, stirring, for 1 minute.

3. Stir in tomatoes and their juice; bring to a boil. Stir in sun-dried tomatoes, seasoning, anchovy paste, artichoke hearts, chicken with any accumulated juices and sugar. Cover and simmer for 10 minutes or until chicken is no longer pink inside.

4. Divide chicken mixture between two 12-cup (3 L) shallow casseroles. (Casseroles can be refrigerated until cool, then covered with foil and refrigerated for up to 1 day.)

5. Bake casseroles, covered with foil, in a 350°F (180°C) oven for about 30 minutes or until bubbly.

6. Orange Gremolata: In a small bowl, stir together garlic, parsley and orange zest. (Gremolata can be covered and refrigerated for up to 1 day.) Sprinkle over casseroles before serving.

orzo walnut pilaf

MAKES 12 SERVINGS

Orzo is a rice-shaped pasta, usually cooked in a large pot of water as you would other pasta. Here it's cooked like a rice pilaf in a smaller amount of chicken stock, which is absorbed for flavour.

1-1/2 cups	walnut pieces	375 mL
2 tbsp	olive oil	25 mL
2	onions, chopped	2
4	cloves garlic, minced	4
3 cups	orzo	750 mL
7 cups	hot chicken or vegetable stock	1.75 L
1-1/2 tsp	dried oregano	7 mL
Pinch	each salt and pepper	Pinch
1/2 cup	chopped fresh parsley	125 mL

1. Toast walnuts in a single layer on a rimmed baking sheet in a 350°F (180°C) oven for 4 to 5 minutes or until fragrant. Let cool.
2. In a large saucepan, heat oil over medium heat; cook onions, stirring often, for 5 minutes or until softened. Reduce heat to low. Add garlic and orzo; cook, stirring, for 3 minutes.
3. Stir in stock (reserving 1 cup/250 mL if making ahead) and oregano; bring to a boil. Reduce heat to low, cover and simmer for about 15 minutes or just until tender. Fluff with a fork; sprinkle with salt and pepper. (To make ahead, transfer to a 12-cup/3 L casserole and let cool, gently stirring occasionally. Cover and refrigerate for up to 1 day. Stir in reserved stock and reheat in a 350°F/180°C oven, stirring occasionally, for about 20 minutes or until heated through.)
4. Just before serving, stir in parsley and walnuts.

VARIATION

TWO-RICE PILAF

In a large saucepan, bring 5 cups (1.25 L) stock and 1 cup (250 mL) wild rice to a boil. Reduce heat to medium-low, cover and cook for 35 minutes. Prepare rest of the recipe as above, using 2 cups (500 mL) long-grain white rice in place of orzo. Add onion-rice mixture to wild rice mixture; cover and cook over medium-low heat until liquid is absorbed, about 20 minutes. (To make ahead, transfer pilaf to a 12-cup/3 L casserole and let cool. Cover and refrigerate for up to 2 days. Reheat as directed.)

vegetable strudel

MAKES 12 SERVINGS

This colourful strudel is an appealing side dish for everyone, yet it's hearty enough for the vegetarians on your guest list.

2 tbsp	olive oil 25 mL
4	cloves garlic, minced 4
3	leeks (white and light green parts only), thinly sliced 3
2	sweet red peppers, diced 2
2 tsp	dried marjoram or oregano 10 mL
1 tsp	dried thyme 5 mL
1/4 tsp	each salt and pepper 1 mL
2	pkgs (10 oz/284 g each) spinach, shredded 2
2	eggs 2
8 oz	cream goat cheese (chèvre) or cream cheese 250 g
16	sheets phyllo pastry 16
1/2 cup	butter, melted 125 mL
1/3 cup	dry bread crumbs 75 mL

1. In a large skillet, heat oil over medium heat; cook garlic, leeks, red peppers, marjoram, thyme, salt and pepper, stirring often, for 5 minutes or until softened.
2. Add spinach in batches, adding more when wilted; cook, stirring, over medium-high heat until all of the spinach is wilted and liquid is evaporated. Remove from heat. In a large bowl, beat eggs and cheese until smooth; stir into spinach mixture. Set aside.
3. Place 1 sheet of phyllo, with long side closest to you, on a damp towel on the work surface, keeping remainder covered with another damp towel to prevent drying out. Brush lightly with some of the butter; sprinkle lightly with some of the bread crumbs. Repeat layering with 7 more sheets.
4. Arrange half of the spinach mixture in a strip 2 inches (5 cm) from the long side of the phyllo and leaving a 2-inch (5 cm) border at each short side. Fold long border over filling; using the towel as an aid, roll up pastry, folding in sides. Place, seam side down, on a greased baking sheet. Brush with butter. Repeat with remaining phyllo and filling to make 2 strudels. (Strudels can be covered and refrigerated for up to 2 days.)
5. Cut 5 slits in the top of each strudel. Bake in the centre of a 400°F (200°C) oven for 25 to 30 minutes or until golden brown. Slice each strudel into 6 servings.

salad of mixed greens, apples and cranberries with cider dressing

MAKES 12 SERVINGS

A light, sweet-and-sour creamy dressing naps this simple green salad that's updated with fruit.

18 cups	torn mixed salad greens or mesclun 4.5 L
1-1/2 cups	dried cranberries 375 mL
1	red onion, thinly sliced 1
1 cup	toasted pecan halves (optional) 250 mL
4	apples, unpeeled 4

CIDER DRESSING

1/4 cup	packed brown sugar 50 mL
1 tbsp	all-purpose flour 15 mL
1 tsp	dry mustard 5 mL
1/2 tsp	salt 2 mL
1 cup	2% evaporated milk 250 mL
1/2 cup	cider vinegar 125 mL
1/2 cup	sour cream 125 mL

1. Cider Dressing: In a small saucepan, stir together sugar, flour, dry mustard and salt; gradually stir in milk and cider vinegar. Bring to a boil over medium-high heat, stirring constantly. Reduce heat to low; cook, stirring, for 2 minutes. Let cool, stirring often. (Dressing can be made to this point up to a week ahead and refrigerated in an airtight container.) Whisk in sour cream.

2. In a large salad bowl, toss together greens, cranberries, onion and pecans (if using). (To make ahead, cover with a damp paper towel and refrigerate for up to 4 hours.) Core, halve and thinly slice apples; add to salad. Toss with dressing to coat.

chocolate caramel tart

MAKES 12 SERVINGS

This decadent sweet must be refrigerated right up until serving time. Its ooey-gooey goodness will send your guests home smiling. I always think a dessert should make this kind of lasting impression.

1 cup	all-purpose flour	250 mL
4 tsp	granulated sugar	20 mL
Pinch	salt	Pinch
1/3 cup	cold butter, cubed	75 mL
1/4 cup	ice water (approx.)	50 mL
6 oz	bittersweet or semi-sweet chocolate, chopped	175 g
3/4 cup	whipping cream	175 mL

CARAMEL FILLING

3/4 cup	granulated sugar	175 mL
1/3 cup	water	75 mL
1/3 cup	whipping cream	75 mL
1/4 cup	butter	50 mL
1/2 tsp	vanilla	2 mL

1. In a large bowl, combine flour, sugar and salt. With a pastry blender or 2 knives, cut in butter until mixture resembles large oatmeal flakes. Sprinkle with water, 1 tbsp (15 mL) at a time, and adding 1 tbsp (15 mL) more if necessary, stirring briskly with a fork until pastry holds together. Press into a disc; wrap in plastic wrap and refrigerate for at least 1 hour until chilled or overnight.

2. On a lightly floured surface, roll out pastry to a 12-inch (30 cm) circle; press into a 9-inch (23 cm) tart tin with removable bottom or a 9-inch (23 cm) pie plate. Fold edge under, leaving pastry slightly above edge of the pan. Refrigerate for 30 minutes or until firm. Prick all over with a fork. Line the shell with foil; fill evenly with pie weights or dried beans. Bake in the bottom third of a 400°F (200°C) oven for 15 minutes. Lift out foil and weights. Bake for 10 to 15 minutes longer or until golden brown. Let cool completely on a rack.

3. Place chocolate in a heatproof bowl. In a small saucepan, bring 3/4 cup (175 mL) cream to a boil. Pour over chocolate, whisking until melted and smooth. Set aside 3 tbsp (45 mL) for garnish. Spread remainder over the pie crust. Refrigerate for 45 minutes or until firm.

4. Caramel Filling: In a heavy saucepan, stir together sugar and water; cook over low heat until sugar is dissolved. Increase heat and boil for 5 to 8 minutes or until golden, swirling pan occasionally. Remove from heat. Holding an arm's length away and averting your face to avoid spatters, whisk in 1/3 cup (75 mL) cream, butter and vanilla. Return to low heat and cook, stirring, for 5 minutes. Transfer to a heatproof bowl; refrigerate, stirring occasionally, for about 20 minutes or until cold but not firm.

5. Spread over chocolate-lined pastry. Drizzle reserved chocolate in a decorative pattern over top. Refrigerate for 1 hour or until firm, or cover and refrigerate for up to 2 days.

our family's christmas eve

Christmas Eve at our house is usually a quiet family affair. Because I've cooked all day to get ready for the big feast on Christmas Day, the menu is very simple, with most things—those that everyone loves—already prepared days in advance.

oysters on the half shell

MAKES 6 SERVINGS

Oysters have a long history as holiday food in Canada, with barrels of fresh oysters brought into Ontario from the coast even in the nineteenth century. This has been our family's traditional Christmas Eve treat for many years. My son, Allen, is our resident oyster shucker after his wife, Cherrie, scrubs the shells. We put out a bottle of Tabasco sauce for anyone who wants an added zip.

36	oysters 36
6	lemon wedges 6
	Large sprigs fresh parsley
	Black pepper

1. Make a bed of crushed ice on a big platter or on 6 deep plates and place in the freezer.
2. Under cold running water, brush oyster shells clean. Shuck the oysters, retaining as much liquor as possible in the cupped bottom shell. Discard the flat upper shell and run the knife under the oyster to loosen it from the bottom shell. Balance oysters in the bottom shells and place on the bed of ice.
3. Garnish platter or each plate with lemon wedges and parsley. Season with pepper to taste.

deep-dish tourtière

MAKES 8 SERVINGS

Tourtière is my favourite Christmas Eve main dish because it is a treat we don't have throughout the year, and I can make it far ahead of that busy day. Serve it with either green tomato relish or chili sauce to temper the richness of pastry plus pork. While tourtière is traditionally made as a double-crust pie, this top-crust version is great for buffets, especially potluck suppers. If you wish, you can mound the pork mixture in a deep 10-inch (25 cm) double-crust pie, or more thinly in two 9-inch (23 cm) double-crust pies. For the latter, you will need to double the amount of pastry.

2	potatoes (1 lb/500 g total)	2
2 lb	lean ground pork, chicken or turkey	1 kg
1 tbsp	vegetable oil	15 mL
6	cloves garlic, minced	6
2	large onions, chopped	2
1	stalk celery, chopped	1
6 cups	sliced mushrooms (about 1 lb/500 g)	1.5 L
1-1/2 tsp	dried thyme	7 mL
3/4 tsp	each salt and dried savory	4 mL
1/2 tsp	black pepper	2 mL
1/4 tsp	each ground cloves and cinnamon	1 mL
2 cups	chicken stock	500 mL
1/4 cup	chopped fresh parsley	50 mL
	Pastry for 1 double-crust pie	
1	egg, beaten	1

1. Peel and quarter potatoes. In a saucepan of boiling salted water, cover and cook potatoes for about 15 minutes or until tender. Drain and return to pan; dry potatoes over low heat for 30 seconds. Mash until smooth.

2. In a Dutch oven or large deep skillet, cook pork over medium-high heat in batches, stirring and scraping up any brown bits from bottom of pan, for about 5 minutes or until no longer pink. Strain through a large sieve set over a bowl. Skim off any fat from the juices; reserve juices and pork.

3. Add oil to the pan; heat over medium heat. Add garlic, onions, celery, mushrooms, thyme, salt, savory, pepper, cloves and cinnamon; cook, stirring often, for about 10 minutes or until softened and liquid is evaporated. Add reserved meat and juices, chicken stock and potatoes; cook for about 5 minutes or until thickened. Stir in parsley. Scrape into 13- x 9-inch (3 L) glass baking dish; refrigerate until cooled.

4. On a lightly floured surface, roll out pastry until slightly larger than the top of the baking dish. Place over filling, letting pastry rise loosely over rim. Tuck under any pastry beyond the rim; press to inner rim. (Tourtière can be covered and refrigerated for up to 1 day. Or, wrap in heavy-duty foil and freeze for up to 2 weeks; thaw in refrigerator for 48 hours or until no longer icy in the middle.) Brush pastry with egg. Cut a steam hole in the centre of the pastry. Bake in the lower third of a 425°F (220°C) oven for about 45 minutes or until golden brown and filling is piping hot. Let stand on a rack for 5 minutes before serving.

tangy cabbage salad

MAKES 12 OR MORE SERVINGS

This delicious coleslaw keeps well for at least two weeks and is one of my favourite ways to have a salad on hand when my house is full of holiday guests.

1	medium cabbage, shredded	1
1	each sweet green and red pepper, chopped	1
1 cup	grated carrot	250 mL
1	onion, chopped	1
1 tbsp	salt	15 mL
	Ice cubes	

DRESSING

1 cup	granulated sugar	250 mL
3/4 cup	white vinegar	175 mL
1/2 cup	vegetable oil	125 mL
1/4 cup	water	50 mL
1 tsp	mustard seed	5 mL
1 tsp	celery seed	5 mL

1. In a large bowl, combine cabbage, green pepper, red pepper, carrot, onion and salt. Cover top with ice cubes and let the mixture stand to crisp for at least 1 hour. Remove any ice and drain cabbage mixture well.
2. Dressing: In a small saucepan, combine sugar, vinegar, oil, water and mustard and celery seeds. Bring to a boil, stirring to dissolve sugar. Pour over cabbage mixture and let cool.
3. Transfer to a large storage container, cover and refrigerate for at least 1 day before using.

apple mincemeat crumble

MAKES 6 SERVINGS

Serve with vanilla ice cream or strained yogurt sweetened with honey and a touch of vanilla or lemon zest for an easy homemade holiday dessert.

4 cups	sliced peeled apples (about 5) 1 L
1-1/2 cups	mincemeat 375 mL
2 tbsp	fresh lemon juice 25 mL
1/2 cup	all-purpose flour 125 mL
1/3 cup	packed brown sugar 75 mL
1/3 cup	rolled oats (not instant) 75 mL
1/3 cup	butter 75 mL
1/2 cup	slivered or sliced almonds or Brazil nuts 125 mL

1. In a 9-inch (2.5 L) square baking dish, combine apples, mincemeat and lemon juice.
2. In a bowl, stir together flour, sugar and rolled oats; cut in butter until mixture resembles coarse crumbs. Stir in almonds. Sprinkle evenly over apple mixture. Bake in a 375°F (190°C) oven for 45 minutes or until apples are tender.

an elegant celebration feast
for two or four

Many family Christmas celebrations are large, with aunts, uncles and cousins gathered around the table. If, however, your family is small or you decide to enjoy an intimate dinner on Christmas Eve before you get together with all of those relatives, this menu is just the answer. Although it has a definite holiday ring to it, it can also be used as an appealing little supper for any time of the year — perhaps to brighten up a cold February night, maybe even around Valentine's Day.

If there are just two of you, most of the recipes can be cut in half without a problem, except for the puddings. In that case, make the four and freeze two for another time.

pickled shrimp on greens

MAKES 4 SERVINGS

Tender shrimp tossed in a piquant dressing, then spooned over crisp greens, make an easy and colourful first course. Serve with lots of crusty bread. The shrimp and vegetable mixture can be prepared the day before and combined a couple of hours before dinner.

2	stalks celery 2
1 tsp	each black peppercorns and mustard seeds 5 mL
4 cups	water 1 L
1	bay leaf 1
1	clove garlic, sliced 1
1 tsp	salt, preferably sea salt 5 mL
1 lb	jumbo shrimp, cleaned and deveined 500 g
1/3 cup	vegetable oil 75 mL
1/4 cup	cider vinegar 50 mL
2 tbsp	drained capers 25 mL
1 tbsp	each tomato paste and Worcestershire sauce 15 mL
2 tsp	Tabasco sauce 10 mL
1 tsp	each dry mustard, paprika and granulated sugar 5 mL
Half	each small sweet red and green pepper, slivered Half
Quarter	white onion, thinly sliced Quarter
6 cups	mesclun 1.5 L

1. Cut in two 1/2 stalk of the celery with leaves. Tie peppercorns and mustard seeds in double thickness of rinsed cheesecloth. In a medium saucepan, combine water, cut celery, cheesecloth bag, bay leaf, garlic and salt. Bring to a simmer, add shrimp, cover and bring back to a simmer until shrimp have turned pink. Watch carefully and do not overcook. Cool slightly, then drain, discarding seasonings; cool shrimp completely. (Shrimp can be covered and refrigerated overnight.)

2. Stir together oil, vinegar, capers, tomato paste, Worcestershire sauce, Tabasco, mustard, paprika and sugar; set aside.

3. Slice remaining celery and combine in a large bowl with peppers and onion. Pour vinegar mixture over vegetables and toss to coat. (Can be covered and refrigerated overnight.)

4. Two hours before serving, combine shrimp with vegetable mixture. Cover and refrigerate.

5. To serve, line 4 salad plates with mesclun and arrange shrimp and vegetables with sauce on top.

rosemary-roasted lamb loins

MAKES 4 SERVINGS

Most of the intensely flavoured sauce for this tender, succulent lamb can be made ahead, leaving last-minute preparation to a minimum. If loins are not available, use loin chops.

1 cup	ruby port	250 mL
2	shallots, minced	2
1	small carrot, minced	1
2	sprigs parsley	2
1	bay leaf	1
1-1/2 cups	lamb or chicken stock	375 mL
4	boneless lamb loins (1-1/4 lb/ 570 g total)*	4
2 tbsp	olive oil	25 mL
	Salt and pepper	
2 tsp	dried rosemary	10 mL
1/4 cup	red wine vinegar	50 mL
1 tbsp	cornstarch	15 mL
2 tbsp	cold water	25 mL

1. In a small saucepan, combine port, shallots, carrot, parsley and bay leaf. Bring to a boil and boil until reduced by half. Add stock, bring back to a boil, and boil until 1 cup (250 mL) liquid remains. Press through a fine sieve into a clean saucepan. (Can be cooled, covered and refrigerated for 1 day.)

2. Dry lamb well with paper towels. Rub all over with half of the oil. Sprinkle with salt, pepper and rosemary, coating well. Heat a heavy ovenproof skillet over high heat. Add remaining oil and brown loins for about 3 minutes, turning to brown all sides. Transfer skillet to 400°F (200°C) oven to roast, uncovered, for about 10 minutes or until a meat thermometer registers 130°F (55°C). (Do not overcook; they still should be pink inside.) Remove to heated platter and tent with foil to keep warm.

3. Add vinegar to skillet and place over high heat; bring to a boil, scraping up any brown bits in the pan. Boil until reduced to 1 tbsp (15 mL); add to port mixture in saucepan. Bring to a boil. Dissolve cornstarch in cold water and stir into sauce; cook, stirring, until thickened and bubbly.

4. Cut loins into diagonal slices and arrange on platter. Serve sauce in heated sauceboat.

* If lamb loins are frozen, thaw them in the refrigerator overnight.

sauté of julienned roots

MAKES 4 SERVINGS

This quick, easy method of cooking seasonal root vegetables brings out their natural sweetness. Best of all, this dish can be prepared hours ahead and reheats beautifully.

1	large leek (white and light green parts only) 1
2	carrots 2
Quarter	rutabaga Quarter
4 cups	cold water 1 L
1 tbsp	fresh lemon juice 15 mL
1	celery root (about 1 lb/500 g) 1
1/4 cup	butter 50 mL
2 tsp	chopped fresh thyme leaves (or 1/2 tsp/2 mL dried thyme) 10 mL
1 tsp	granulated sugar 5 mL
3/4 tsp	salt 4 mL
1/4 tsp	black pepper 1 mL
1 tbsp	snipped chives or green onion tops 15 mL

1. Trim root end from leek, cut in half lengthwise, then wash leek thoroughly under cold running water. Cut leek into 3- x 1/4-inch (8 cm x 5 mm) strips. Keeping vegetables separate, peel carrots and rutabaga, then cut into strips the same size as the leeks.

2. Stir together water and lemon juice in a large bowl. Peel celery root, then cut into strips the same size as the other vegetables, dropping pieces into the water as you work. (Vegetables can be wrapped separately—keep celery root in the bowl of water and lemon juice—then refrigerated for up to 24 hours.)

3. Melt the butter in a large skillet over medium-high heat. Add carrots, rutabaga and thyme; stir-fry for 2 minutes. Drain celery root and add to skillet; stir-fry for 1 minute. Add leeks; stir-fry for 2 minutes. Reduce heat to low and stir in sugar, salt and pepper; cook, covered, for about 10 to 12 minutes, stirring occasionally, until vegetables are tender. (Vegetables can be cooled, covered and refrigerated for up to 8 hours. Just before serving, reheat over low heat, gently stirring often, until piping hot.)

4. Spoon into a warm serving dish; sprinkle with chives and serve at once.

sweet fennel and pomegranate salad

MAKES 4 SERVINGS

Seasonal pomegranate lends its seeds to add holiday sparkle to a simple salad of thinly sliced sweet fennel (often misnamed anise in supermarkets). Soaking the fennel in cold water reduces the sharp licorice edge.

1	fennel bulb	1
1	large pomegranate	1
2 tsp	chopped fresh parsley	10 mL
3 tbsp	extra virgin olive oil	45 mL
2 tsp	white wine vinegar	10 mL
	Salt and pepper	

1. Cut the top from the fennel bulb and trim the base, cutting out core. Cut bulb crosswise into the thinnest slices you can to produce rings. Soak in cold water for 10 minutes; drain and soak again in fresh cold water for 10 minutes. Drain well and dry in salad spinner. Arrange in a deep platter or shallow salad bowl. Sprinkle with the seeds of the pomegranate and parsley. (Salad can be covered and refrigerated for up to 4 hours.)

2. Whisk together oil and vinegar; pour over salad. Sprinkle with salt and a generous amount of freshly ground black pepper.

individual cranberry-orange puddings

MAKES 4 SERVINGS

These British-style puddings, made of cake batter that is steamed instead of baked, are a lighter alternative to most traditional holiday desserts. Serve them hot with the Orange Hard Sauce that follows, or with dollops of softly whipped cream. The easiest way to chop cranberries is to pulse them in a food processor or mini-chopper.

3/4 cup	cranberries (fresh or frozen), chopped 175 mL
1/4 cup	dried cranberries 50 mL
2 tbsp	Grand Marnier or orange juice 25 mL
2 tsp	grated orange zest 10 mL
	Butter and granulated sugar
3/4 cup	all-purpose flour 175 mL
1 tsp	baking powder 5 mL
1/2 tsp	salt 2 mL
1/4 cup	butter, softened 50 mL
1/3 cup	granulated sugar 75 mL
1	egg 1
1/2 tsp	almond extract 2 mL
1/4 cup	fresh orange juice 50 mL
1/4 cup	blanched slivered almonds 50 mL

1. Combine chopped cranberries, dried cranberries, Grand Marnier and orange zest; set aside while preparing the cups and the rest of the ingredients.
2. Butter four 1-cup (250 mL) custard cups, moulds or ramekins. Sprinkle with granulated sugar. Cut rounds of waxed paper the size of the bottom of each cup and press 1 into each cup. Cut rounds the size of the top of each cup and set aside.
3. Sift or stir together flour, baking powder and salt. Set aside.
4. In a large bowl, cream butter; add sugar and beat together until fluffy. Beat in egg and almond extract. Stir in flour mixture alternately with orange juice, making 3 additions of dry ingredients and 2 of liquid. Stir in almonds and spoon batter into prepared cups. Place round of waxed paper on top of each cup. Make a small pleat in a piece of foil to cover each cup. Tie foil in place with string. Place cups on a rack in a small roasting pan and pour in enough boiling water to come two-thirds of the way up the cups. Cover and simmer over medium-low heat for about 45 minutes or until a tester inserted into the centre of each cup comes out clean. Remove cups from pan and let stand for 5 minutes. Unmould onto serving platter. (Puddings can be made up to 2 months ahead, wrapped well and frozen, or made up to 2 days ahead, covered and refrigerated. Thaw in refrigerator overnight if frozen. To reheat, bring to room temperature, cover with a microwaveable bowl and heat at High for about 4 minutes or until hot. Or, return to cups and steam until hot, about 20 minutes.)
5. Serve hot with Orange Hard Sauce or another pudding sauce of your choice.

orange hard sauce

MAKES 3/4 CUP (175 ML) SAUCE

1/4 cup	butter, softened 50 mL
1 cup	icing sugar 250 mL
1 tbsp	grated orange zest 15 mL
1 tbsp	Grand Marnier or orange juice 15 mL

1. In a bowl, beat butter until creamy. Gradually blend in sugar; stir in zest and Grand Marnier. Transfer to a pretty serving bowl and refrigerate until firm. (Sauce can be made up to 2 days ahead, covered and refrigerated.) Let stand at room temperature for 30 minutes before serving.

index